THE

BAMPTON LECTURES

FOR M.DCCC.LXXX.

THE ORGANIZATION

OF THE

Early Christian Churches

EIGHT LECTURES

Delivered before the University of Oxford, in the Year 1880

On the Foundation of the late Rev. John Bampton, M.A.
CANON OF SALISBURY

BY

EDWIN HATCH, M.A.

VICE-PRINCIPAL OF ST. MARY HALL
AND GRINFIELD LECTURER IN THE SEPTUAGINT, OXFORD

Wipf & Stock
PUBLISHERS
Eugene, Oregon

Wipf and Stock Publishers
199 W 8th Ave, Suite 3
Eugene, OR 97401

The Organization of the Early Christian Churches
Eight Lectures Delivered before the University of Oxford, in the Year 1880.
By Hatch, Edwin
ISBN: 1-57910-245-X
Publication date 5/6/1999
Previously published by Rivingtons, 1881

PREFACE.

THE author of the following Lectures is very sensible of the complexity of the facts with which he has had to deal, and of the importance of the issues which he has raised. Nor is he so confident in his own powers of historical analysis as to think that the conclusions at which he has arrived will be in every case the ultimate verdict of those who are competent to decide upon the evidence. The only title to attention which he ventures to urge is that he has endeavoured faithfully to collect, sift, and compare the available evidence, and to draw the conclusions to which that evidence seems to point, without reference to other hypotheses, however venerable from their antiquity, or however widely diffused in the Christian world. And the only claim which he makes from those who pass judgment upon his conclusions is, that which is in fact the postulate of all historical enquiry, that such judgments shall be formed with reference to the evidence, and not with reference to current or counter hypotheses.

Of that evidence only a small portion could, in most cases, be given in the notes. The author has for the most part confined himself, in those notes, to mentioning facts which, as far as he is aware, have not hitherto been collected, or the bearings of which upon ecclesiastical history have not been appreciated, and to stating the patristic or other authorities for facts which are likely to be unfamiliar to those who have not made ecclesiastical history their study. Where the evidence is fully and accurately stated in other works, he has thought it sufficient to refer to those works; in the notes to the last lecture he has been indebted for some facts of mediaeval history to the valuable, but as yet unfinished, work of Professor Hinschius, *Das Kirchenrecht der Katholiken und Protestanten in Deutschland;* and in some cases he has thought it sufficient to refer to, instead of partially reprinting, his own contributions to the second volume of the *Dictionary of Christian Antiquities.* But he has not attempted to give the bibliography of any portion of the subject, partly because to have done so completely would have extended the volume to an inconvenient length, and partly also because he wishes to avoid even the semblance of sharing in the prevalent confusion of idea between the knowledge of a subject in itself and an acquaintance with the books which have been written about it.

The author takes this opportunity of expressing his obligations to the friends who on one or two points outside the range of his own studies have corrected his imperfect information, and to the officers of the Bodleian Library for their special and courteous attention.

OXFORD,
January 26, 1881.

SYNOPSIS OF CONTENTS.

LECTURE I.

THE METHOD OF STUDY.

(1) In patristic literature there is (i) the difficulty which arises from the fact that late Latin and Greek are very imperfectly known, (ii) that which arises (*a*) from the tendency to confound the theological or homiletic value of a Father with his value as a witness to fact, (*b*) from the tendency to ignore the question of his probable means of observation. . . pp. 5–7

(2) In conciliar literature there is the difficulty which arises, in all but the Œcumenical Councils, from the question of the extent to which a canon of a local council proves the existence of a general rule. This difficulty is increased by the fact of the distinctions between the various local councils having been to a great extent obliterated by their incorporation in the code of Canon Law. . . . . pp. 7–9

And in regard to all the evidence, whether patristic, or conciliar, or otherwise, there are two primary distinctions the ignoring of which has contributed more than any other single cause to the existing divergences of opinion: these are

(1) The distinction of *time*. The period which Christian history covers is so large a portion of the whole field of recorded history that in a survey of it the wide differences between one century and another are apt to be overlooked: and yet until the exact historical surroundings of a given fact are known, its significance cannot be known. . . pp. 9–11

(2) The distinction of *locality*. The space over which Christianity has extended has been the whole civilized world, with its great varieties of race and national character: the significance of a fact varies widely according as it belongs to one country or another. . . . . pp. 11–12

III. These are the preliminary steps: they are followed by the comparison of the facts, so ascertained and so localized, with other facts, with the view of ascertaining their causes: nor is such an enquiry barred. . . . . pp. 12–14

This comparison is made on two principles:

(1) Any given group of facts has to be compared with preceding and succeeding facts of the same kind, with the view of finding out the law of their sequence. The main difficulty of that process in the present enquiry arises from the fact of the per-

LECTURE II.

BISHOPS AND DEACONS.

LECTURE III.

PRESBYTERS.

LECTURE IV.

THE SUPREMACY OF THE BISHOP.

LECTURE V.

CLERGY AND LAITY.

LECTURE VI.

THE CLERGY AS A SEPARATE CLASS.

LECTURE VII.

COUNCILS AND THE UNITY OF THE CHURCH.

LECTURE VIII.

THE PARISH AND THE CATHEDRAL.

I. *The Parish.*

II. *The Cathedral.*

In other words, the Lectures tend to establish the view that in the organization of the Christian Church, as in the formation of the natural world, God has been pleased to act by an economy of slowly-operating causes. Nor is it legitimate to allow an *a priori* theory

LECTURE I.

INTRODUCTORY: THE METHOD OF STUDY.

I PROPOSE in these Lectures to examine the history of the organization of the Christian Churches from the times of the Apostles until the fall of the Western Empire. How that organization began, and what causes gave it shape, are questions of extreme obscurity: and in the uncertainty of many of the data upon which the answers have to be based, some of the answers themselves must be more or less problematical. Nor is it easy to enter upon the consideration of these questions with an unbiassed judgment, because the fierce heats of the controversies which once raged round them have not even now sufficiently cooled down to enable the data to be dealt with, as we should deal with data that were wholly new, by the simple canons of either logical inference or literary criticism. Nor should I feel justified in approaching a subject which is in itself so complicated, and which before now has divided kingdoms, and overthrown dynasties, and sent theologians to the stake, if it were not for the strong conviction that the time has come at which the area of disputable points may be lessened by the discovery of new facts and the use of a more certain method of enquiry.

For we have seen the growth in our own day, and to no slight extent in our own community, of a method of treating historical questions which, if it does not abolish controversy, at least limits it. We have seen the growth of a method which deals with the facts of history by processes analogous to those which have been applied with surpassing success to the phenomena of the physical world, and which have there vindicated their accuracy as methods of research by proving to be methods of discovery. We have seen the growth, in short, of historical *science*. We have seen the growth, as the result of the pursuit and application of that science, of a habit of mind which stands in the same kind of relation to the facts of history as the habit of mind of a practised judge in relation to evidence in a court of law, and which estimates the several items not by some roughly generalized rule, but in the subtle balances of a matured experience. We have seen the growth, in short, not only of historical science, but also of the historical temper.

Hitherto that method and that temper have been applied almost exclusively, in this country at least, to the facts of civil history: but if we assume, as I propose to assume, that—at least for purposes of study—the facts of ecclesiastical history, being recorded in the same language, and in similar documents, and under the same general conditions of authorship, belong to the same category as the facts of civil history, it is not too much to maintain the existence of a presumption that the application of historical science and the historical temper to a field of historical phenomena which they have hitherto left comparatively unexplored, may be followed by new results.

I propose therefore, in dealing with the great questions which I have indicated, to deal with them by the help of modern methods. It is not necessary for me to vindicate those methods. On the comparatively neutral ground of civil history scholars are virtually agreed as to the kind of evidence for which they should look, and as to the manner in which they should deal with it. On the assumption which I have made that the phenomena are cognate the methods will presumably be cognate also.

But since every field of research has its special difficulties, and since this particular field has been often traversed, and since, moreover, the chief ground for challenging the verdict which more than one generation has passed upon the facts, is that the method of study has been imperfect, it seems appropriate, before we begin the detailed consideration of the subject, to consider what are the special difficulties which we must expect to encounter, and what have been the chief causes which have led to the existing divergences of opinion.

The first step in historical science is the testing of the documents which contain the evidence. In some fields of historical enquiry the difficulty of that step lies in the scantiness of the evidence: in the present enquiry, on the other hand, the difficulty arises from its extent. We find ourselves at the outset face to face with a mass of literature which has come to us in many forms and through many channels, under varying conditions of authentication, and with varying claims to attention. It is as impossible to accept each document for what it purports to be, as it would be impossible to accept *en bloc* the historical literature of England. There are forgeries and counter-forgeries: there are documents of great value which we can only put together from the chance quotations of an opponent: there are anonymous works which the enthusiasm of a later age has fastened upon some great name: there are books which were the growth of successive generations, and which the last reviser recast and unified, so that the separation of the new from the old is as difficult as it would be to rebuild an ancient tower from its chipped and battered stones after they have been worked into the structure of a modern wall. Upon this vast accumulation of centuries of busy thought and changing circumstance, of vigorous polemic and sometimes blind belief, literary criticism has barely begun its work. There are vast tracts of ecclesiastical literature which are like vast tracts of unexplored morass: because although patches of solid ground exist here and there, there is hardly a moment of our passage through them at which we may not find ourselves sinking in the mire. And yet there is scarcely a single item in the whole complex mass which we can afford to lose. A document which is proved to be spurious is not thereby proved to be valueless. That at which a historian has to look is not so much authorship as date. The Apostolical Constitutions, for example, are no more the work of the Apostles than is the Apostles' Creed, and yet they are the most valuable evidence that we possess of the internal life of the Eastern Churches from the third century to the fifth. The Isidorian Decretals are known to be mostly forgeries, and yet they throw a flood of light upon the state of the Church in the Frankish domain in the middle of the ninth century.

This *testing* of evidence is followed by the *weighing* of evidence: in other words, assuming that we have found out who the witnesses are, the next point is to estimate the value of what they say. And here we are encircled by a new class of difficulties. The internal evidence for the history of the organization of Christianity ranges itself into two classes—patristic literature and conciliar literature. For some periods, and in some cases, patristic literature is our only guide. The interest of that literature is so great as almost to fascinate us. Much of it was written by men whose saintly lives and spiritual insight seem to place them upon a higher level than that upon which we ordinarily move. We listen to them, as it were, with bated breath, and their words seem almost to fall from the lips of inspired evangelists. But for the purposes of constitutional history, and when investigating questions not of doctrine but of fact, we have to make a clear distinction between their value as theologians and their value as witnesses. We have to scan what they say with a close scrutiny. There is the initial and preliminary difficulty of finding out exactly what they mean. The science of patristic philology has hardly yet begun to exist. The words are for the most part familiar enough to a Greek or Latin student; but the meaning which attaches to those words is often very remote from that which seems to lie on the surface. And assuming that we understand their meaning, we have to make what scientific observers call the 'personal equation.' We have to realize to ourselves their personal character, their varying natures—passionate and impressionable, imaginative and mystical, cool-headed and practical. We have to place ourselves in the midst of the circumstances which surrounded them—their struggles for existence or for independence, the rush and storm of their controversies, the flatteries of their friends, and the calumnies of their opponents. We have to remember that they were all of them advocates, and many of them partizans. And even when, after subtracting from what they say that which belongs not to the witness but to the advocate or the partizan, we come upon a statement which cannot reasonably be questioned, we have to consider their nearness in time to the fact which they attest. In ecclesiastical as in civil history the lapse of a generation, though it does not invalidate testimony, compels us to distinguish carefully between what the witnesses know of their own knowledge and what they know only at second-hand. When they state what is clearly not of their own knowledge we have to consider what were their probable sources of information, or whether what they state is a conjecture.

But wherever it is possible, we have to base our inferences not upon the Fathers, but upon the Councils. Just as the historian of the constitution of our own country looks primarily to the Statute-book, so the historian of the constitution of the Church looks primarily to the decrees of Councils. But though in passing from patristic to conciliar literature, we pass to firmer ground, we by no means emerge from cloudland into light. We are confronted at the outset by a difficulty which has probably done more to produce erroneous views as to the history of ecclesiastical organization than all other causes put together. Comparatively early in the history of the Church the decrees of Councils were gathered together into collections. Almost every great group of Churches had its own collection of rules. About the beginning of the fifth century in the East, and about the end of the same century in the West, the provincial collections were merged into general codes. In these general codes the decrees of local as well as of oecumenical councils had a place. Side by side with the decrees of the great parliaments of Nicaea and Chalcedon were placed the resolutions of obscure provincial assemblies, which were essentially local and temporary, which had originally no validity outside the limits of their provinces, and which until exhumed by the care of the antiquary were unknown to the greater part of Christendom. In addition to this, almost all the collections were singularly imperfect. From at least the beginning of the fourth century provincial assemblies were held, often year by year, over a large part of the Christian world. A complete collection of the resolutions of such assemblies would have enabled us to frame a complete history of the organization of the several provinces. But when only one assembly in fifty has left a record, a factitious importance attaches to those which remain. The prevalence of the ideas or usages which they adopted tends to be greatly exaggerated. It is as though only a few fossils remained of a great geological epoch: valuable as such fossils would be, they would yet be misleading, because they would tend to be regarded as typical, whereas they might be only unimportant specimens of the fauna and flora of their time.

This difficulty of the heterogeneity and imperfection of the collections has been increased to an almost incalculable degree by the fact that these collections came in time to be regarded as a legal code, and to have the authority of legislative enactments. They constitute the nucleus of what is known as Canon Law. The various items of which they were composed were regarded as standing upon the same level. The distinctions of place and time which existed between those items was practically ignored. For having, as they had, the force of law, the duty of a canonist was not to investigate their origin, but to interpret their meaning. And consequently since Canon Law has had, and has still, an important and recognized place in European jurisprudence, there has been a tendency on the part of ecclesiastical historians to regard conciliar enactments as a canonist would regard them. Since the clauses of the code were of equal, or nearly equal, value as laws, they came to be regarded as being of equal, or nearly equal, value as facts: and hence it has come to pass that over the enormous varieties of constitution which have prevailed in different ages, and in different parts of Christendom, there has been spread the hypothesis of an ideal uniformity, which covers them as the whitewash covers frescoes of various ages and by various masters upon a cathedral wall.

But the virtue of a canonist is the vice of a historian. Historical science, like all science, is the making of distinctions; and its primary distinctions are those of time and space.

These distinctions are even more important in the subject which lies before us than they are in the secular history of either mediaeval or modern times, on account of the magnitude of the scale upon which Christianity has existed. For the history of Christianity covers more than three-fourths of the whole period of the recorded history of the Western world. It goes back year by year, decade by decade, century by century, for more than fifty generations. If we compare what we are and what we believe, the institutions under which we live, the literature which we prize, the ideas for which we contend, in this present year, with the beliefs, the institutions, the literature, the prevalent ideas, of a hundred years ago, we shall begin to realize the difference between one century and another of these eighteen centuries of Christian history. The special difficulty of studying any such period of history arises from the fact that the centuries which are remote from our own seem, in the long perspective, to be almost indistinguishable. It is as though we stood upon some commanding height in a country of mountains and valleys, and as we saw fold over fold of the purple hills recede farther and fainter into the distant haze, failed to realize that between each of those far faint lines were valleys filled with busy industries, or, it might be, breadths of pasture land, or, it might be, only the torrent-sounding depths of deep ravines. So the far centuries of Christian history recede until they are lost in the sun-lit haze of its dawn. Between the third century and the fourth, for example, or between the fourth and the fifth, there seems to all but the scholars who have trod the ground to be an hardly appreciable difference. If a writer quotes in the same breath Eusebius and Sozomen, or St. Hilary of Poitiers and St. Leo the Great, he seems to many persons to be quoting coeval or nearly coeval authorities. And yet in fact between each of these authorities there is an interval of a hundred years of life and movement, of great religious controversies, of important ecclesiastical changes. The point is not merely one of accuracy of date; it is rather that usages and events have at one time as compared with another a widely varying significance. For different centuries have been marked in ecclesiastical as in social history by great differences in the drift and tendency of ideas. Our many-sided human nature tends to develop itself by the exaggerated growth of one side at a time: and this tendency exhibits itself in great secular movements—such as were, for example, the great movement of the fourth century in the direction of monasticism, or the great movement of the sixteenth century in the direction of simplicity of worship. Now a usage or an event which is of great significance at one stage of such a movement may be of slight importance at another. In the constitutional history of our own country, for example, no one would fail to see the importance of noting whether the Toleration Act was passed in the reign of William and Mary, or in the reign of Elizabeth: and similarly, in the constitutional history of Christianity, until we are able to see the surroundings of any given fact we may wholly mistake its value.

Nor are these distinctions of time the only ones of which we have to take accurate note. We have also to recognize distinctions of place. In the constitutional history of our own country we at once recognize the importance of distinguishing between the local usages, for example, of Wales and those of the Scotch Lowlands; and we should at once reject as absurd any attempt to erect such usages into universal rules of the British constitution. But in the case of the Christian Church, the magnitude of the scale upon which it has existed makes the adequate recognition of the distinction vastly more important. The Church has been spread not only over eighteen centuries of time, but over the greater part of the civilized world,—over countries peopled by different races, with different institutions, varying widely in intellectual and moral force, in the arts of civilized life, and in the institutions of social order. Even in those early centuries with which alone I propose to deal it existed among a placid peasantry on the grey slopes of the Batanean hills, in villages which were always scattered, and which, as the great highways of Roman commerce closed, gradually decayed into a silent death. It existed in the thriving municipalities of Gaul, where rhetoric and philosophy flourished, where the civil law was studied and practised by skilled jurists, and where the elaborate framework of the municipal institutions of the Empire was strong enough to withstand the tempest of Teutonic invasion. It existed in the rude septs of Ireland, where Roman organization was practically unknown. It existed also in the busy commercial centres of Africa, where the competition of life was keen and the sense of individuality strong. It is obvious that we cannot ignore these distinctions, and regard a rule which was good for and valid in one country as having been equally good for and valid in another country. In other words, what is true of distinctions of time is true also of distinctions of place; we cannot determine the value of any item of evidence until we have localized it.

I have dwelt upon these distinctions at what may have seemed an unnecessary length because, as I ventured to indicate at the outset, no small part of the differences of opinion which have arisen respecting the course of Christian history may be traced to an inadequate appreciation of their importance. There is a kind of glamour attaching to ecclesiastical literature from the spell of which few of us are wholly emancipated. A quotation from an ancient Father, or from an early Council, is to many persons an end of all controversy. But it is a primary duty of the historian to go behind the quotation, to enquire into its precise meaning and its precise value, and to endeavour to fit it into its exact place in the vast mosaic of Christian history.

So far as we have yet gone, so far, that is to say, as in any particular case we have tested the evidence and estimated its value, and assigned it to its proper country and its proper time, we are in the position of a palaeontologist who, wishing to study certain fossils, ascertains—which is a comparatively easy task—that they are fossils and not forgeries, and then proceeds to ascertain the precise strata and the precise locality of each of them.

But just as neither a palaeontologist nor any one else who applies himself to the systematic study of any phenomena, is content with however precise a verification and localization of facts, but is led on by an inevitable bent of his nature to compare one group of facts with another, to find out the law of their sequence, and to reach at length, if he can, the common causes of all of them, so our work is only begun when we have ascertained what the facts are and what is the precise place of each of them in the strata of Christian history. We are impelled to proceed to enquire into probable causes of these phenomena. There may be those to whom the answer to any such enquiry seems easy and obvious. Just as in the early days of the physical science to which I have alluded, there were some pious persons who, not being yet ripe for that larger conception of creation which is gradually opening up to us, explained the appearance of fossils in this place or in that by an inscrutable fiat of the divine will, which had determined that fossils should be and fossils were: so it is possible that there may be persons still living to whom it is a sufficient explanation of the facts of Christian organization to say that God so willed them.

But most of us cannot be so easily satisfied, nor can we believe that enquiry is barred. In this, as in other fields which lie open to our view, we cannot resist, nor do we see any ground of either reason or revelation for attempting to resist, the enquiry into sequences and causes. We go on from the ascertainment of facts to the framing of inductions in reference to those facts.

Now there are two, and only two, ways in which any phenomena, which have existed through successive periods of time, can be legitimately viewed for the purposes of such inductions. They may be treated by comparison of the whole of the phenomena which coexist at any one time: and they may be treated by tracing each group through its successive periods of existence. The palaeontologist, for example, makes his inferences partly by putting together all that he can find about the fauna and flora of each stratum, and partly by tracing each type of animal or plant through successive strata, so as to arrive at a conclusion respecting the order and succession of life upon the earth.

It is so in the enquiry which lies before us.

In the first place, we have to view the facts in their relation to preceding and succeeding facts of the same kind; in other words, as constituting a series. We cannot, of course, assume at the outset that that series is progressive: but neither on the other hand can we assume that the links which compose it are of precisely the same kind throughout. The danger to which inferences of this kind are exposed arises more from the latter assumption than from the former. If we deal with an institution or an office which has wholly passed away—like the Athenian *βουλὴ* or the Roman praetorship—we endeavour to form an idea of the functions of that institution or of that office simply by putting together whatever we can find out from contemporary evidence. But if we are dealing with an institution which, under whatever modifications, has remained to the present day, we tend almost inevitably to carry back with us into past times those conceptions of it which we have derived from our modern experience. The tendency is assisted by a fact of language which cannot be too steadily borne in mind. By the slow and silent alchemy of time institutions change: but, while they change, the words which designate those institutions frequently remain permanent. We consequently tend to make the more or less unconscious assumption that the same word designated in past times what it designates now. Whereas what we have in fact to do with every name which we meet with in ancient records, is to treat it altogether independently of the accident that it has remained to our own times.

In other words, instead of reading the series of historical facts reversely, and interpreting each factor of the series as we go backwards by what we know of its modern use, we have to begin at the beginning, and find out by careful induction what the function of the institution or the office was at the earliest period at which we find it, and, as we trace it through succeeding centuries, add on step by step the new elements which attached themselves to it, until we reach, and so account for, the meaning which it bears now.

In the second place, we have to view the facts of ecclesiastical organization at any given time in their relation to all the other ascertainable facts of that time. To a certain extent that comparison is so inevitable that all writers on the subject of Christian organization have made it. It is inevitable for the reason that, with probably no single exception, the names of Christian institutions and Christian officers are shared by them in common with institutions and officers outside Christianity. It follows, from the mere conditions of the case, that those names were given by virtue of some resemblance in the Christian institutions and officers to institutions and officers which bore the same names already. These resemblances have always been admitted, and have to some extent long been investigated. But evidence which has not been thoroughly investigated until recent years, and evidence which has only within recent years come to light—especially in the unimpeachable form of inscriptions—has shown that the resemblances are not merely general but minute. The points of comparison which have been hitherto known have to be supplemented by a large number of other points, in which the close relation between Christian and non-Christian organizations has hitherto been hardly suspected. The importance of such a comparison lies in the fact that we cannot avoid going on to the further question, how far the similar phenomena are the product of the same causes. If we find in the Roman Empire civil societies with organizations analogous to those of the Christian societies, civil officers with the same names and similar functions to those of ecclesiastical officers, the question arises and must be answered, whether the causes which are sufficient to account for them in the one case are not equally sufficient to account for them in the other.

It has been contended, and it will no doubt continue to be contended, that the phenomena of ecclesiastical history are unique, and that an attempted comparison between them and the phenomena of civil history is vitiated at the outset by the fact that the resemblances are accidental and superficial, and that the two groups of phenomena are in reality incommensurable.

And no doubt those phenomena are so transcendent in their interest, and so stupendous in their importance, that few of us can fail to have a profound, if not an absorbing, sympathy with the sublime exaggeration which characterizes many descriptions of them. We, like the inspired dreamer of earlier days, can see the new City of God coming down bodily from the sky, invisible to the carnal sight, but to the eye of faith the only reality in a world of shadows. We can conceive, as ancient lovers of symbols often conceived, that no earthly mother gave birth to the spouse of Christ, but that, as Eve was taken from the side of the First Adam, so from the side of the Second Adam there sprang into instantaneous and immortal life the Virgin 'without spot or blemish' who should be His mystic Bride[1].

But when we descend from poetry to fact, from the dreams of inspired and saintly dreamers to the life of incident and circumstance which history records, and in which we ordinarily dwell, then, if the evidence shows, as I believe it to show, that not only did the elements of the Christian societies exist, but that also the forces which welded them together and gave them shape are adequately explained by existing forces of human society, the argument from analogy becomes so strong that, in the absence of positive proof to the contrary, it is impossible to resist the inference that in the divine economy which governs human life, as it governs the courses of the stars, by the fewest causes and the simplest means, the Christian societies, and the confederation of those societies which we commonly speak of in a single phrase as "the visible Church of Christ," were formed without any special interposition of that mysterious and extraordinary action of the divine volition, which, for want of a better term, we speak of as 'supernatural.' The inference is a presumption and not a demonstration. It is of the same kind as all inferences except those of the purely ideal sciences.

[1] e.g. Tertull. *De Anima*, 43: *Acta Petri et Pauli*, 29 ap. Tischendorf, *Acta Apostolorum Apocrypha*, p. 12. The symbolism probably accounts for the frequency with which the creation of Eve is represented in early Christian art.

But it is strong enough to throw the onus of proof not upon those who make, but upon those who deny it. For those who infer from a group of resembling facts a relation of identity in kind, have a presumption in their favour which is not enjoyed by those who infer from those facts a relation of difference.

There are some, no doubt, who will think that to account for the organization of the Church in this way is to detract from the nobility of its birth, or from the divinity of its life. There are some who can see a divinity in the thunder-peal, which they cannot see in the serenity of a summer noon, or in the growth of the flowers of spring. But I would ask those who think so to look for a moment at that other monument of divine power, and manifestation of divine life, which we bear about with us at every moment. Out of the dust of the earth, if we listen to the Hebrew poet who first sang the inspired song of Genesis; out of earlier types of organized beings, if we listen to those who tell us—or think that they tell us—the story of the earth from the records which the earth contains: but, in either view, from antecedent and lower forms, came into being these human bodies with their marvellous complexity of structure, with their almost boundless capacity of various effort, with their almost infinitely far-reaching faculty of observation. And so, it may be—nor is it a derogation from its grandeur to say that it *was*—out of antecedent and, if you will, lower forms, out of existing elements of human institutions, by the action of existing forces of human society, swayed as you will by the breathing of the Divine

Breath, controlled as you will by the Providence which holds in its hand the wayward wills of men no less than the courses of the stars, but still out of elements, and by the action of forces, analogous to those which have resulted in other institutions of society, and other forms of government, came into being that widest and strongest and most enduring of institutions which bears the sacred name of the Holy Catholic Church. The divinity which clings to it is the divinity of order. It takes its place in that infinite series of phenomena of which we ourselves are part. It is not outside the universe of Law, but within it. It is divine, as the solar system is divine, because both the one and the other are expressions and results of those vast laws of the divine economy by which the physical and the moral world alike move their movement and live their life.

It is by these methods, and with, as I believe, these general results, that I propose to consider the early organization of the visible Church of Christ.

I propose to begin at the beginning, and to take into consideration as we go on the conditions of the society in which the Christian communities grew as well as the facts of their growth.

But I do not propose to occupy your time by a preliminary discussion of the ecclesiastical polity of the New Testament, because I believe that that polity will be best understood by the light of subsequent history. At the time when the majority of the sacred books were written that polity was in a fluid state. It had not yet congealed into a fixed form. It seems, as far as can be gathered from the simple interpretation of the text, without the interpretation which history has given it, to have been capable of taking several other forms than that which, in the divine economy, ultimately established itself. It has the elements of an ecclesiastical monarchy in the position which is assigned to the Apostles. It has the elements of an ecclesiastical oligarchy in the fact that the rulers of the Church are almost always spoken of in the plural. It has the elements of an ecclesiastical democracy in the fact, among others, that the appeal which St. Paul makes to the Corinthians on a question of ecclesiastical discipline is made neither to bishops nor to presbyters, but to the community at large. It offers a sanction to episcopacy in the fact that bishops are expressly mentioned and their qualifications described: it offers a sanction to presbyterianism in the fact that the mention of bishops is excluded from all but one group of Epistles. It supports the proposition that the Church should have a government in the injunctions which it gives to obey those who rule. It supports on the other hand the claim of the Montanists of early days, and the Puritans of later days, in the preeminence which it assigns to spiritual gifts.

Which of these many elements, and what fusion of them, was destined in the divine order to prevail, must be determined, not by exegesis, but by history. That history will unfold itself before us in subsequent lectures. We shall see those to whom the Word of Life was preached gradually coalescing into societies. We shall see those societies organizing themselves as charitable associations in the midst of great poverty and depression[2]. We shall see them organizing themselves as disciplinary associations, held together by the force of a strong moral law, in the midst of social disorder and laxity[3]. We shall see them passing from a condition of oligarchy or democracy to that of virtual monarchy[4]. We shall see the individual communities ultimately confederated together into a world-wide association[5]. We shall see that world-wide association and its separate components recognized by the State, and trace the effect upon it of the close neighbourhood and the supporting arm of the civil power[6]. We shall see its officers gradually formed into a class standing apart from the mass of the Christian community, invested with attributes of special sanctity, and living, or supposed to live, by a higher rule of life than that of those to whom they ministered[7]. We shall see the heads of the separate organizations exercising jurisdiction outside their proper communities over adjacent and outlying communities, so as to establish a relation of subordination between the latter and the former[8]. We shall pause at length upon the threshold of that period, alike of glory and of shame, when this grand confederation of Christian societies, arrogating to itself the name of that Catholic Church the belief in which is part of all Christian creeds, became the greatest corporation upon earth, stronger than the Roman Empire itself in its moral influence upon civilized society and hardly inferior to it in political power, sitting like

[2] Lecture II. [3] Lecture III. [4] Lecture IV. [5] Lecture VII.
[6] Lecture VI. [7] Lectures V and VI. [8] Lecture VIII.

a queen upon her throne, with her feet upon the necks of kings, and using the majesty of her sublime consolations, and the prestige of her long traditions, and the wealth of her splendid charities, to enslave rather than to free the world.

But upon a subject on which misconception is so easy and so prevalent, it seems necessary to add one word more, and to draw your attention explicitly and once for all to that which I have implied throughout, that the subject which lies before us is not the Christian faith, but the organization of the Christian Churches. In whatever I may have to say about the latter, I do not propose to touch the former. With doctrine, and with the beliefs which underlie doctrine, we shall have in these lectures no direct concern. Out of the tangled mass of truths and tendencies, of institutions and practices, which make up what we sometimes speak of collectively as Christianity, I shall endeavour to extricate a single thread, and to deal with it as far as possible in isolation. It is true that, except in the purely ideal sciences of metaphysics and geometry, the perfect isolation of any subject is impossible. It is true that there are many points at which the history of organization links itself almost inextricably with the history of doctrine. But I will ask those who listen to me to put upon themselves the same intellectual self-restraint which I endeavour to put upon myself, and to keep a fixed attention upon the immediate point in hand, apart from its innumerable side-issues and its far-reaching relations.

No doubt for all our self-restraint there will loom out before us continually as we go on the majestic vision of that stupendous work which these organizations have effected, and are effecting, in the midst of human society. We shall be like a student who makes it his temporary task to explore some great historic cathedral with a view only to its architecture. At every step he treads on hallowed ground. On every side are the memorials of saintly lives, and heroic deeds, and immortal genius. From their silent tombs there seem to rise up the shadows of the holy dead, gazing at him with their beatified faces, and stretching out hands of ghostly fellowship. He is tempted at every moment to throw aside his study, and to yield to the fascination of the place, and to gain some new hope for his own sad life from the weird and whispered tale of what they did and suffered for Christ and for the world. But his present concern is with the architecture, and the soft and solemn voices that bid him linger in sympathy or in dream fall upon deafened ears.

And so, in the lectures that will follow, it will not be in forgetfulness, but only because their limits are too brief for even the single subject which they propose to compass, that we shall turn our eyes from the saintly souls of these early centuries, and from the sublime truths they taught, to consider only the framework of that vast society to which they and we alike belong,—that society into which for eighteen centuries have been gathered the holiest and the noblest of our race,—that society which links together the ages by the mystic tie of spiritual communion,—that society which, though to some men it has seemed a crushing despotism, has been to you and me and the world at large a beneficence and a salvation.

LECTURE II.

BISHOPS AND DEACONS.

AMONG the many parallels which can be drawn between the first centuries of the Christian era and our own times, there is probably none more striking than that of their common tendency towards the formation of associations. There were then, as now, associations for almost innumerable purposes in almost all parts of the Empire. There were trade guilds and dramatic guilds; there were athletic clubs, and burial clubs, and dining clubs; there were friendly societies, and literary societies, and financial societies: if we omit those special products of our own time, natural science and social science, there was scarcely an object for which men combine now for which they did not combine then[1].

[1] Associations occupy a much larger place in epigraphical monuments than in literary history: of the kinds mentioned above, i. trade-guilds are found among almost every kind of workmen and in almost every town of the Empire of which inscriptions remain; e.g. among the raftsmen at Geneva (Mommsen, *Inscriptiones Confoederationis Helveticae*, No. 75), among the wool-carders of Ephesus (Wood, *Discoveries at Ephesus*, Append. viii. No. 4), among the litter-bearers of a remote colony in Wallachia (*Corpus Inscr. Lat.* vol. iii. No. 1438), and among the shoemakers of a market-town in Spain (*ibid.* vol. ii. No. 2818): ii. dramatic guilds, in

There was more than one attempt at repression. The State feared lest the honeycombing of the Empire by organizations which in their nature were private, and so tended to be secret, might be a source of political danger: but the drift of the great currents of society towards association was too strong for even the Empire to resist [2].

The most important among them were the *religious* associations. Almost all associations seem to have had a religious element: they were under the protection of

e.g. Le Bas et Waddington, *Inscriptions Grecques et Latines*, vol. iii. Nos. 1336, 1619 (cf. Foucart, *De Collegiis scenicorum artificum apud Graecos*, Paris, 1873; Lüders, *Die dionysischen Künstler*, Berlin, 1873): iii. athletic clubs, in e.g. *Corpus Inscr. Graec.* Nos. 349, 5804, Wilmanns, No. 2202 (cf. Herzog, *Gallia Narbonensis*, p. 247): iv. burial clubs, in e.g. Orelli-Henzen, No. 6086 = Wilmanns, No. 319 (cf. Boissier, *Etudes sur quelques colleges funeraires romains* in the *Revue Archéologique*, 1872, vol. xxiii, p. 82; De Rossi, *I collegii funeraticii famigliari e loro denominazioni* in the *Commentationes philologicae in honorem Th. Mommsenii*, p. 705): v. dining clubs, in e.g. Orelli, No. 4073; Tertullian, *Apol.* 39: vi. friendly societies, in e.g. Le Bas et Waddington, vol. iii. No. 1687; Plin. *Epist.* 10. 94; Renier, *Inscriptions d'Algerie*, No. 60, 70 = Wilmanns, *Exempla Inscr. Lat.*, Nos. 1481, 1482: vii. literary societies, in e.g. Orelli, No. 4069 = Wilmanns, No. 2112: viii. financial societies, in e.g. Wilmanns, No. 2181 (cp. the well-known 'societates publicanorum'), the 'Ambubaiarum collegia' of Hor. *Serm.* I. 2. 1, and the 'latronis collegium' of Apul. *Metam.* 7. 137 may be caricatures: but the extent of the tendency is shown by the fact that sometimes the slaves on an estate (*Corpus Inscr. Lat.* vol. vi. No. 404), or even in a household (Orelli, No. 2414), formed an association.

[2] The repression began under the Republic, Cic. *in Pison.* 4 (cf. Asconius *ad loc.* ap. *M. T. Cic. Schol.* ed. Orelli, p. 7); Jos. *Ant.* 14. 10. 8; Suet. *Caes.* 42, and was continued by Augustus, Suet. *Octav.* 32, and others, e.g. by Trajan, Plin. *Epist.* 10. 34 (43). The allegation that they tended to become political clubs is supported by the inscriptions on the walls of Pompeii, *Corpus Inscr. Lat.* vol. iv. Nos. 202, 710, 787. For the question of the precise amount of legality which they had under the Empire, see Huschke in the *Zeitschrift f. geschicht. Rechtswissenschaft*, Bd. xii, pp. 207, sqq.; Mommsen, *ibid.* Bd. xv, p. 353 sqq.; Walter, *Geschichte des römischen Rechts*, 3te Aufl. § 348, and especially Cohn, *Zum römischen Vereinsrecht*, Berlin 1873. Alexander Severus seems to have been the first Emperor who saw in them a conservative rather than a revolutionary force, and encouraged instead of repressing them, Lamprid. *Alex. Sev.* c. 33.

a tutelary divinity, in the same way as at the present day similar associations on the continent of Europe invoke the name of a patron saint[3]: and their meetings were sometimes called by a name which was afterwards consecrated to Christian uses—that of a 'sacred synod[4].' But in a considerable proportion of them religion was, beyond this, the basis and bond of union. Inside the religion of the State, and tolerated by it, were many forms of religion and many modes of worship. Then, as now, many men had two religions, that which they professed and that which they believed: for the former there were temples and State officials and public sacrifices; for the latter there were associations: and in these associations, as is shown from extant inscriptions, divinities whom the State ignored had their priests, their chapels, and their ritual[5].

[3] Of the Latin associations some were under the protection of one or more of the greater gods: e.g. most of the trades-unions at Rome claimed the patronage of Minerva, Ovid, *Fast.* iii. 819-832, the physicians of Turin that of Aesculapius and Hygia, *Corpus Inscr, Lat.* vol. v. No. 6970: others had a 'genius' of their own, e.g. *ibid.* vol. iii. 1424, vol. v. No. 7595. Some associations, in even closer correspondence with modern confraternities, had their banners for fête-days and processions, 'Vexilla collegiorum,' Vopisc. *Aurel.* 36; *Gallien.* 3; Eumen. in *Grat. Act.* 8: and the lodge-room or guild-hall, *schola,* of almost all associations seems to have had a chapel, *templum,* or at least an altar, *ara,* e.g. *Corp. Inscr. Lat.* vol. iii. No. 633, vol. v. No. 7906: the fact is the more noteworthy because De Rossi (*Bulletino di Arch. Christ.* 1864, ann. ii. p. 60, *Roma Sotteranea*, vol. iii. p. 475), maintains that some of the primitive churches were *scholae.* For the Greek associations see e.g. Schömann, *Griech. Alterthumer*, Bd. i. 3te Aufl. pp. 541-6, who rightly says that the religious element was invariable.

[4] The expression ἱερὰ σύνοδος for an association, or its meeting, is found, e.g. in Le Bas et Waddington, vol. iii. No. 1336, 1619; *Corpus Inscr. Graec.* No. 4315 n.

[5] The data for the above statements will be found, for the Greek religious associations in the inscriptions collected by Foucart, *Des Associations religieuses chez les Grecs*, Paris, 1873: for the Latin associations in Wilmanns, *Exempla Inscriptionum Latinarum* (see the Index in vol. ii. pp. 631 sqq.). Other inscriptions, and further details, will be found in Mommsen, *De Collegiis et Sodaliciis Romanorum*, Kiel, 1843; Wescher, *Revue Archéologique*, vol. x, 1864, p. 160, vol.

When the truths of Christianity were first preached, especially in the larger towns of the Roman Empire, the aggregation of those who accepted those truths into societies was thus not an isolated phenomenon. Such an aggregation does not appear to have invariably followed belief. There were many who stood apart: and there were many reasons for their doing so. The rule of Christian life was severe. It involved a sharp separation from the common pursuits of ordinary society; it sometimes involved also a snapping asunder of the ties of family and home. A man might wish to be Christ's disciple, and yet shrink from 'hating father and mother, and wife and children, and brethren and sisters, yea and his own life also.' We consequently find that the union of believers in associations had to be preached, if not as an article of the Christian faith, at least as an element of Christian practice. The Epistle to the Hebrews urges this especially on the ground that the 'day' was approaching[6]. The Epistle of St. Jude condemns those 'who separate themselves,' and charges them with walking 'after their own ungodly lusts[7].' The Shepherd of Hermas speaks of those who were sound in the faith and yet 'lived with the Gentiles and did not cleave to the saints[8].' The Epistle of Barnabas exhorts Christians not to withdraw themselves and live lives apart, but to meet together and

xii, 1865, p. 214, vol. xiii, 1866, p. 245; Boissieu, *Inscriptions antiques de Lyon*, pp. 373 sqq.; Boissier, *La Religion Romaine*, vol. ii. pp. 267 sqq.; Duruy, *Histoire des Romains*, vol. v. pp. 149 sqq.; Marquardt, *Römische Staatsverwaltung*, Bd. iii. pp. 76, 131 sqq.

[6] Heb. x. 25.

[7] St. Jude 19.

[8] Herm. *Sim.* 9. 26. 3: so in effect 8. 8. 1; 8. 9. 1; 9. 20. 2; *Vis.* 3. 6. 2.

consult about common interests[9]. The Epistles of Ignatius make the exhortation to association especially prominent. The chief purpose of those much controverted, and most valuable, monuments of early Christianity seems to be not, as has sometimes been supposed, to exalt the episcopate at the expense of the presbyterate, but, accepting the episcopate as an established institution in the Asiatic Churches, to urge those who called themselves Christians to become, or to continue to be, or to be more zealously than before, members of the associations of which the bishops were the head[10]. After the sub-apostolic age these exhortations cease. The tendency to association had become a fixed habit. The Christian communities multiplied, and persecution forged for them a stronger bond of unity. But to the eye of the outside observer they were in the same category as the associations which already existed. They had the same names for their meetings, and some of the same names for their officers[11]. The basis of association, in the one case as the other, was the profession of a com-

[9] Barn. 4. 10.

[10] It is clear from the letters to the communities at Ephesus (c. 5, 3), at Magnesia (cc. 4. 7, 1), at Tralles (cc. 2. 7), at Philadelphia (cc. 3. 7), and at Smyrna (c. 7, 2), that there were Christians in those cities who did not come to the general assembly or recognize the authority of the bishop, presbyters, and deacons: it is also clear from *Ephes.* 20. 2, *Philad.* 4, *Smyrn.* 7. 2, that this separation from the assembly and its officers went to the extent of having separate eucharists: it is consequently clear that attachment to the organization of which the bishop was the head was not yet universally recognized as a primary duty of the Christian life.

[11] *ἐκκλησία* is used of the meeting of an association in e.g. Le Bas et Waddington, vol. viii. No. 1381, 1382; Le Bas, vol. iv. No. 1915 = *Corp. Inscr. Graec.* No. 2271: so *συναγώγη*, *Corp. Inscr. Graec.* No. 2448, 3069; Wescher, *Revue Archéologique*, 1865, vol. xii. p. 216: so *σύνοδος*, *Corpus. Inscr. Graec.* Nos. 126, 3067, 3069; Le Bas et Waddington, Nos. 1143, 1336, 1619: so *τὸ κοινόν*, which is in ordinary use for the general body of an association, is used, e.g. in Euseb. *H. E.* 6. 19. 16; 7. 32. 27, for the general body of a church.

mon religion. The members, in the one case as in the other, contributed to or received from a common fund[12], and in many cases, if not universally, shared in a common meal[13]. Admission was open, in the one case as in the other, not only to free-born citizens, but to women and strangers, to freedmen and slaves[14]. Consequently when a Roman governor found the Christian communities existing in his province he brought them under the general law which was applicable to such associations[15]; and the Greek satirist of the second century

[12] The contribution to a common fund was of the essence of a Greek ἔρανος (cf. Harpocrat. s. v. ἐρανιστής): it was payable every month, and was strictly exacted (*Corpus Inscr. Attic.* vol. ii. Nos. 610, 630; cf. Foucart, pp. 42, 599). In the Roman 'collegia tenuiorum' monthly contributions were also of the essence ('stipem menstruam conferre,' *Digest.* xlvii. 22. 1; cf. Mommsen, *De Collegiis*, p. 87; Marquardt, *Röm. Staatsverw.* Bd. iii. 139). The fund so formed was the common property of the association, and a member who left under compulsion could claim his share (*Digest. ibid.*). The funds of both Greek and Roman associations were frequently increased by benefactions.

[13] The institution of a common meal seems also to have been general: in the Greek associations it is implied in the constant provision for a sacrifice at the stated meetings: in the Latin associations regulations respecting it are given at length in the extant bylaws (which are printed, e.g. Orelli-Henzen, Nos. 4947, 6086; Wilmanns, Nos. 318, 319). Philo says that at Alexandria the associations, under the pretext of religion, were merely convivial meetings (in *Flaccum*, ii. pp. 518, 537): and Varro complains that college-dinners sent up the prices of provisions at Rome (*De Re Rustica*, iii. 2–16). Josephus, *Ant.* 14. 10. 8, describes the exemption of the Jewish communities at Rome from the general suppression of unauthorized societies by Julius Caesar, by saying μόνους τούτους οὐκ ἐκώλυσεν οὔτε χρήματα εἰσφέρειν οὔτε σύνδειπνα ποιεῖν.

[14] The evidence for the admission of these classes into the Greek associations is collected by Foucart, pp. 6 sqq. For the Latin associations the proofs are, e.g. i. that in the *album* of a college of the *Cultores Silvani* at Philippi, almost all the names are those of freedmen or slaves (*Corpus Inscr. Lat.* vol. iii. No. 633): ii. the dictum of the jurist Marcian 'servos quoque licet in collegio tenuiorum recipi volentibus dominis' (*Digest.* xlvii. 22. 3, § 2). On one other important point the evidence is too scanty to enable a general statement to be made: but in one of the few extant codes of bylaws, the association requires its officers to test a candidate for admission as to whether he is 'chaste, and pious, and good' (*Corp. Inscr. Graec.* No. 126 = Foucart, No. 20, who reads ἁγνὸς for ἅγιος).

[15] Plin. *Epist.* 10. 96 (97). 7.

invented for their bishop that which would have been an appropriate title for their head [16].

What then, if we look at these Christian communities simply on their human side as organizations in the midst of human society, was their point of peculiarity and difference?

Before I attempt to answer this question I will ask you to consider briefly the circumstances of the society in which those communities existed.

The economical condition of the Roman Empire during the early centuries of the Christian era was for the most part one of intense strain [17]. The great political disruptions which preceded the creation of the Empire, and the great political dissensions which accompanied its consolidation, left their inevitable result in a disturbance, which proved to be permanent, of the social equilibrium. Hardly any of the elements of an unsound state of society were absent. Large tracts of

[16] Lucian, *De Morte Peregrini*, 11, referring expressly to Christians, though perhaps, not expressly to either Ignatius or Polycarp (cf. Keim, *Celsus*, p. 145; Zahn, *Ignatius von Antiochien*, p. 517), speaks of the head of the community as *θιασάρχης καὶ ξυναγωγεύς* (the former of these words is a substitute, which does not occur elsewhere, for *ἀρχιθιασίτης*, *Corpus Inscr. Graec.* No. 2271, standing to it in the relation of *tricliniarchus*, Petron. *Satyr.* 22, to *ἀρχιτρίκλινος* S. John 2. 8: it implies that the Christian communities, like those of the Jews at Rome, Jos. *Ant.* 14. 10. 8, and of the Essenes, Philo, ii. 458 ed. Mang, were regarded as *θίασοι*).

[17] The evidence as to the internal state of the Roman Empire during the second and third centuries has not hitherto been collected, and is too extensive to be compressed into a note: some of it, and sufficient to corroborate the statements made above, will be found in Herzberg, *Die Geschichte Griechenland unter der Herrschaft der Römer*, Bd. ii. 189–210; Finlay, *History of Greece*, ed. Tozer, vol. i. chap. 1; Mommsen, *Ueber den Verfall des römischen Münzwesens in der Kaiserzeit*, in the *Berichte der königl. sächsischen Gesellsch. der Wissenschaft, phil-hist. Classe*, 1850, Bd. ii., esp. pp. 229, sqq.; Burckhardt, *Die Zeit Constantins des Grossen*, Abschn. iii, v, vii; Duruy, *Histoire des Romains*, vol. vi. pp. 284–317.

country had gone out of cultivation. The capital which should have rendered them productive was employed to a great extent not in agriculture but in luxury. The absentee landlords of the great estates wasted their substance in the encouragement of a debased Art, in demoralizing largesses, and in the vanishing parade of official rank. The smaller landowners were crushed by the weight of an unequal and oppressive taxation. Wealth tended to accumulate in fewer hands, and the lines which separated the poor from the rich became more and more sharply defined, until the old distinction between citizen and foreigner, or citizen and freedman, was merged in a new distinction between the better classes and the lower classes [18]. The municipalities vied with one another in the erection of the massive buildings whose ruins survive not only to tell the traveller or the historian of a departed greatness, but also to point the moral of the economist as to the results of wasteful expenditure. In order to pay for them they sometimes ran heavily into debt: sometimes they endeavoured to make the future pay for the present by borrowing at usurious interest: sometimes they debased the coinage. So great was the mischief that the emperors were often obliged to send commissioners with extraordinary powers to rearrange municipal finances, and that at last they asserted the right of veto upon projected public works, and took the coinage into their own hands [19].

[18] On this distinction see Duruy, *Memoires de l'Academie d'Inscriptions*, Tom. xxix. pp. 253, sqq. (reprinted as an appendix to vol. v. of his *Histoire des Romains*).

[19] For the *curatores* or λογισταὶ see Marquardt, *Röm. Staatsverw.* Bd. i. 358, 487: for the veto on public works see Macer in the *Digest.* L. 10. 3, § 1, and

But this action on the part of the emperors was palliative and not remedial. It may have postponed, but it did not avert, the final decay. In the meantime, in the age which preceded the final decay, the pressure of poverty was severely felt. There was not that kind of distress which is caused by a great famine or a great pestilence: but there was that terrible tension of the fibres of the social organism which many of us can see in our own society. It was the crisis of the economical history of the Western world. There grew and multiplied a new class in Graeco-Roman society—the class of paupers. And out of the growth of a new class was developed a new virtue—the virtue of active philanthropy, the tendency to help the poor. Large sums were bequeathed to be expended in annual doles of food. The emperor Trajan had established in Italy a great system for the maintenance and education of children [20]. Rich men and municipalities and succeeding emperors followed his example. The instinct of benevolence was fairly roused [21]. And yet to the mass of men

Ulpian, ibid. I. 16. 7 § 1: for the abolition of the local mints, see Mommsen, *Geschichte des röm. Münzwesens*, pp. 728, 831.

[20] The institution of 'alimenta,' which was begun by Nerva (Aurel. Vict. *Epit.* 12), was extended and organized by Trajan. The bronze tablets containing the regulations, and a list of the investments, for two districts of Italy, which were discovered near Piacenza in 1747, and near Benevento in 1831, have been printed, e.g. by Mommsen, *Inscr. Regn. Neap.* No. 1354; Wilmanns, No. 2844, 2845; Haenel, *Corpus Legum*, pp. 69-70. (cf. Desjardins, *De Tabulis alimentariis*, Paris, 1854; Henzen *Tabula alimentaria Baebianorum*, Rome, 1845; Borghesi, *Oeuvres*, vol. iv. 119, 269). The extent to which the example of the Emperors was followed by private persons is shown, not only by numerous extant inscriptions, but also by the fact that Severus and Caracalla discontinued the exemption of such endowments from the operations of the *Lex Falcidia*, and required them to be administered by the provincial governor (Marcian in *Digest.* Lib. xxxv. 2. 89).

[21] Cf. *Corpus Inscr. Graec.* No. 3545, for the almost Christian sentiment ἐν βίῳ καλὸν ἔργον ἓν μόνον εὐποιΐα.

life was hardly worth living. It tended to become a despair.

Such was the state of society when those who accepted Christian teaching began to be drawn together into communities. They were so drawn together in the first instance, no doubt, by the force of a great spiritual emotion, the sense of sin, the belief in a Redeemer, the hope of the life to come. But when drawn together they 'had all things common.' The world and all that was in it were destined soon to pass away. 'The Lord was at hand.' In the meantime they were 'members one of another.' The duty of those who had 'this world's goods' to help those who were in need was primary, absolute, incontrovertible. The teaching of our Lord Himself had been a teaching of entire self-sacrifice. 'Sell that thou hast and give to the poor, and thou shalt have treasure in heaven [22].' And the teaching of the earliest Christian homily which has come down to us elevates almsgiving to the chief place in Christian practice: 'Fasting is better than prayer, almsgiving is better than fasting: blessed is the man who is found perfect therein, for almsgiving lightens the weight of sin [23].'

It was in this point that the Christian communities were unlike the other associations which surrounded them. Other associations were charitable: but whereas

[22] S. Matt. 19. 21.

[23] 2 Clem. Rom. 16, apparently following Tobit xii. 8, 9. Similar sentiments are not infrequent in patristic literature: e.g. Lactant. *Inst.* 6. 12, 'magna est misericordiae merces cui Deus pollicetur peccata se omnia remissurum'; S. Chrys. *Hom.* 6 *in Tit.* c. 3, Opp. ed. Migne xi. 698, *αὕτη φάρμακόν ἐστι τῶν ἡμετέρων ἁμαρτιῶν.* Const. Apost. 7. 12, *ἐὰν ἔχῃς διὰ τῶν χειρῶν σου δὸς ἵνα ἐργάσῃ εἰς λύτρωσιν ἁμαρτιῶν σου· ἐλεημοσύναις γὰρ καὶ πίστεσιν ἀποκαθαίρονται ἁμαρτίαι.*

in them charity was an accident, in the Christian associations it was of the essence [24]. They gave to the religious revival which almost always accompanies a period of social strain the special direction of philanthropy. They brought into the European world that regard for the poor which had been for several centuries the burden of Jewish hymns. They fused the Ebionism of Palestine with the practical organization of Graeco-Roman civilization.

I have dwelt at length upon the circumstances under which the early Christian communities grew, because those circumstances seem to account for, and to explain, that which it is our more immediate task to examine—the form which the organization of those communities took, and the titles which their officers bore.

It is clear from the nature of the case that in communities which grew up under such circumstances, and in which the eleemosynary element was so prominent, the officers of administration and finance must have had an important place.

If we turn to the contemporary non-Christian associations of Asia Minor and Syria—to the nearest neighbours, that is to say, of the Christian organizations—we find that the officers of administration and finance were chiefly known by one or other of two names, not far distant from one another in either form or meaning. The one of these was ἐπιμελητής—which has this additional interest, that it was the designation of the

[24] Cf. St. Chrys. *Hom.* '32 *in Hebr. c. xii.* Opp. ed. Migne, vol. xii. 224 οὐδὲν οὕτω χαρακτηριστικὸν Χριστιανοῦ ὡς ἐλεημοσύνη.

chief officers of the Essenes[25]: the other was the name which became so strongly impressed on the officers of the Christian societies as to have held its place until modern times, and which in almost all countries of both East and West has preserved its form through all the vicissitudes of its meaning—the Greek *ἐπίσκοπος*, the English *bishop*[26]. There is this further point to be noted in reference to these names, that they were used not only in private associations, but also in municipalities[27]: and that they were there applied not only to permanent or quasi-permanent officers, but also to the governing body, or a committee of the governing body, when

[25] Ἐπιμελητής, which has undoubtedly a large contemporary use in the general sense of 'commissioner' or 'superintendent,' is used specially of the administrative officers of a religious association; in e.g. *Corpus Inscr. Graec.* No. 119, 120 (= Hicks, *Greek Inscriptions in the British Museum,* Part i. No. 21), 3438, 5892: and of the officers of the Essenes, Josephus, *B. J.* 2. 8. 5, 6. It is also used of the officer of a temple, Le Bas et Waddington, Nos. 4596*a*, 5892 (of the temple of the colony of Gazaeans at Portus Trajani): and of the financial officer of the mysteries at Andania in Messenia, Le Bas, *Voyage Archéologique,* vol. ii. ed. Foucart, No. 326 *a*.

[26] *Ἐπίσκοπος* is used of the financial officer of an association in the Theran inscription published by Wescher, *Revue Archéologique,* 1866, vol. 13, p. 246 *ἀ[ποδε]ξαμένος τὰν ἐπαγγελίαν τὸ μ[ὲν ἀρ]γύριον ἐγδανεῖσαι τὸς ἐπισκό[πος] Δίωνα καὶ Μελέϊππον.* 'It is resolved that the *ἐπίσκοποι* Dion and Meleippus shall accept the offer and invest the money.' It is used of the financial officers of a temple in several inscriptions which have been found in the Haurán, e.g. in that which was first printed by Mr. Porter in the *Transactions of the Royal Society of Literature,* 2nd Ser. vol. v. p. 248, and afterwards by Wetzstein in the *Abhandlungen der Berlin. Akademie,* 1863, No. 47, and Le Bas et Waddington, No. 1990 (the inscription belongs to Christian times, but its Pagan character is shown by the preliminary formula Ἀγαθῇ Τύχῃ).

[27] Ἐπιμελητὴς is used of a municipal officer, e.g. at Sparta (in the time of Hadrian), *Corpus Inscr. Graec.* No. 1241, at Amyclae, *ibid.* No. 1338, at Coronea, No. 1258: *ἐπίσκοπος* at Erythrae, *ibid.* No. 73; Kirchhoff, *Corpus Inscr. Att.* vol. i. No. 10. The former was the title of the special officer who was sent by the Spartans to subject states, the latter that of the officer so sent by the Athenians: cf. Boeckh, *C. I. G.*, vol. i. p. 611 b.; Hicks, *Greek Inscriptions in the British Museum,* Part i. No. 3.

entrusted with the administration of funds for any special purpose. The βουλευταὶ of a city or a division, or a committee of them, were for the time being, in relation to such administration, ἐπιμεληταὶ or ἐπίσκοποι[28].

Now in the Christian communities there appears to have been from very early times a body of officers: it must be inferred from the identity of the names which were employed that those officers were in relation to the Christian communities what the senate was in relation to a municipality, and what the committee was in reference to an association. They were known collectively by a name which is common in both relations—that of *ordo*[29]: they were known individually as well as collectively by a name which was common to the members of the Jewish συνέδρια and to the members of the Greek γερούσιαι of Asia Minor—that of πρεσβύτεροι[30]: they were also known—for I shall here assume what the weight of evidence has rendered practically indisputable—by the name ἐπίσκοποι[31]. In

[28] E.g. Le Bas et Waddington, No. 2309, 2310, at Soada in Batanea ἐπισκοπούντων βουλευτῶν φυλῆς Βιταιηνῶν 'the councillors of the tribe of the Bitaeeni acting as ἐπίσκοποι': *ibid.* No. 2412 *e*=Wetzstein, No. 184, at Kanata in the Haurân, ἐπισκοποῦντος βουλευτοῦ 'the councillor acting as ἐπίσκοπος': similarly *ibid.* No. 2072 at Philippopolis in Batanea ἐπιμελουμένων . . . βουλευτῶν, 'the councillors acting as ἐπιμεληταί.' (A third word of equivalent meaning is sometimes found, προνοητής, e.g. *ibid.* No. 2413 *c*=Wetzstein, No. 177, at Agraba in the Haurân: *ibid.* No. 1984 *d*=Wetzstein No. 53, at Ayoun.)

[29] *Ordo* is of frequent occurrence in inscriptions: (1) for a municipal senate, e.g. Mommsen, *Inscr. Regn. Neap.* No. 1115; *Corpus Inscr. Lat.* vol. ii. No. 1956: (2) for the committee of an association, e.g. Orelli, No. 2417, 4104=Wilmanns, Nos. 320, 1743. In relation to the Christian communities it is sometimes used by itself in contrast, as in the Latin *collegia,* with *plebs,* i.e. the mass of ordinary members, Tertull. *De Exhort. Castit.* c. 7, sometimes with a defining epithet '*ordo ecclesiasticus,*' *id. De Monog.* c. 11.

[30] See below, Lecture III, Note 25.

[31] For a clear summary of the evidence on this point see Bishop Lightfoot,

their general capacity as a governing body they were known by names which were in current use for a governing body: in their special capacity as administrators of Church funds they were known by a name which was in current use for such administrators.

I propose in a future lecture to enter into the question of the causes which led to that great change in Christian organization by which the functions of this original plurality of probably coordinate officers came practically to pass into the hands of a single officer. I propose now to suggest reasons for the fact that this single officer came in time to monopolize the name which had hitherto been shared by the members of the governing body in common, and which had reference to financial and administrative functions rather than to his position as president: in other words, to answer the question, why was the single head of the Christian communities called, at first commonly and at last exclusively, by the name *bishop*?

The key to the answer to this question seems to be furnished by the fact, which we learn first from Justin Martyr, that the offerings of Christians were made, not privately but publicly, and not directly to those who had need, but to the presiding officer in the general assembly [32]. The presiding officer who received

St. Paul's Epistle to the Philippians, ed. 3, pp. 93 sqq., and Gebhardt and Harnach's note to 1 Clem. Rom. i. 3, in their *Patrum Apostolicorum Opera*, ed. alt. fasc. 1. p. 5. The admissions of both mediaeval and modern writers of almost all schools of theological opinion have practically removed this from this list of disputed questions.

[32] The offerings were of two kinds, but both were made to the presiding officer, and both solemnly dedicated. 1. The offerings which were made by those who

them solemnly dedicated them to God, and uttered over them, in the name of the assembly, words of thanksgiving and benediction. Part of them were at once distributed among those who were present, part of them were reserved for distribution afterwards, whether to the Church officers or to the poor. In a significant and graphic phrase some of the sub-apostolic writers call the widows and orphans and poor of the Christian communities a θυσιαστήριον—an altar of sacrifice[33]. They were in the new economy what the great altar of the Temple Court had been in the older economy. Just as the new Temple of God was the temple of the regenerate soul, so the new altar of God was the altar of human need. That

were present at the eucharistic service, some of which were consumed at the time, others carried home, others taken to those who were absent, and others sent in token of goodwill to foreign churches (S. Justin M. *Apol.* 1. 65. 67; S. Iren. ap. Euseb. *H. E.* 5. 24. 17, cf. Vales. *ad loc.*; Tertull. *Apol.* 30, *ad Uxor.* 2. 5, *de Orat.* 19; S. Cyprian, *De Lapsis*, 26, p. 256; Conc. Laod. c. 14). At first these offerings seem to have been of various kinds: but afterwards a rule was made limiting them to bread and wine, or corn and grapes (*Can. Apost.* 3): and, still later, those which were not consumed at the time were divided in fixed proportions among the clergy (*Const. Apost.* 8. 30). The practice of making them personally to the president or bishop lingered longer in the West than in the East as is shown by the earliest form of the *Ordo Romanus* (printed in Hittorp, *De divinis Catholicae Ecclesiae Officiis*, Cologne, 1568, p. 17; Mabillon, *Mus. Ital.* vol. ii. p. 10, cf. *ibid. Comm. Praev.* pp. xliv–xlvii., and for the probable date, Merkel in the *Theologische Quartalschrift*, 1862, vol. xliv. p. 59), in which the bishop goes round the church to receive the offerings, followed by acolytes with a linen sheet for carrying the collected loaves, and by a deacon with a bowl, into which the flasks of wine were emptied. 2. The freewill offerings for the clergy and the poor were, first as a matter of practice (S. Justin. M. *Apol.* 1. 67), and afterwards as a matter of rule, (*Const. Apost.* 2. 25), made not directly to the intended recipients but to the bishop, and by him solemnly offered to God (*ibid.* 2. 25. 34: cf. *Conc. Gangr.* c. 7, 8, which anathematizes any one who makes his offerings to any one but the bishop or his commissary).

[33] S. Polycarp, *ad Phil.* 4; *Const. Apost.* 2. 26; 4. 3; pseudo-Ignat. *ad Tars.* 9; cf. Tertull. *ad Uxor.* 1. 7.

which was given to 'the least of the little ones' was given also to God.

When the president became a single permanent officer he was, as before, the person into whose hands the offerings were committed and who was primarily responsible for their distribution. He thus became the centre round whom the vast system of Christian charity revolved. His functions as supreme almoner tended to overshadow his functions as president of the council. The names which were relative to his functions as president, though they never completely passed away, fell gradually into disuse. The title which clung to him was that which was relative to his administration of the funds, *ἐπίσκοπος* or bishop. In the same way his functions were chiefly known by names which were relative to his administration—*οἰκονομία, διακονία*[34]. They were the analogue in the Church of the administrative services which citizens rendered to the State, and were called by the same name, *λειτουργία*[35]. And sometimes by a metaphor which almost startles us by its boldness the bishop is compared to God—the Supreme Administrator, *ὁ πάντων ἐπίσκοπος*, who gives to every man severally as he has need[36].

[34] Οἰκονομία is used of a bishop's administration, e. g. Euseb. *H. E.* 4. 4; διακονία, S. Ignat. *ad Philad.* 1, *Epist. Eccles. Vienn. et Lugd.* ap. Euseb., *H. E.* 5. 1. 29.

[35] Λειτουργία of a bishop's administration, e. g. Euseb. *H. E.* 3. 22; 5. 28. 7; 6. 11. 1; 6. 29. 1. It was the common word for public duties; e. g. for the duty which at Rhodes the citizens discharged at their own cost, rather than at the cost of the state, of providing for the needy poor, Strab. 2. 14. 5.

[36] S. Ignat. *ad Magnes.* 3; cf. Philo. i. 449, 454, 457, *πατέρα τῶν ὅλων καὶ ἐπίσκοπον*, and the frequent stoical phrase ὁ διοικῶν τὰ ὅλα, e. g. Epict. *Diss.* 1. 12. 7; 2. 16. 33. M. Anton. 6. 42; 10. 25.

If we look at the internal economy of the Christian communities during the earlier centuries of their existence, we shall see that the functions of an administrator were so various in kind and so considerable in amount as to be not inadequate to account for the importance which was attached to them, and that, as years went on that importance rather increased than diminished.

The Christian communities grew up, as we have seen, in the midst of poverty. They had a special message to the poor, and the poor naturally flowed into them. And the poverty in the midst of which they grew was intensified by the conditions of their existence. Some of their members were outcasts from their homes: others had been compelled by the stern rules of Christian discipline to abandon employments which that discipline forbad [37]. In times of persecution the confessors in prison had to be fed: those whose property had been confiscated had to be supported: those who had been sold into captivity had to be ransomed [38]. Above all there were the widows and orphans [39]. In such times as those which we are con-

[37] Cyprian, Epist. 2. (61) p. 467, ed. Hartel, says that an actor who has been forced to abandon his profession is to be placed 'inter ceteros qui ecclesiae alimentis sustinentur.'

[38] 1 Clem. Rom. 55. 2; Herm. *Mand.* 8. 10, *Sim.* 1. 8; Dionys. Corinth. ap. Euseb. *H. E.* 4. 23. 10; Clement. *Epist. ad Jacob.* 9; Tertull. *ad Martyr.* 1; S. Cyprian, *Epist.* 7 (36), p. 485, 62 (60), c. 4, p. 700. *Const. Apost.* 4. 9. 5. 1. Lucian, *De Morte Peregrini*, 12, caricatures the practice: cf. Libanius, *Orat.* 16 in Tisam. *Orat.* de Vinctis, ii. 258, 445. So much stress was laid upon it that Ambrose (*De Offic.* 2. 28) defended, and Justinian (*Cod.* 1. 2. 22) legalized, the sale of the eucharistic vessels in order to obtain the necessary funds.

[39] Herm. *Mand.* 8. 10, *Sim.* 1. 8: 5. 3: 9. 26, 27; S. Ignat. *ad Smyrn.* 6, *ad Polyc.* 4; S. Polycarp. *ad Philipp.* 4; S. Justin M. *Apol.* 1. 67; Clement. Epist. *ad Jacob*, 8; Tertull. *ad Uxor.* 1. 8; S. Cyprian, *Epist.* 7 (36), p. 485; *Const. Apost.*

sidering the poverty of widows and orphans is necessarily great, because men have in their lifetime a less than ordinary chance of saving, and after their death their children have a less than ordinary chance of success in the social struggle. But in this respect again the Christian communities tended to intensify the evils which they cured. In the ordinary course of society orphan girls would have married, and many widows would have found for themselves a second home. But there grew up in the Christian communities a tendency, which many of the great preachers fostered, towards perpetual virginity and perpetual widowhood. To marry was indeed not a sin, but it was a confession of weakness: to marry a second time was almost to lapse from grace [40]. The numbers of virgins and widows for whom the Church had to provide consequently multiplied in an increasing ratio [41]. In addition to these were the strangers who passed in a constant stream through the cities of all the great routes of commerce in both East and West. Every one of those strangers who bore the Christian name had therein a claim

frequently, e.g. 2. 26: 3, 4, 6, 7, 14: 4. 2, 3, 8: 8. 29. The claims of women to special provision had been acknowledged by non-Christian communities: e.g. Le Bas et Waddington, Nos. 226, 227, 228 = *Corpus Inscr. Graec.* Nos. 2886, 2883 *c*, 2885 *d*, are inscriptions in honour of those who had made distributions *ταῖς ἐκ ναοῦ γυναιξὶ καὶ ταῖς παρθένοις.*

[40] Athenag. *Deprec.* 28 *ὁ δεύτερος [γάμος] εὐπρεπής ἐστι μοιχεία*: so in effect Origen, *Hom. xvii. in Luc.* Tom. iii. p. 953 ed. De la Rue.

[41] In addition to providing for widows who were in need, the Church officers had frequently to take charge of the property of those who had it (e.g. S. Ambros. *De officiis Ministr.* ii. 29; cf. 2 Macc. 3. 10, which shows that Jewish widows had been in the habit of taking their money to the Temple), or to defend them in the civil courts (e.g. Conc. Sardic. c. 7). The civil and the canon law combined to make the functions which grew out of this an important part of a bishop's duties in later times.

to hospitality. For Christianity was, and grew because it was, a great fraternity. The name 'brother,' by which a Jew addressed his fellow-Jew, came to be the ordinary designation by which a Christian addressed his fellow-Christian [42]. It vividly expressed a real fact. For driven from city to city by persecution, or wandering from country to country an outcast or a refugee, a Christian found, wherever he went, in the community of his fellow-Christians a welcome and hospitality. The practice of hospitality was enjoined as the common virtue of all Christians: in the New Testament itself stress is laid upon it by St. Paul, St. Peter, and St. John [43]. But it was a special virtue of the ἐπίσκοπος. It was for him not so much a merit as a duty [44]. Travelling brethren, no less than the poor of his own community, were entitled to a

[42] 'Brother,' of one Jew in relation to another, frequently in the Old Testament; e.g. Deut. 15. 12: 17. 15; cf. Philo, ii. 285, ἀδελφὸν τὸν ὁμόφυλον εἶπεν, and Clem. Alex. *Strom.* 2. 18, p. 473, ed. Pott.: so also in the New Testament, e.g. S. Matth. 5. 47: 18. 15. For its use of Christians, see e.g. S. Justin M. *Apol.* 1. 65; Tertull. *Apol.* 30, Iren. 2–31. 2; Clem. Alex. *Strom.* 2–9, p. 450: cf. Lucian, *De Morte Peregrini*, 13. The word was also used of the fellow-members of non-Christian associations, e.g. *Corpus Inscr. Lat.* vol. iii. No. 2509. (But after the Arian controversy it was superseded in general use by the word 'fidelis,' which, according to Mone, *Lateinische u. Griechische Messen*, p. 89, is invariable in St. Augustine.)

[43] Rom. 12. 13, 'given to hospitality': Heb. 13. 2, 'Be not forgetful to entertain strangers': 1 Pet. 4. 9, 'Use hospitality one to another without grudging:' 3 John 5–7, commends Gaius for his charity to strangers which went forth for His name's sake, 'taking nothing of the Gentiles.' It was a special qualification of a widow, 'if she have lodged strangers,' 1 Tim. 5. 10. So in sub-Apostolic literature: Clement of Rome, 1. c. 2, speaks of the splendid hospitality of the Corinthians, and holds up before them, c. 10–12, for their encouragement the examples of the hospitality of the patriarchs.

[44] 1 Tim. 3. 2: Titus 1. 8: cf. the description of a good bishop in Herm. *Sim.* 9. 27: so e.g. S. August. *Serm.* 355 (*De Divers.* 49), Opp. ed. Migne, vol. v. 1570, 'vidi necesse esse habere episcopum exhibere humanitatem quiscunque venientibus sive transeuntibus.'

share in his distribution of the Church funds [45]. It is natural to find that such a system was abused. The common weaknesses of human nature asserted themselves. Even in Apostolic days there were 'false brethren:' and later on the Apostolical Canons say in reference to the practice that 'many things are done in a spirit of plunder [46].' But the abuses increased the responsibility and the importance of the bishop. A rule was adopted that although the bodily necessities of travellers might continue to be relieved, no one should be admitted to hospitality, in the fuller sense of earlier times, without a certificate of membership from his own community [47]. The officer who gave this certificate was the ἐπίσκοπος—who in all probability also kept the roll: and his responsibility in relation to it became greater when in course of time it became necessary to draw sharper lines of definition round the circle of admissible beliefs.

In addition to the poor, the widows and orphans, and the travelling brethren, there was the care of such of the church officers as, not having means of their own, were

[45] Can. Apost. 41. Conversely, when one church differed with another, its bishop refused to admit the travelling members of that church to communion, and if the difference were considerable he denied them even 'board and lodging' ('tectum et hospitium,') as in the case of the difference between the African churches and Stephen of Rome, *Epist. Firmil.* ap. S. Cyprian, Op. *Epist.* 75. 25, p. 826.

[46] Gal. 2. 4: Can. Apost. 33 πολλὰ γὰρ κατὰ συναρπαγὴν γίνεται.

[47] The system of giving such letters, which seems to have also prevailed in the philosophical Schools, Epict. *Diss.* 2. 3. 1; Diog. Laert. 8. 87, dates from Apostolic times: Acts 18. 27: 2 Cor. 3. 1: but it does not seem to have been obligatory earlier than the Council of Antioch, A.D. 341, c. 7, afterwards incorporated in Can. Apost. 12. 33. The Apostolical Constitutions, 2. 58, require the deacon to question even those who bring commendatory letters as to their soundness in the faith, before assigning them a place in the church, and so admitting them to communion.

dependent on the Church funds for their subsistence [48]. The roll of these, as of others, was probably kept by the bishop: and in the great cities the number of those who were entered upon it was large even when measured by a modern standard. We have some indication, though a late one, of those numbers in the regulation of the Emperor Justinian which limited the number of officers for the four great churches of Constantinople to 525, and enacted that if the bishop ordained more he should provide for them at his own expense [49].

Of this vast system of ecclesiastical administration the ἐπίσκοπος was the pivot and the centre. His functions in reference to it were of primary importance. He had no doubt other important functions, of which I propose to speak on a future occasion: he was the depositary of doctrine, and he was the president of the courts of discipline. But the primary character of these functions of administration is shown by the fact that the name which was relative to them thrust out all the other names of his office, and that most of the abstract names for his office are names which directly connote administration.

There are two other considerations which so strongly confirm this view that I regret that the necessary limits of a lecture prevent me from doing more than indicating them.

1. In the first place, there is the argument from the abuses of the office. Just as in the science of physiology

[48] E.g. S. Cypr. *Epist.* 41 (108), p. 588: Can. Apost. 4, Const. Apost. 2. 28.

[49] Justin. *Novell.* 3 c. 1, 2: the numbers were to be sixty presbyters, a hundred deacons, forty deaconesses, ninety sub-deacons, a hundred and ten readers, twenty-four singers, a hundred doorkeepers.

the nature of the functions of an organ is often shown by its lesions, so the nature of the functions of an office is often shown by its abuses. But the larger proportion of all the abuses of the episcopal office which are provided against in both civil and canon law are relative to the administration of the Church funds [50].

2. In the second place, there is the argument from current conceptions of the nature of the office. No small part of the eulogies upon bishops, whether by contemporary writers, or by their biographers, or upon their epitaphs, are relative to their care of the distressed, and to their protectorate of the widow and orphan [51].

[50] The offerings were in early times at the free disposal of the church officers: and scandals appear very early, e.g. in the case of the presbyter Valens, at Philippi (Polycarp, *ad Phil.* 11), and of the deacons mentioned by Hermas (*Sim.* 9. 26): cf. Origen, *Hom.* 16 *in Matth.* c. 22, vol. iii. p. 752. In the fourth century, when administration had come to be centred in the bishops, the Apostolical Constitutions remind them that though there is no human check, they are responsible to God, (*Const. Apost.* 2. 24): the Council of Antioch, c. 25, the Apostolical Canons, c. 38–41, the African Code, c. 33, the code known as 'Statuta Ecclesiae Antiqua' (=4 Conc. Carth.) c. 31, 32, all find it necessary to remind the bishop that he is a trustee for the poor, and that he is not at liberty to enrich himself or his family out of the church funds. In time two checks were devised: (1) the bishop was compelled to appoint a steward (*οἰκονόμος*), Conc. Chalc. c. 26, so that the administration of the funds should not be without a witness, and the property of the church be scattered: (2) the offerings were divided in the West according to a recognized scale, which, however, varied in different churches and at different times: Conc. Aurel. A.D. 511, c. 14, 15; 2 Conc. Brac. A.D. 563, c. 7; S. Greg. M. *Epist.* 4. 12; 12. 31; Conc. Emerit. A.D. 666, c. 14; ps.-Gelas. *Epist. ad Episc. Lucan.* c. 27, ap. Hinschius, *Decretales pseudo-Isidorianae,* p. 650, which embodied the ultimate rule of the canon law. In the civil law, the chief enactments are those of Justinian, *Cod.* 1. 2. 14; 1. 3. 4; 2. 8. 7, and especially Novell. 3. 69, which requires that none but childless persons shall be appointed, to prevent the alienation of church property in favour of a bishop's children.

[51] In lives of bishops, e.g. S. Pontii *Vita S. Cyprian,* c. 6; *Hymnus in Natale S. Zenon.*, Op. ed. Ballerini, p. cxciv; S. Paulin. *Vita S. Ambros,* c. 30; Possid. *Vita S. Augustin,* c. 23: Uranii *Epist. de obitu S. Paulin. Nolan,* c. 6, 7; Venant. Fortun. *Vit. S. German. Paris.* c. 74; Joann. Diac. *Vita S. Greg. M.*, ii. 55, 57; Pauli Emerit. *De Vita patrum Emerit,* c. 8 (ap. Migne, *Patr. Lat.*, vol. lxxx. 135); Anon. *Vita S. Desider. Cadurc.* c. 9 (ap. Migne, vol. lxxxvii. 227); Anon.

They are summed up in the emphatic declaration of St. Jerome: 'The glory of a bishop is to relieve the poverty of the poor [52].'

There was probably a time in the history of the Christian Church at which these functions of administration were the functions of a single class of officers. The conception of the nature of Church office which is found in the New Testament divides itself into two parts—that of presidency and that of ministry. But the two parts are not yet divided: the favourite terms by which St. Paul designates himself and his work are those of 'minister' and 'ministry [53].' But very soon a division of labour became imperative. Early in the history of the community at Jerusalem 'seven men of honest report' were appointed to relieve the Apostles of the 'business' of serving tables. No title is given

Vita S. Elig., ii. 25 (ap. Dachery, *Spicilegium*, vol. ii. 113), where the people are represented as crying out at his funeral 'O Eligi, dulcedo tu pauperum, fortitudo debilium, tu protector et impar egentium consolator: quis post te eleemosynam sicut tu dabit largam: vel quis nostri erit protector sicut tu, bone pastor?' On epitaphs, e.g. ap. De Rossi, *Bulletino di Arch. Christiana*, 1864, p. 55 'Haec mihi cura fuit nudos vestire petentes, Fundere pauperibus quidquid concesserat annus:' S. Tetricus of Dijon, ap. Le Blant, *Inscriptions Chrétiennes de la Gaule*, No. 3, 'Esca inopum, tutor viduarum, cura minorum, Omnibus officiis omnia pastor eras:' a bishop of Gaeta, circ. A.D. 529, ap. Mommsen, *Inscr. Regni Neapolitani*, No. 4138, 'Hospitibus gratus se ipsum donavit egenis, Illosque eloquio hos satiavit ope.'

[52] S. Hieron. *Epist.* 52 (2) *ad Nepot.* c. 6. vol. i. p. 261, ed. Vall. A third consideration may probably be added to the above, viz. that the Gnostics seem to have had no organized system of philanthropy, and, as a corollary of this, they, with the exception of the Marcionites, had neither bishops nor deacons: cf. (Munter) *Versuch über die kirchl. Alterthumer der Gnostiker*, p. 12; nor did they recognize the Pastoral Epistles, S. Hieron. *Prol. in Comm. in Ep. ad Titum*, Opp. vol. vii. 685, ed. Vall. The contrast between orthodox and heterodox teachers in this respect is probably made first by S. Ignat. *ad Smyrn.* 6. 2.

[53] διάκονος, διακονία, Rom. xi. 13; 1 Cor. iii. 5; 2 Cor. iii. 6; iv. 1; vi. 3, 4; xi. 8, 23; Ephes. iii. 7; Col. i. 23, 25.

to these men: their work, like the work of Matthias, or the work of Archippus, is spoken of as a 'ministry:' but they themselves are only 'the seven [54].' But they served as the prototype of a class of officers who were soon forced into existence, and who have since been permanent in the Christian Churches. Before the Apostolic age had passed we find not one class of officers but two. The one was that of those of whom I have spoken—the *ἐπίσκοποι*: the other was that of the ministers—or *διάκονοι*. The two classes are in close relation: they are for the most part spoken of together: they are so much alike that in the Pastoral Epistles the qualifications of the one are difficult to distinguish from the qualifications of the other.

If we pass from the Apostolic age to that which succeeded it, the nature of the division of labour between these two classes of officers becomes clearly defined.

The landmarks amid a sea of floating evidence are Justin Martyr and Polycarp in the middle of the second century, and the Clementines at the beginning of the third.

1. In the general meetings of the community, as they are described by Justin Martyr, the offerings were received and blessed by one officer, but they were distributed among the people by others [55]. The name which those who distributed bore (*διάκονοι*) was

[54] Acts vi. 3, 'seven men of honest report,' *ib.* 21. 8, 'one of the seven:' *διακονία* is used of 'the daily ministration:' *ib.* vi. 1, and of 'the ministry of the word:' *ib.* vi. 4, cf. *διακονεῖν τραπέζαις*, 'to serve tables,' *ib.* 6. 2: it is also used, with *ἀποστολή*, of the office of Matthias, *ib.* 2. 25, and of Archippus, Col. 4. 17.

[55] Justin M. *Apol.* 1. 55, 57.

not only a common name for those who served at table, but seems to have been specially applied to those who at a religious festival distributed the meat of the sacrifice among the festival company [56]. In this respect the deacons held a place which they have never lost: in all Churches which have been conservative of ritual, those who assist the presiding officer at the Eucharist are known—whatever be their actual status, archbishop, bishop, or presbyter—as deacon and subdeacon.

2. Outside the general meetings, as we gather from clear statements of the Clementines, the division of labour was closely analogous. The alms for the relief of those who were in distress were in the hands of the bishop: but the officers who actually sought them out and relieved their necessities were the deacons [57].

3. But both the Clementines and the letter of Polycarp show, what must also be inferred from the Pastoral Epistles, that the deacons shared with the bishop and his council the duties not only of administration but of discipline. Of the nature of that discipline something will be said in the succeeding Lecture: the relation of the deacons to it was analogous to their relation to administration: in the latter sphere of action the bishop was in the position of a chairman and treasurer, the deacons in that of outdoor relieving officers: in the former the bishop and his council were in the position

[56] An inscription at Anactorium (*Corpus Inscr. Graec.* No. 1793 *b. add.*) gives a list of the officers of the festival: they are the *ἱεροθύτης*, who sacrificed the victims, the *μάγειρος*, who cooked or carried the portions that were to be eaten, the *διάκονος*, who distributed the flesh, the *ἀρχιοινόχοος*, who distributed the wine. Deacons and deaconesses are also found as officers of a temple at Metropolis, in Lydia, *C. I. G.*, No. 3037.

[57] Clement, *Epist. ad Jacob.* 5, *Hom.* 3. 67: cf. *Const. Apost.* 3. 19.

of superintendents and judges, the deacons in that of officers of enquiry [58].

Between these two classes of officers the relation was necessarily one of subordination: though the subordination was by no means so great as it afterwards became [59]. The status of the deacons came to be affected by two circumstances: in the first place, when the analogy between the Christian ministry and the Mosaic priesthood asserted itself, the deacons were regarded as corresponding to the Levites, and as being thereby subordinate to presbyters, in the same way as Levites

[58] S. Polycarp. *ad Philipp.* 5, *ὁμοίως διάκονοι ἄμεμπτοι κατενώπιον αὐτοῦ τῆς δικαιοσύνης, ὡς Θεοῦ καὶ Χριστοῦ διάκονοι καὶ οὐκ ἀνθρώπων· μὴ διάβολοι, μὴ δίλογοι, ἀφιλάργυροι, ἐγκρατεῖς περὶ πάντα, εὔσπλαγχνοι, ἐπιμελεῖς, πορευόμενοι κατὰ τὴν ἀλήθειαν τοῦ Κυρίου ὃς ἐγένετο διάκονος πάντων.* These characteristics, which closely resemble those given in 1 Tim. 3. 8–12, clearly imply disciplinary duties: the deacons are to be 'blameless,' in order that they may be themselves, like the bishops, free from the faults which they are to note in others; they are to be 'not slanderers, nor double-tongued,' because they stood in the relation of accusers. Their functions in this respect are clearly stated in the Clementines, *Epist. ad Jacob.* 12: they are to be the bishop's 'eyes,' reporting to him any one who seems to be in danger of sinning, 'in order that being admonished by the president he may perhaps not accomplish his sin': *ibid. Hom.* 3. 67, they are to go about among the brethren and report to the bishop about the souls as well as the bodies of the brethren. Similarly in the Apostolical Constitutions, e.g. 3. 19, 'you deacons ought to keep watch over all who require watching, and also in the case of those who are in distress, and to report to your bishop': the lighter cases the deacon might, on the deputation of the bishop, decide by himself, *ibid.* 2. 44. The existence of disciplinary powers on the part of the deacons is also clearly implied in S. Cyprian, *Epist.* 14 (5), p. 512, ed. Hartel, 16 (9), p. 520; 17 (11), p. 522: they might in certain cases readmit penitents, *ibid.* 18 (12), p. 524. There is the same combination of functions in the Damasine inscription on a Roman archdeacon, 'primus levitarum,' which has recently been brought to light again by De Rossi (*Roma Sotteranea*, vol. iii. p. 242):

'Non illum sublimis honor non extulit ordo
Edomuit rigidos plus pietate magis,
Justiciae cultor, vitae servator honestae,
Pauperibus dives, sed sibi pauper erat.'

[59] The Apostolical Constitutions, 2. 30, compare the relation to that which existed between Moses and Aaron.

had been to priests: in the second place, the increase of the scale upon which the Christian Churches existed, and the increase, which was in a still greater proportion, of the number of those for whom the Christian Churches undertook to provide, brought about a change, which has since become permanent, in the mode of relieving the distressed. In primitive times every case of poverty or suffering had been separately known to the bishop, and personally relieved by the deacon; in later times grew up the system of institutions. The sick Christian, at least in the great cities, was no longer visited by the deacon bringing him from the church his share in the church offerings: the whole body of the sick poor were gathered together into hospitals: orphans were gathered into orphan-homes: infants into infant-asylums: the aged into almshouses: the poor into poor-houses: and strangers into guest-houses [60]. Each of these institutions was managed by its appropriate officers [61]. The deacons do not appear to

[60] Νοσοκομεῖα are mentioned in Pallad., *Vit. S. Chrysost.*, c. 5, Justin. *Cod.* I. 2. 15: first established in the West by Fabiola according to S. Hieron. *Epist.* 77 (30) *ad Ocean.* vol. i. 461, ed. Vall.: ὀρφανοτροφεῖα, Cod. Justin. *Cod.*, I. 2. 19; *Novell.* 7. 1: Leo, *Novell.* 84: βρεφοτροφεῖα, Justin. *Cod.* I. 2. 19, 22; *Novell.* 7. 1: γεροντοκομεῖα, Justin. *Cod.* I. 2. 19: *Novell.* 7. 1: πτωχοτροφεῖα, πτωχεῖα, S. Basil. *Epist.* 142 (374), c. 8, p. 235; S. Greg. Naz., *Epist.* 211, vol. II, p. 176, ed. Ben.; Sozom. *H. E.* 4. 20; Conc. Chalc. c. 8; Justin. *Cod.* I. 2. 15, I. 2. 19, I. 2. 33, § 7; ξενοδοχεῖα S. Chrys. *Hom.* 45 *in Act. Apost.* c. 4: Op. ed. Migne, vol. ix. 319; Epiph. *Haeres.* 75, p. 905; Justin. *Cod.* I. 2. 15, 19, 22, 33; *Novell.* 59. 3; 131. 10; Theodoret. *H. E.* 5. 19; S. Augustin, *Tract.* 97 *in Joann.* c. 4; Op. ed. Migne, vol. iii. 1879; S. Hieron. *Epist.* 66 (26) *in Pammach.* c. 11, Op. vol. i. 401. For the splendid foundation of Basil, see S. Greg. Naz. *Orat.* 43 *in laudem Basil. M.* c. 63, Op. vol. i. 816, Sozom. *H. E.* 6. 34: and for the imitation of the Christian practice by Julian, see his Epist. 49: Sozom. 5. 16.

[61] We find mention of *νοσοκόμοι, ὀρφανοτρόφοι, βρεφοτρόφοι, γεροντοκόμοι. πτωχοτρόφοι,* and *ξενοδόχοι* in connexion with the several institutions mentioned in the preceding note: some of these officers were bishops (Sozom. *H. E.* 6. 34),

have had any special relations to them in the East, nor permanently in the West. Their outdoor work was narrowed; they gradually lost their ancient share in discipline; and the main conception of their functions which came to exist was that they were subordinate officers of public worship. But they were still conceived, as they had been conceived in primitive times, to be in a closer relation to bishops than to presbyters: and when, like each of the other grades of officers, they came to form a college, with a president, or *arch*deacon, at its head, that officer was conceived to be, in an especial sense, the bishop's assistant in ecclesiastical administration, and, sometimes, to be next to him in rank. These functions and this status were so important that in time, though probably not until the ninth century, it was found inconvenient to limit them to deacons, and the earlier rule which enacted that an archdeacon on becoming a presbyter ceased to be an archdeacon fell into disuse. But the presbyter-archdeacon of later times has preserved in some important respects the original conception of the deacon's office, and is still, as in primitive days, the bishop's 'eye' and 'heart.'

some presbyters (S. Greg. Naz. *Epist.* 211: it is probable from Pallad. *Lausiac.* c. 1, that at Alexandria this was always the case), some monks or laymen (Justin. *Cod.* I. 3. 33, § 7). There is no trace in the East of any special connexion with the diaconate. In Italy, on the contrary, similar institutions were originally called *diaconiae*, which are found not only at Rome, but also at Pesaro (S. Greg. Max. *Epist.* 5. 28, vol. ii. 756), and at Naples (*ibid.* 10. 21, vol. ii. p. 1054). Mabillon (*Mus. Ital.* vol. ii. *Comm. praev.* p. xvii), advances the probable view that at Rome there was one of these *diaconiae* in each of the seven ecclesiastical districts, and that it was originally under the charge of the deacon of that district (see *infra*, Lect. VIII): but it is clear from the *Liber Pontificalis* (*Vit. Greg. IV*, p. 464, *Vit, Steph. II*, p. 229), that by that time the *diaconiae* were rather churches than poor-houses: and it also appears from the *Ordo Romanus I* (ap. Mabillon, *Mus. Ital.* vol. ii. p. 7), that the 'pater diaconiae' might be not even a clerk.

Such, in respect of their primary functions, were the bishops and deacons of the early Churches, and such, in outline, were the relations of the early Churches to the social strain in the midst of which they grew. It is the task rather of the economist than of the historian to enquire how far the Christian Churches themselves increased the evils which they tended to cure, and how far the vast system of organized mendicity which they fostered was an inevitable result of the conditions of society, or the spurious offspring of a deceived philanthropy. This enquiry has not yet been made by scientific investigators. But it may be permitted so far to anticipate their verdict as to advance the assertion that the apparent and admitted evils which were wrought were counterbalanced, even from the economical point of view, by the forces which Christian organization kept in motion. Those forces have been among the strongest conservative forces of society. They have arrested decay. They have prevented the disintegration, and possibly the disintegration by a vast and ruinous convulsion, of the social fabric. Of those forces the primitive bishops and deacons were the channels and the ministers. They shone through the darkness of social distress as lights of solace and of sympathy. They bridged over the widening interval between class and class. They lessened to the individual soul the weight of that awful sadness of which, then as now, to the mass of men, life was the synonym and the sum.

LECTURE III.

PRESBYTERS.

THE patriarchal state of society, in which families lived apart, and the head of the family was its administrator and judge, was succeeded in many parts of the world by the communal system, in which the government of an aggregation of families was in the hands of a council of heads of families—the elders of the commune. And just as the patriarchal system survived through many modifications of social circumstances, as an underlying theory of domestic government which has not wholly passed away even from modern society, so the communal system survived through many varieties of political organization as a system of local administration.

It is found, for example, on the banks of the Nile: long after Egypt had been so far Hellenized that official documents were drawn up in Greek, we find from an extant papyrus that the presence of the elder of a village is necessary to the validity of an administrative act[1]. It is found also in Palestine, and its

[1] Leemans, *Papyri Graeci Mus. Ant. publ. Lugduni-Batavi*, Leyden 1843, p. 3: *Corpus Inscr. Graec.* vol. iii. p. 294: possibly the same officers may be intended in the Theban inscription, *C. I. G.* No. 4717.

presence there had so important a bearing upon the early organization of the Christian Churches as to render some account of it a necessary preliminary to the further consideration of that organization.

It is recognized both in the Mosaic legislation and throughout the Old Testament history. It is the elders of a city who are to deliver up a wilful murderer to the avenger of blood: and it is into their ears that an unwitting homicide is to declare his cause [2]. It was the elders of the city who thrust out Jephthah as the son of a strange woman from his father's house [3]. It was before the elders of the city sitting in the city gate that the kinsman refused, and Boaz took, the redemption of Elimelech's inheritance [4]. It was to the elders of Jezreel that Jezebel wrote and procured the condemnation of Naboth for blasphemy [5]. It was also to the elders of Jezreel that Jehu wrote to cause the slaying of Ahab's sons [6]. The elders of those early times were probably like the sheykhs who have continued to the present day both among the Bedouins of the desert and in the settled villages of the Arabian peninsula. Their tenure of office rested rather upon general consent than upon formal appointment, and the limits of their authority were but loosely defined. But in the interval between the close of the Old Testament and the beginning of the New, a more definite form seems to have been given to this primitive institution. It may be gathered from the Talmud that out of the elders or chief men of every community a certain number had

[2] Deut. 19. 12; Jos. 20. 4.
[3] Judges 11. 5, 7.
[4] Ruth 4. 2.
[5] 1 Kings 21. 8.
[6] 2 Kings 10. 1.

come to be officially recognized, and that definite rules were laid down for their action. Side by side with the synagogue of a town, but distinct from it, was the συνέδριον or local court. The former was the general assembly or 'congregation' of the people: the latter was the 'seat' of the elders. The two institutions were so far in harmony with one another that the meetings of the local court were held in the synagogue, and that in the meetings of the synagogue for its own proper purposes the elders of the local court had seats of honour—the πρωτοκαθεδρίας which our Lord describes the Pharisees as coveting [7]: and hence the word synagogue is sometimes used where the word synedrion would be more exact: but the distinction between the two is clearly established and is of great importance [8].

So firm was the hold which this system obtained upon the Jews that they carried it with them into the countries of the dispersion. In those countries they lived apart from the rest of the community. Then, as now, they were a separate class. They preserved, and were so far privileged as to be allowed to preserve, not only their own usages and their own forms of worship, but also their own administration [9].

[7] S. Matth. 23. 6; S. Mark 12. 39; S. Luke 11. 43; 20. 46.

[8] For the Rabbinical and other authorities for the above statements, see Herzfeld, *Geschichte des Volkes Jisrael*, 2te Aufl. Bd. ii. pp. 391 sqq.; Leyrer in Herzog, *Real-Encyclopädie*, s. vv. *Synagogen der Juden* and *Synedrium*; Derenbourg, *Essai sur l'histoire et géographie de la Palestine*, c. 6; Jost, *Geschichte des Judenthums*, erste Abth. pp. 270–287; Schürer, *Lehrbuch der neutestamentlichen Zeitgeschichte*, pp. 402–418, 468–471; Hausrath, *Neutestamentliche Zeitgeschichte* (Eng. Trans. vol. i. pp. 83 sqq.).

[9] Strabo ap. Joseph. *Ant.* 14. 7. 2, says that at Cyrene there were four divisions of the population, citizens, farmers, metoeci, and Jews: Philo ii. 568 speaks of the Jews as forming a separate colony in the Trastevere at Rome. In each colony they

At Alexandria, for example, they had their own governor and council[10]: and at Rome the recent discovery of the Jewish cemeteries on the Appian Way enables us to gather from the unimpeachable records of inscriptions a detailed account—which singularly confirms what is more vaguely known from other sources—of their internal organization[11].

It seems certain upon the evidence that in these Jewish communities, to which in the first instance the Apostles naturally addressed themselves, there existed a governing body of elders whose functions were partly administrative and partly disciplinary. With worship and with teaching they appear to have had no direct concern. For those purposes, so far as they required officers, another set of officers existed. In other words, the same community met, probably in the same place,

were subdivided into smaller communities, 'synagogues,' which were recognized by the State under the ordinary designation of *θίασοι*, or religious associations, and allowed by Julius Cæsar to exist when similar associations were dissolved (Jos. *Ant.* 14. 10. 8). In the same way other Semitic settlers preserved their nationality and their religion by forming associations: the Syrians at Puteoli had a subvention from Tyre, like an English chaplaincy abroad, *Corpus Inscr. Graec.* No. 5853, cf. Mommsen in the *Berichte der königl. sächs. Gesellschaft der Wissensch.* phil. hist. Klasse, 1850, Bd. ii. p. 57: so, also at Puteoli, the settlers from Berytus, Mommsen, *Inscr. Regn. Neap.* 2488, 2476, Wilmanns, 2002, 2003: so the Syrians at Malaga, *Corpus Inscr. Lat.* vol. ii. p. 252: so the Gazaeans at Portus Trajani, *C. I. G.* No. 5892: so the Tyrians at Delos, *ibid.* No. 2271.

[10] Strabo ap. Joseph. *Ant.* 14. 7. 2 (writing of the Jews of Alexandria), *καθίσταται δὲ καὶ ἐθνάρχης αὐτῶν ὃς διοικεῖ τὸ ἔθνος καὶ διαιτᾷ κρίσεις καὶ συμβολαίων ἐπιμελεῖται καὶ προσταγμάτων ὡς ἂν πολιτείας ἄρχων αὐτοτελοῦς.* (On the title *Alabarch*, which is sometimes, erroneously, given to the Jewish ethnarch, see Schürer, *Die Alabarchen in Aegypten* in the *Zeitschrift f. wissenschaftl. Theologie*, 1875, Bd. xviii. pp. 13 sqq.)

[11] These inscriptions, with some others, have been collected and published (chiefly after Garrucci) by Schürer, *Die Gemeindeverfassung der Juden in Rom in der Kaiserzeit*, Leipsig, 1879. Some of them will also be found in the *Corpus Inscr. Graec.* Nos. 9902-9910.

in two capacities and with a double organization. On the sabbath there was an assembly presided over by the ἀρχισυνάγωγος or ἀρχισυνάγωγοι for the purpose of prayer and the reading of the Scriptures and exhortation: on two other days of the week there was an assembly presided over by the γερουσιάρχης or ἄρχοντες or πρεσβύτεροι for the ordinary purposes of a local court [12]. Each community, whether assembling for the one class of purposes or the other, appears to have been in most cases independent. At Alexandria, where the State gave the Jewish colony exceptional privileges, the separate synagogues seem to have been all subject to the ethnarch: but at Rome and elsewhere there are no signs of their having been linked together by any stronger tie than the fellowship of a common creed and a common isolation from the Gentiles [13].

Consequently, when the majority of the members of a Jewish community were convinced that Jesus was the Christ, there was nothing to interrupt the current of their former common life. There was no need for secession, for schism, for a change in the organization. The old form of worship and the old modes of government could still go on. The weekly commemoration of the Resurrection supplemented, but did not supersede, the ancient sabbath. The reading of the life of Christ and of the letters of Apostles supplemented, but did

[12] ἀρχισυνάγωγος (ἄρχων τῆς συναγωγῆς S. Luke 8. 41) in the singular, S. Mark 5. 35, 36, 38; S. Luke 8. 49; 13. 14; Acts 18. 8, 17: in the plural, S. Mark 5. 22; Acts 13. 15; Mischna *Joma* 7. 1, *Sota* 7. 7; S. Justin M. Dial. c. Tryph. 137; Acta Pilati I. ap. Tischendorf, *Evang. Apocryph.* p. 221, 270; S. Epiphan. *Haeres.* 30. 11. 18; Cod. Theodos. 16. 8. 4, 13, 14.

[13] See Schürer, *Die Gemeindeverfassung*, &c. pp. 18–24.

not supersede, the ancient lessons from the prophets, and the ancient singing of the psalms[14]. The community as a whole was known by the same name which had designated the purely Jewish community. It was still a παροικία—a colony living as strangers and pilgrims in the midst of an alien society: and even when the sense of alienation lessened, the word was retained, though it was used in a new relation to signify that upon earth none of us has an abiding city[15]. The same names were in use for the court of administration and for the members of that court[16]: and even the weekly

[14] The Apostolical Constitutions (2. 57) direct the reading of two lessons from the historical books of the O. T. and from the prophets, the antiphonal singing of the Psalms of David, and the reading of the Acts, the Epistles of Paul, and the Gospels: cf. Justin. M. *Apol.* 1. 67.

[15] παροικία, πάροικος, and παροικεῖν are used in the sense of 'sojourning,' or 'a colony of sojourners' in the LXX.: e.g. Gen. 37. 1 κατῴκει δὲ Ἰακὼβ ἐν τῇ γῇ οὗ παρῴκησεν ὁ πατὴρ αὐτοῦ 'Jacob dwelt as an inhabitant in the land where his father had dwelt as a sojourner:' Ezra 8. 35 υἱοὶ τῆς παροικίας, of those who had returned from the captivity. So in the N. T. Acts 7. 29; Ephes. 2. 19; Heb. 11. 9, and in early patristic Greek, e.g. 1 Clem. Rom. inscr.; Polycarp, *Epist. ad Phil.* inscr., *Epist. Eccles. Smyrn.* ap Euseb. *H. E.* 4. 15. 3. The relation to contemporary and civil society which this implies is important: cf. Origen, *c. Cels.* 8 ἡμεῖς ἐν ἑκάστῃ πόλει ἄλλο σύστημα πατρίδος κτισθὲν λόγῳ Θεοῦ ἐπιστάμενοι: and Le Blant, *Le détachment de la patrie* in the *Comptes rendus de l'Academie d'Inscriptions*, 1872, Tom. i. p. 388. In the other sense mentioned above the words are also found in early times, e.g. 2 Clem. R. 5. 1; Testam. xii. Patr. *Levi* 11, and in later times they are sometimes found on tombstones, *C. I. G.* 9474, 9683.

[16] συνέδριον is used, i. of the Jewish local councils and of the chief council at Jerusalem, S. Matt. 10. 17; 26. 59; S. Mark 13. 9; Joseph. *Ant.* 14. 9. 3; 15. 6. 2; 20. 9. 6; Mischna *Sanhedrim*, 1: ii. of the Christian councils, S. Ignat. *ad Philad.* 8. 1; *ad Magnes.* 6. 1; *ad Trall.* 3. 1, and by the Fathers of the fifth and sixth centuries, e.g. S. Greg. Naz. *Orat.* 42. 11. vol. 1. p. 756; S. Basil. M. *Epist.* 28, vol. iv. p. 107, ed. Ben. Πρεσβυτέριον is similarly used, i. of the Jewish councils, S. Luke 22. 26; Acts 22. 5: ii. of the Christian councils, 1 Tim. 4. 14, and frequently in Ignatius and later writers. Πρεσβύτεροι is used of the members of the Jewish councils in e.g. Judith 6. 16, 21; 7. 23; 1 Macc. 1. 26: it is not found in the Jewish inscriptions which are collected by Schürer: but it occurs in those of the catacombs at Venosa which are printed by Ascoli, *Iscrizioni di antichi sepolcri Giudaici*, IV. A. No. 17 in the *Atti del IV congresso internazionale degli Orientalisti*, vol. i. p. 292, Florence, 1880.

court-days remained the same[17]. There is no trace of a break in the continuity: and there is consequently a strong presumption, which subsequent history confirms, that the officers who continued to bear the same names in the same community exercised functions closely analogous to those which they had exercised before; in other words, that the elders of the Jewish communities which had become Christian were, like the elders of the Jewish communities which remained Jewish, officers of administration and of discipline.

The origin of the presbyterate in those Christian communities which had been Jewish is thus at once natural and simple: its origin in those communities of which the members or a majority of the members were Gentiles is equally natural, though rather more complex. Two elements have to be accounted for: (1) the fact of government by a council or committee, (2) the fact that the members of such council or committee were known by a name which implies seniority.

(1) In regard to the first of these elements, the evidence shows that government by a council or committee was all but universal in the organizations with which Christianity came into contact. The communal idea which underlay the local government of Palestine

[17] The weekly court-days of the local synedria were Monday and Thursday (Bab. Talmud, *Baba Kamma,* 82 a Mischna *Kethuboth* i. 1 (Jerus. Talmud, *Megilla,* iv. 1), which were perhaps chosen as being also the usual market-days. There is a further point of similarity in the fact that the minimum number of presbyters in a church was originally two, forming with the bishop a court of three: Ambrosiast. *in Epist.* 1 *ad Timoth.* vv. 12, 13, vol. ii. p. 295: 'aliquantos presbyteros (esse oportet) ut bini sint per ecclesias et unus in civitate episcopus.' So also the minimum number of the members of a local synedrium was three, of whom one was the president (Bab. Talmud, *Sanhedrin* 1).

had in fact survived in the Graeco-Roman world. Every municipality of the Empire was managed by its curia or senate [18]. Every one of the associations, political or religious, with which the Empire swarmed had its committee of officers [19]. It was therefore antecedently probable, even apart from Jewish influence, that when the Gentiles who had embraced Christianity began to be sufficiently numerous in a city to require some kind of organization, that organization should take the prevailing form; that it should be not wholly, if at all, monarchical, not wholly, though essentially, democratical, but that there should be a permanent executive consisting of a plurality of persons. It was as natural that this should be so as that the management of a new society in our own day should be entrusted not wholly to an irresponsible chairman or president, nor on the other hand to periodical meetings of the whole body of members, but to a council or committee. And this we find to have been the case. The names of the governing body varied: but they all imply presidency or government, and they are always used in the plural [20].

(2) In regard to the second element, we find the idea of respect for seniority in many places and in many forms. So strong was this idea that the terms which

[18] i.e. all provincial municipalities in the West were organized on the model of Rome, and those of the East on that, which in this respect did not differ from Rome, of Athens or of Sparta: for the details see Marquardt, *Römische Staatswerwaltung*, Bd. i. pp. 501, 518.

[19] This statement is in fact a corollary from the preceding one: the associations were organized on the model of the states within which they existed.

[20] See below, Lecture V.

were relative to it were often used as terms of respect without reference to age. In the philosophical schools the professor was sometimes called ὁ πρεσβύτερος [21]. In the ascetic communities of Egypt and Palestine respect for seniority was strongly marked, not only in the common usages of life, but also and especially in the assemblies— where the members sat in ranks, the younger beneath the elder, and where it was the task of the eldest and most experienced to discourse about divine things [22]. Within the Christian communities themselves respect for seniority was preached from the first as an element of Christian order [23]. Both in the Epistles of the New Testament, and in the extra-canonical Epistle of Clement of Rome, the submission of the younger to the elder is enjoined, and the idea of age and the idea of rank so pass into one another as to make it sometimes difficult to determine which of the two was the more prominent in the writer's mind [24].

[21] Schweighaüser ad Epictet. *Diss.* I. 9. 10.

[22] Philo, ii. 458, says of the Essenes that at their weekly meetings they sat according to age, the younger below the elder, and, ii. 476, that the eldest and most experienced discoursed: elsewhere, ii. 481, he explains that the word 'elder' was used in reference not to length of years, but to mental and moral development.

[23] It seems probable that, in at least some Christian communities in the earliest stages of their existence, the word elder was used in its proper rather than in its acquired meaning, and that the governing body, i.e. the elders in the official sense, consisted of a section of the elders in the natural sense. Hence the defining phrases in 1 Tim. 5. 17, 'that rule well,' and in Herm. *Vis.* 2. 4, 'that preside over the Church,' mark off not so much senior from junior members of the community, but those elders who formed part of the governing body from those who did not.

[24] See e.g. 1 Pet. 5. 1–4: 1 Clem. Rom. 1. 3: 3. 3: 21. 6: so in Clem. Alex. ii. p. 958, ed. Pott. (quoted by Euseb. *H. E.* 3. 23), πρεσβύτερος at the beginning of the narrative is equivalent to πρεσβύτης later on, and both are interchanged with ἐπίσκοπος. The MSS. sometimes interchange πρεσβύτερος and πρεσβύτης, e.g. in Theodotion's text of the story of Susanna.

There was thus an antecedent probability, apart from Jewish influence, not only that the Christian communities, when organized, would be governed by a council, but also that in the appointment of the members of such a council seniority would be a prime qualification. And this we find to have been in fact the case. Out of the several names which the members of the Christian councils bore one ultimately survived the rest: they continue to be known to modern times as presbyters.

There is a remarkable contemporary parallel to this drift of Christian organization, which both confirms the antecedent probability and illustrates the fact. It is well known that the councils or senates of the Greek cities, though they sometimes still retained the name *γερουσία*, had come, like other senates, to be councils of 'old men' only in name. But it appears from some inscriptions which have been found within recent years that there was in some states of Asia Minor a tendency to revert to the original theory of a senate. The *γερουσία* was distinct from the *βουλὴ* [25]: the evidence points to the inference that the *γερουσία* was the committee of the *βουλή*, standing to it in something like the same relation as that in which the Cabinet stands to the Privy Council in England [26], and that the members of

[25] This is proved by the fact of their being mentioned separately, e.g. at Stratonicea in Caria, *ὁ δῆμος καὶ ἡ βουλὴ καὶ ἡ γερουσία*, *Corpus Inscr. Graec.* No. 2724, at Aphrodisias, *ibid.* No. 2775, at Nysa, *ibid.* No. 2944, at Ephesus, Wood, *Discoveries at Ephesus*, Append. vi. p. 36. The presiding officers are also mentioned separately, e.g. at Branchidae, *βούλαρχος καὶ προστάτης γερουσίας*, *C. I. G.* No. 2881.

[26] This is an inference from the fact that at Ephesus the *ψήφισμα* of the *γερουσία* and *ἐπίκλητοι* was laid before the *βουλὴ* and passed, in the same way as at Athens the *προβούλευμα* of the *βουλὴ* itself was laid before the *ἐκκλησία*: *περὶ ὧν οἱ νεωποῖαι*

the γερουσία bore the same name as the members of the committee of the Christian Churches — that of πρεσβύτεροι [27].

If we put the evidence together, it will appear probable that the presbyterate in the Gentile Churches had a spontaneous and independent origin. This hypothesis accounts for the fact which is not easily explained on the hypothesis of the direct transference of the Jewish office to the Gentile communities, namely, that the members of the governing council were known by various names, and that the names which were in use for the Jewish officers did not at once uniformly

καὶ οἰκουρῆτες κατασταθέντες διελέχθησαν τῇ βουλῇ καὶ τὸ ψήφισμα ἤνεγκαν τῆς γερουσίας καὶ τῶν ἐπικλήτων ὑπὲρ Εὐφρονίου πολιτείας, δεδόχθαι τῇ βουλῇ . . . Wood, *Discoveries at Ephesus*, Append. ii. p. 29. The existence of such a committee is rendered probable by the unwieldy size of most Eastern councils: e.g. Josephus, *Ant.* 13. 13. 3, mentions 500 βουλευταὶ at Gaza, and, *B. J.* 2. 21. 9, 600 at Tiberias: Libanius, in the fourth century, speaks of the municipal council of Antioch in times before his own as having consisted of 600 members (Op. vol. i. p. 182, ii. pp. 527, 528 ed. Reisk.), and this was also the normal number at Cyzicus (Böckh in *Corpus Inscr. Graec.* vol. ii. p. 920). But whether the precise relation of the γερουσία to the βουλὴ be that which is stated above, or not, the general proposition, that there was a tendency to give the elder members of a community or municipality a separate and integral share in its administration, is sufficiently shown by the fact, which is stated in the preceding note, that the γερουσία is co-ordinated with the βουλὴ and the δῆμος, in certain municipal acts, e.g. *C. I. G.* Nos. 2814, 2820, 3417, 3462, and also by the distinction which is made between οἱ γέροντες (ἡ γερουσία) and οἱ νέοι, e.g. Dio Chrys. *Orat.* 34, vol. ii. p. 27, ed. Dind., *C. I. G.* Nos. 2781, 2930. So in Africa the old Roman distinction between 'seniores' and 'juniores' was retained or revived, Renier, *Inscr. Romains d'Algérie*, Nos. 91, 1525, 3096, Wilmanns, Nos. 139, 1401.

[27] This is an inference from the fact that ἡ γερουσία and οἱ πρεσβύτεροι are evidently used as interchangeable terms, and both distinguished from ἡ βουλή, at Philadelphia, *Corpus Inscr. Graec.* Nos. 3417, 3422, and at Ephesus, Wood, *Discoveries at Ephesus*, Append. vi. pp. 10, 24, 66, Append. vii. p. 6. But οἱ πρεσβύτεροι is sometimes used to designate the members of a γερουσία even when there is no evidence of a distinction between it and the βουλή: e.g. of the members of the senate at Rome, Sozomen, *H. E.* 2. 3, and of the πρεσβυτικὸν at Chios, *C. I. G.* Nos. 2220, 2221.

prevail. But when, in the course of the second century, the distinction between the Christian communities which had once been Jewish and those which were originally Gentile tended to pass away, the Jewish conception of the nature of the governing council undoubtedly became dominant.

It is clear from the exhortation of Polycarp to the presbyters of Philippi that those presbyters had the supreme oversight of all matters of administration[28]. It was their duty to visit the sick, to provide for the widows and orphans and poor, to turn back those who had gone astray from the error of their ways, to sit in merciful judgment upon those who had committed wrong. Nor does it appear that any of these duties ever wholly ceased to be the duties of the presbyterate. The presbyters were, in theory, the council of the bishop, even after the bishop had asserted a virtual autocracy[29].

But it is equally clear that out of these varied duties those which came to be in practice the chief or only duties of the Christian councils were those which had been the chief duties of the Jewish synedria. The building in which they assembled came to be called a *basilica* or court-house : the part of it in which they sat was a *tribunal* or judgment-seat[30] : they were chiefly courts of discipline.

[28] S. Polycarp. *ad Philipp.* 6 : *καὶ οἱ πρεσβύτεροι δὲ εὔσπλαγχνοι, εἰς πάντες ἐλεήμονες, ἐπιστρέφοντες τὰ ἀποπεπλανημένα, ἐπισκέπτομενοι πάντας ἀσθενεῖς, μὴ ἀμελοῦντες χήρας ἢ ὀρφανοῦ ἢ πένητος . . . . ἀπεχόμενοι πάσης ὀργῆς, προσωποληψίας, κρίσεως ἀδίκου, μακρὰν ὄντες πάσης φιλαργυρίας, μὴ ταχέως πιστεύοντες κατά τινος, μὴ ἀπότομοι ἐν κρίσει, εἰδότες ὅτι πάντες ὀφειλέται ἐσμὲν ἁμαρτίας.*

[29] See below, Lecture IV. p. 107.

[30] For the use of *basilica* in relation to the early Christian churches see De Rossi,

Now there were two ways in which the Jewish synedria exercised authority. They had jurisdiction, on the one hand, in breaches of the ecclesiastical law, and on the other hand between man and man in cases of wrong. They had in their several localities the same powers which for graver cases and for national rather than local questions were possessed by the central court—the great Sanhedrin—at Jerusalem [31]. They could enforce their decisions by the moral punishment of excommunication, and by the physical coercion of scourging and imprisonment. Outside Palestine the same kinds of authority remained [32]: although as their jurisdiction was consensual and not of legal force the *ultima ratio* was exclusion from the community or excommunication. But it is remarkable as a proof not only of the existence of these courts but of their permanence, that at the end of the fourth century the Christian emperors Arcadius and Honorius, following the general tradition of imperial policy, gave to the synedria the protection of the state, and required provincial judges to carry out their decisions [33].

Roma sotteranea, Tom. iii. p. 461: for the use of βῆμα or 'tribunal' in the same relation, see De Rossi, *ibid.* iii. 486. The facts of the case are by no means sufficiently explained by the hypothesis that the use of the terms arose from the transfer of some civil *basilicae* by Constantine to the Church.

[31] The respective jurisdictions of the local councils and of the central council at Jerusalem are defined in Mischna *Sanhedrin* 1, 2 (translated into Latin in Ugolini, *Thesaurus*, vol. xxv).

[32] The existence of Jewish courts in the midst of Gentile communities is shown, e.g. at Sardis, Jos. *Ant.* 14. 10. 7, at Alexandria, Strab. ap. Jos. *Ant.* 14. 7. 2, and is probably implied at Corinth in the expression ὄψεσθε αὐτοί, Acts 18. 15: that they had a certain power of coercion is implied in Acts 9. 22: 22. 19: 26. 11. Cf. Origen, *ad African.* 14. vol. i. p. 28. ed. De la Rue.

[33] Cod. Theodos. 2. 1. 10, which however shows not only that the jurisdiction

The main functions of the Christian council of presbyters were closely analogous.

1. They exercised discipline. There was indeed this difference between Christian and Jewish discipline that it was of a severer kind. It is difficult for us in modern times, with the widely different views which we have come to hold as to the relation of Church government to social life, to understand how large a part discipline filled in the communities of primitive times. Those communities were what they were mainly by the strictness of their discipline. The tie of a common belief was looser than the tie of a common ideal and a common practice. The creed was as yet vague: the moral code was clear. For the kingdom of God was come which was a kingdom of righteousness. Each organized gathering of believers seemed to itself to be the visible realization of that Holy City of which the greatest of Hebrew poets had sung and which the divinest of Christian seers had seen. Between that City of God, and the diseased and decaying society which surrounded it, there was a perpetual and sharp antithesis [34]. And that antithesis was the sharper because the one and the other were in close and daily contact. The profound moral reaction which had set in was in itself not confined to Christianity.

was consensual, but also that it had come to be confined, if not originally confined, to civil matters: 'si qui per compromissum ad similitudinem arbitrorum apud Judaeos vel patriarchas ex consensu partium in civili duntaxat negotio putaverint litigandum, sortiri eorum judicium judicio publico non vetentur: eorum etiam sententias provinciarum judices exsequantur tanquam ex sententia cognitoris arbitri fuerint attributi.'

[34] Cf. e.g. 2 Clem. Rom. 6. 3 ἔστιν δὲ οὗτος ὁ αἰὼν καὶ ὁ μέλλων δύο ἐχθροί· οὗτος λέγει μοιχείαν καὶ φθορὰν καὶ φιλαργυρίαν καὶ ἀπάτην, ἐκεῖνος δὲ τούτοις ἀποτάσσεται.

The spirit of asceticism was, so to speak, in the air, and other ascetic communities had been formed [35]. But those ascetic communities had solved the difficulties of the world by withdrawing from it. They would not face ordinary society. They lived as the Christian ascetics lived in aftertime, when the level of Christian life was lower, apart from ordinary men in the solitude of the wilderness. The Christian communities on the other hand were in the world. Their members were brought face to face day by day with the seething mass of corruption from which divine grace had rescued them [36]. The very fact that they could not share the common sins of their neighbours exposed them to the ready taunt that their garb of superior sanctity was but a cloke for still darker forms of wickedness. In the midst of 'a crooked and perverse nation' they could only hold their own by the extreme of circumspection. Moral purity was not so much a virtue at which they were bound to aim as the very condition of their existence. If the salt of the earth should lose its savour, wherewith should it be salted? If the lights of the world were dimmed, who should rekindle their flame? And of this moral purity the officers of each community were the custodians. They 'watched for souls as those that must give account.' Week after week, and in some cases, as the Jewish synagogues had done, on two days in a week, the assembly met not only for prayer but

[35] See below, Lecture VI.

[36] The point of view of the early Christians is here assumed: but it is probable that their opinion of the vices of contemporary society, as represented by the Apologists, was exaggerated.

for discipline [37]. 'We come together,' says Tertullian, 'to call the sacred writings to remembrance, if so be that the character of the present times compel us either to use admonition or recollection in anything. In any case, by these holy words we feed our faith, raise our hopes, establish our confidence; nor do we the less strengthen our discipline by inculcating precepts. For our judgment also cometh with great weight, as of men well assured that they are under the eye of God: and it is a very grave forestalling of the judgment to come if any shall have so offended as to be put out of the communion of prayer, of the solemn assembly, and of all holy fellowship. The most approved elders preside [38].' And about the same time Origen, refuting a calumnious statement of Celsus in reference to the indiscriminate character of the Christian congregations, says, 'There are men appointed among us to examine closely into the lives and characters of those who come to us, that they may prevent those who do what is forbidden from entering our common assembly, and that by receiving those who do otherwise they may make them better day by day [39].' And in a similar way the Clementines put these words into the mouth of St. Peter: 'Do ye as elders of the Church adorn with discipline the bride of Christ—and by the bride of Christ I mean the whole assembly of the Church—in moral purity: for if she be found pure by the Bridegroom King, she herself will attain the height of honour, and ye, as guests at the marriage-

[37] See above, note 18. [38] Tertull. *Apol.* 39. [39] Origen, *c. Cels.* 3. 51.

feast, will gain great delights: but if she be found to have sinned, she herself will be cast out, and ye will suffer punishment because, it may be, the sin has happened through your neglect[40].'

2. The Christian like the Jewish presbyters exercised a consensual jurisdiction in matters of dispute between Christian and Christian. It was only when a severer punishment was necessary than such a consensual jurisdiction admitted that any Gentile court had been allowed to interfere between Jew and Jew[41]. And the recognition of such a jurisdiction became for the Christian an obligation, because it rested on a divine command. In one of the only two passages in which our Lord speaks expressly of the Church, He speaks of it in this relation: 'If thy brother shall trespass against thee, go and tell him his fault between thee and him alone: if he shall hear thee, thou hast gained thy brother. But if he will not hear thee, then take with thee one or two more, that in the mouth of two or three witnesses every word may be established. And if he shall neglect to hear them, tell it unto the Church: but if he neglect to hear the Church, let him be unto thee as an heathen man and a publican[42].' And hardly had the organization of the Christian communities begun before St. Paul looked upon it as an intolerable scandal that 'brother goeth to law with brother, and that before the unbelievers.' He deprecates litigation of any kind: the Christian rule was a rule

[40] Clementin. *Epist. Clem. ad Jacob.* c. 7.

[41] Mekhiltha and Midrash *Thanhuma* ad Exod. 21. 1: Mischna *Gittin* 9. 10.

[42] S. Matth. 18. 15–17: the other passage in which our Lord uses the word church is *ib.* 16. 19.

not of litigation but of forgiveness: but if litigation became inevitable he asks indignantly, 'Dare any of you, having a matter against another, go to law before the unjust and not before the saints [43]?' In those early days it may have been the case that the assembly itself, or persons chosen by the assembly, acted as arbitrators: and to this St. Paul's words point: 'If then ye have judgments of things pertaining to this life, set them to judge who are least esteemed in the Church [44].' But when the organization of the churches was more complete it is clear that the jurisdiction belonged to the council of presbyters. 'Let not those who have disputes,' say the Clementines, 'go to law before the civil powers, but let them by all means be reconciled by the elders of the Church, and let them readily yield to their decision [45].'

These two great functions of the early council of presbyters have been modified in many important particulars as the circumstances under which the Church itself has existed have themselves undergone material change.

1. In the first place, the relations of the Church to discipline were of necessity altered when the Church began to fill a larger place in history. That which had been possible in a small community became impossible in a larger. The stern self-restraint which had linked men arm to arm in the grim struggle for existence relaxed its tension. The close supervision

[43] 1 Cor. 6. 1. Cf. 5. 12. [44] 1 Cor. 6. 4.
[45] Clement. *Epist. Clem. ad Jacob.* 10.

with which the officers of the Church had watched the failings and backslidings of their small communities could exist no longer in a vast and complex society. And again: the transition of any community from a state of repression to a state of supremacy tends to change the character of the offences of which it takes cognizance. It accentuates the organization. It elevates the by-laws to a new prominence. It makes offences against those by-laws important. And we have but to compare the early monument which is known as the Constitutions of Clement[46] with the post-Constantinian code which is known as the Apostolical Canons[47], to see how wide was the chasm which in the Christian Church severed the ethics of the age of struggle from the ethics of the age of supremacy. And again: Christianity had no sooner become the religion of the Roman world, than it found itself swung round and round in a vast eddying swirl of intellectual currents — doubts and half-beliefs and rationalizings of divine truths—through which it was almost impossible to steer. Those times of intense crisis were no times for scanning too narrowly the characters of those who manned the ship. There was no condonation of flagrant and open sin: but at the

[46] This work is printed under the title Αἱ διαταγαὶ αἱ διὰ Κλήμεντος καὶ κανόνες ἐκκλησιαστικοὶ τῶν ἁγίων ἀποστόλων printed by Bickell, *Geschichte des Kirchenrechts*, Bd. I. Beil. I: Lagarde, *Juris Ecclesiastici reliquiae*, pp. 74 sqq.: Pitra, *Juris Ecclesiastici Graecorum hist. et mon.* vol. i. pp. 77 sqq.: and under the title 'Judicium Petri' by Hilgenfeld, *Novum Testamentum extra canonem receptum*, Fasc. iv. to which reference may be made for a clear, though not conclusive, discussion of its origin.

[47] The date of the Apostolical Canons, at least in their present form, is very uncertain: but since they embody decrees of councils of the fourth century, especially those of the Council of Antioch, they must at least be post-Constantinian.

same time soundness in the faith may have covered many a minor fault, and unsoundness in the faith was not atoned for by the highest Christian virtue. In the meanwhile a new code of Christian morality was being formed. The ascetic communities laid an abnormal stress upon certain special forms of virtue and the corresponding special forms of vice. They dreamed in their seclusion of all imaginable sins: and the *coup de grace* to the earlier Christian morality was given when the ghastly catalogues of those imagined possibilities of sin, each with its specific penalty, came to be looked upon as the code of Christian morals and the rule of Christian life [48].

2. In the second place, the recognition of Christianity by the State tended to narrow the broad border-line between the Church and the world. The fact that the Christians were no longer a παροικία, a colony of strangers in a strange land, that the local judges were Christian, and that the emperors who were the ultimate court of appeal were also Christian, diminished the force of the reason for submitting disputes 'in things pertaining to this life' to the Church officers. The consensual jurisdiction of the Church courts came to be limited to disputes in which Church officers were themselves concerned. That jurisdiction was recognized by the State, but it was viewed with a jealous eye. Out of it grew that long line of contests

[48] The reference is to the books known as 'Penitentials,' the most important of which will be found in Wasserschleben, *Die Bussordnungen der abendländische Kirche*, Halle, 1851; Kunstmann, *Die lateinische Pönitentialbücher der Angelsachsen*, Mainz, 1844; Haddan and Stubbs, *Councils and Ecclesiastical Documents*, vol. iii.

between State and Church with which many of us are familiar, but which passes far beyond the limits of the present subject—the Church constantly claiming and the State constantly endeavouring to limit this ecclesiastical and consensual jurisdiction[49]. Inside these contests was another struggle—the struggle on the part of the bishops to act as sole judges, without the *συνέδριον* or 'consilium' of presbyters, of which in early times they had been merely the presidents. But there are at least two significant indications that the original conception of the presbyterate never wholly passed away: the one is the fact that in all the Ordinals of the Latin Church, in both the prayers and the addresses to the people at the ordination of presbyters, Church government is a leading element in the conception of the presbyter's office[50]; the other is the fact that, after the parochial system had come to prevail, the presbyter who was put in charge of a parish was said to be sent not to teach but to rule ('ad regendum'); the conception of his office which underlies this ex-

[49] See below, Lecture VI.

[50] The chief petition of the prayer entitled 'consecratio,' the importance of which may be inferred not only from its place in the service, but also from the fact of its having lasted, with only slight verbal changes, from the time of the earliest surviving Sacramentaries until now, is as follows: 'Da, quaesumus, omnipotens Pater, in hos famulos tuos presbyterii dignitatem: innova in visceribus eorum spiritum sanctitatis; ut acceptum a te, Deus, secundi meriti munus obtineant, censuramque morum exemplo suae conversationis insinuent. Sint providi cooperatores ordinis nostri; eluceat in eis totius forma justitiae ut bonam rationem dispensationis sibi creditae reddituri aeternae beatitudinis praemia consequantur.' (The text here given is that of the modern Roman Pontifical: the text of the Leonine and Gelasian Sacramentaries will be found in Muratori, *Liturgia Romana Vetus*, vol. i. pp. 425, 513.) The form of the address to the people, or to the ordinands, has passed through several changes: but even the latest form, that of the modern Pontifical, preserves the early statement that the presbyters are appointed to help the bishop as the seventy elders were appointed to help Moses.

pression is preserved to us even in modern times in the familiar title of 'Rector [51].'

In the meantime, other functions which in early times were in the background came to the front. It will no doubt have been observed that the functions which have been described are all such as could be exercised by and were appropriate to a college or council of officers [52]. What powers, if any, were possessed by a single presbyter acting alone there is no evidence to show. But by one of those slow and silent revolutions which the lapse of many centuries brings about in political as well as in religious communities, the ancient conception of the office, as essentially disciplinary and collegiate, has been superseded by a conception of it in which not only is a single presbyter competent to discharge all a presbyter's functions, but in which also those functions are primarily not those of discipline, but 'the ministration of the Word and Sacraments [53].'

1. In regard to the first of these functions it is clear that the presbyters of the primitive Churches did not necessarily teach. They were not debarred from

[51] e.g. Conc. Cabill. A.D. 649, c. 5, Statt. *Eccles. Antiq.* (= 4 Conc. Carth.) c. 36: so also when a parish priest resigns his office he is said 'ab ordine et titulo et regimine plebis se exuere,' Conc. Remens. A.D. 874, c. 1. The title 'Ecclesiae rector,' seems first to occur in the ninth Council of Toledo, A.D. 655, c. 2.

[52] The minimum number of presbyters appears to have been two, forming with the bishop a court of three, which was the minimum number of a Jewish *συνέδριον* (Talmud Bab. *Sanhedrin* 2). See above, note 18.

[53] It is probable that even in the Jewish communities the distinction between the presbyters and the *ἀρχισύναγωγοι*, i.e. between the *συνέδριον* and the *συναγωγή*, became gradually obliterated: since in Justinian. *Novell.* 146. 1, the names appear to be identified, *παρ' αὐτοῖς ἀρχιφερεκῖται ἢ πρεσβύτεροι τυχὸν ἢ διδάσκαλοι προσαγορευόμενοι.*

teaching, but if they taught as well as ruled they combined two offices[54]. In the numerous references to presbyters in sub-apostolic literature there is not one to their being teachers, even where such a reference might have been expected, as for example in the enumeration of the duties of presbyters which is given by Polycarp in the form of an exhortation to fulfil them[55]. But the Clementine literature of the beginning of the third century makes the distinction, that whereas the bishops are to teach doctrine, the presbyters are to teach morals: in other words, they might inculcate what they were bound to require[56]. About the same time in the memoirs of two African martyrs, and later in the same century in a letter of Cyprian, we find the recognition of the combination of the two functions in the phrase 'presbyteri doctores[57]:' still later, St. Chrysostom makes it evident that the functions were still separable when he says that baptism was in his time entrusted to the less intelligent presbyters, the word of teaching to the wiser[58].

2. In regard to the second of these functions, the

[54] This is a clear inference from 1 Tim. 5. 17: so *ποιμένες* are distinct from *διδάσκαλοι* in Ephes. 4. 11, and *ἐπίσκοποι* (probably identical with *πρεσβύτεροι*) from *διδάσκαλοι* in Herm. *Vis.* 3. 5. 1: so also *πρεσβύτεροι* and *διδάσκαλοι* are mentioned separately in Hippol. ap. S. Epiphan. *Haeres.* 42. 2, and in Euseb. *H. E.* 7. 24. 6.

[55] S. Polycarp. *ad Philipp.* 7. There is the more positive evidence that the 'Constitutions of Clement' distinctly contemplate the existence of an unlettered presbyter (*Διατ. Κλήμ.* c. 16).

[56] Clementin. *Hom.* 3. 65: cf. Clem. Alex. *Strom.* 7. 1. p. 829, ed. Pott. *τὴν μὲν βελτιωτικὴν οἱ πρεσβύτεροι σώζουσιν εἰκόνα τὴν δὲ ὑπηρετικὴν οἱ διάκονοι.*

[57] S. Cyprian, *Epist.* 29 (24) p. 548, ed. Hart.: *Acta SS. Perpetuae et Felicitatis*, ap. Ruinart, *Acta Martyrum Sincera*, c. 13, p. 99: cf. Dodwell, *Dissertationes Cyprianicae, No.* 6, *De presbyteris Doctoribus*, Oxford, 1684.

[58] S. Chrys. *Hom.* 3 *in Epist.* 1 *ad Corinth.* c. 3, Op. vol. x. p. 19, ed. Montf.

theory upon which the public worship of the primitive Churches proceeded was that each community was complete in itself, and that in every act of public worship every element of the community was present. When the episcopal system had established itself, there was a bishop wherever in later times there would have been a parish church. From the small province of proconsular Asia, which was about the size of Lincolnshire, 42 bishops were present at an early council [59]: in the only half-converted province of North Africa 470 episcopal towns are known by name [60]. It is therefore reasonable to expect that the bishop, as the chief officer of the community, presided whenever the community met together. The offerings at the Eucharist were made to him: they were distributed by the deacons: in the account of the Eucharist which is given by Justin Martyr the presbyters have no place at all [61]: and in the later and more elaborate ritual which is preserved in the Apostolical Constitutions their place is altogether insignificant [62]. They probably had no more than the place which the Jewish presbyters had in the synagogue—seats of honour and dignity, but no official part in the service.

But in course of time, under the influence of altered

[59] The reference is not to the earlier but to the later (i.e. post-Diocletian) *Asia Proconsularis*: in this province Hierocles, *Synecdemus*, p. 658, mentions in all 42 towns; of these 32 are represented by their bishops in the subscriptions to the Council of Ephesus, and 39 in those to the Council of Chalcedon, ap. Mansi, *Concilia*, vol. iv. pp. 130, 2007, 1710: cf. Kuhn, *Die stadtische u. bürgerliche Verfassung des römischen Reichs*, 2er Theil, p. 276.

[60] Kuhn, *ibid.* p. 436: Gams, *Series Episcoporum*, p. 463.

[61] S. Justin M. *Apol.* I. 67.

[62] *Const. Apost.* viii. 1–14.

circumstances, the original system underwent a great change. There grew up the system of forming smaller communities within the territory of a city, or in outlying country places, which though separate in locality were still one in theory with the original community, and which were under the supervision of its bishop and council. From among the presbyters of that original community one or more was detached to take the oversight of the new congregation[63]. The functions of such a presbyter were for a long time narrowly limited. Baptism by a presbyter, and the celebration of the Eucharist by a presbyter, had no doubt been valid from the very first. But as a matter of Church order a presbyter could baptize only in emergencies: and it is not certain that he had an original right of celebrating the Eucharist[64]. As years went on, as the number of bishops was diminished and the number of detached congregations multiplied, the functions of the presbyters of such congregations became more and more independent. Their right to teach and their right to celebrate the Eucharist became ordinary and unquestioned: but one familiar instance shows that the primitive theory has never wholly passed away: the bishops of the Western Church have preserved to the present day their share in the complex ceremonies of

[63] See below, Lecture VIII.

[64] See the passages of Tertullian quoted in Lecture V. notes 22, 23: they are confirmed, in regard to baptism by S. Hieron. *Dial. c. Lucifer.* 9, Op. ed. Migne, vol. ii. 164: 'inde [i.e. from the necessity of unity] venit ut sine chrismate et episcopi jussione neque presbyter neque diaconus jus habeat baptizandi: quod frequenter, si tamen necessitas cogit, scimus etiam licere laicis': and in regard to the Eucharist by S. Ignat. *ad Smyrn.* 8. 1: *ἐκείνη βεβαία εὐχαριστία ἡγείσθω, ἡ ὑπὸ τὸν ἐπίσκοπον οὖσα, ἢ ᾧ αὐτὸς ἐπιτρέψῃ.*

baptism: no baptism is theoretically complete until a bishop has taken that part in it which once followed immediately upon immersion, but which has now come to have the semblance of a separate rite, and is known as Confirmation [65].

The change has been inevitable. The functions of the primitive presbyters are relative to a state of society which has long since passed away. The penitential system, which has been sometimes regarded as its modern counterpart, arose out of different circumstances, and involves a different principle. Between the *chiffonier* of the conscience, raking among the garbage of diseased thoughts and despicable actions, and the primitive college of disciplinary officers, there is barely the resemblance of a grotesque caricature. The counterpart, if counterpart be sought, must be found rather in the officers of those smaller bodies which have from time to time sprung up within the wide area of Christianity, and which have failed within even their own narrow limits as soon as the enthusiasm of their first founders has been crystallized into written rules of discipline. For in modern times, though the mainsprings of human conduct may have remained the

[65] The separation of the two chief elements of the baptismal rite, immersion and imposition of hands, had already begun to prevail in the West in the time of Jerome; but the latter was reserved for the bishop as a mark of respect to his dignity, and not as of necessity: 'ad honorem potius sacerdotii quam ad legem necessitatis' (S. Hieron. *Dial. c. Lucifer.* c. 9, Op. ed. Migne, vol. ii. 164.); when, in the controversy between the Eastern and Western Churches in the ninth century, the Latin theologians had to defend the separate existence of 'confirmation' by arguments, they were not able to cite early authorities (see e.g. the treatise of Aeneas of Paris in Dachery, *Spicilegium*, vol. i. p. 141).

same, the conception of the nature of morality, and of the forces which act upon conduct, has undergone significant change. We have come again to the conviction, which is not new but old, that the virtues which can be rewarded, and the vices which can be punished, by external discipline are not, as a rule, the virtues and the vices that make or mar the soul. The inner world of moral action knows no other tribunal than that of the conscience: and the education of the conscience, which is another phrase for moral growth, is the result of many internal forces—and not least of all of that force which the humblest of the Church's ministers may set in motion, when he holds up before the souls of men that ideal of a divine Life which was once an incarnate reality, and which is not now a vanished dream.

LECTURE IV.

THE SUPREMACY OF THE BISHOP.

WITH the exception—which is probably rather apparent than real—of two passages in the Pastoral Epistles, all general references to Church officers in Apostolic and sub-Apostolic literature speak of them in the plural [1]. The names by which they are designated are various but interchangeable: and their variety is probably to be explained by the fact that the same officers, or officers having equivalent rank, had various functions.

But in the course of the second century, although, for the most part, the same names continue to be used in the plural, one of them is appropriated to a single officer, who evidently stands above the rest, and in any enumeration of Church officers is mentioned separately.

I have already suggested reasons for the fact that this single officer had, as his ordinary designation, one rather than another of the names by which Church

[1] The exceptions are 1 Tim. 3. 2; Tit. i. 7: they are probably apparent rather than real because the article is probably generic: but the question of its precise significance has an important bearing on the wider question of the date of the Epistles.

officers had been known. I approach to-day the more difficult question how it was that such a supremacy came to exist. I approach this question with the greater diffidence because a hypothesis has long been current which does not admit of direct refutation, and which assigns the origin of this quasi-monarchical government to an institution of either our Lord Himself or the Apostles acting under His express directions. But in spite of the venerable names by which for many centuries, and in many Churches, this hypothesis has been maintained, and in spite also of the disadvantage under which any one labours who declines the short and easy road which it seems to offer, and winds his way through a dense undergrowth of intricate facts, it is impossible, at least for some of us, to accept the belief that the episcopate forms an exception to the general course of the divine government of the world, and to refrain from proceeding to the enquiry whether any causes were in operation which are adequate to account for its supremacy, without resorting to thehypothesis of a special and extraordinary institution.

I will ask you to look at two groups of facts: on the one hand the organization of contemporary associations, on the other the internal condition of the Christian communities themselves.

1. If we look at contemporary organizations, we find that the tendency towards the institution of a president was almost, if not altogether, universal. The evidence for the existence of this tendency does not consist of

a few facts, such as in a large mass of historical records may be collected together in support of almost any hypothesis: it is considerable in amount, it is various in character, it has no important exceptions. Whether we look at the municipal councils, at the private associations, religious and secular, with which the East was honeycombed, at the provincial assemblies, at the boards of magistrates, at the administrative councils of the Jews both in Palestine and in the countries of the dispersion, or at the committees of the municipal councils whose members sometimes bore in common with the Christian and the Jewish councils the name of 'elders' (*πρεσβύτεροι*), we find in every case evidence of the existence of a presiding officer [2].

[2] The following are instances: i. in the municipal councils there was a *βούλαρχος* at Termessus, *Corpus Inscr. Graec.* No. 2264, at Branchidae, *ibid.* No. 2881, at Aphrodisias, *ibid.* No. 2811, at Thyatira, *ibid.* No. 3494: a *πρέσβυς* at Sparta, Le Bas, *Voyage Archéologique*, 2me partie, ed. Foucart, No. 173 *a*: ii. in the private associations, there was an *ἀρχιερανιστὴς* at Athens, *C. I. G.* No. 126 (= *Corpus Inscr. Att.* vol. iii. No. 23), an *ἀρχιθιασίτης* at Delos, *ibid.* No. 2271, a *προστάτης τῆς συνόδου* *ibid.* No. 4893 in Upper Egypt: iii. in the provincial assemblies the president took his name from the province, e.g. *Συριάρχης* of the president of the *κοινὸν* of Syria, Cod. Justin. 5. 27. 1, *Βιθυνιάρχης* of that of Bithynia, Le Bas et Waddington, No. 1142 (cf. Marquardt, *Römische Staatsverwaltung*, Bd. i. p. 374, who gives a complete list of such presidents and identifies the office with that of *ἀρχιερεὺς*: so Kuhn, *Verfassung d. röm. Reichs*, 1er Th. pp. 106 sqq.): iv. in boards of magistrates there was a *πρεσβὺς τῆς συναρχίας* and also a *πρεσβὺς τῶν ἐφόρων* at Sparta, in imperial times, and board is sometimes spoken of as *οἱ περὶ τὸν δεῖνα*, *C. I. G.* 1241, 1249, 1268, 1326, 1347, 1375 (cf. Böckh's note, *ibid.* vol. i. p. 610): v. in the Jewish councils there was a *γερουσιάρχης* at Rome, *C. I. G.* 9902, and in Campania, Mommsen, *Inscr. Regn. Neap.* No. 2555 (cf. Schürer, *Die Gemeindeverfassung d. Juden in Rom*, p. 18): vi. in the committees of municipal councils there was an *ἀρχιπρύτανις* at Miletus and at Branchidae, *C. I. G.* Nos. 2878, 2881: an *ἀρχιπρόβουλος* at Termessus, *ibid.* No. 4364: and the office is implied in the expression *ἄρξαντα τοῦ πρεσβυτικοῦ* at Chios and at Sinope, *ibid.* Nos. 2220, 2221, 4157. It may be added to what is stated above that in Egypt from the time of the Macedonian kings, every class of functionaries, small and great, seems to have been organized on the basis of subordination to a chief officer: for some instances see Böckh in the *Corpus Inscr. Graec.* vol. iii. p. 305.

Now although the existence of such a general drift in contemporary organizations by no means proves that the Christian communities were borne along with it, still it establishes a basis of probability for the inference that communities which were so largely in harmony with those organizations in other respects, were in harmony with them also in this. The inference is strengthened by the fact that the localities in which there is the earliest contemporary evidence for the existence of a president, are also the localities in which the evidence for the existence of a president in other organizations is most complete. Both the one and the other are chiefly found in the great cities, and in the East even more than in the West. So strong is the inference when the facts are closely examined, that if we did not know as a matter of history that the Christian Churches did come to have a single head, it would be as necessary to account for the non-existence of such a head, as it would be in modern times to account for the singularity of a newly-formed group of associations which had neither president, nor governor, nor chairman.

2. If we look at the internal condition of the Christian communities, we shall see that several causes were at work to foster that which, if it be not inherent in all societies, was at any rate the dominant tendency of all societies at the time. Whether we look at them in their eleemosynary character as communities in which the widows and poor were supported from a common fund, or in their disciplinary character as communities which were bound together by the tie of

a holy life and in which moral offences were strictly judged, or in their character as communities which met together for public worship and required in such public worship some rule and leadership, in any of these characters there would be, as time went on, a convenience which in large communities would almost amount to a necessity, for a centralized administration —for at least a chairman of the governing body.

There are, besides these antecedent probabilities, two groups of known causes which operated in the same direction.

1. In the first place, there were some cases in which an Apostle had been supreme during his lifetime, and in which the tradition of personal supremacy lingered after his death: there were others in which the oversight of a community had been specially entrusted by an Apostle to some one officer: there were others in which special powers or special merits gave to some one man a predominant influence. Rome, Antioch, Ephesus, are examples of such cases. It is, indeed, wholly uncertain how far they are typical: and there is a probability that, where such supremacy existed, it was personal rather than official, inasmuch as those who exercised it do not appear to have had as such any distinguishing appellation. In later times they were entitled 'bishops:' the Clementines speak of James, 'the Lord's brother, as 'archbishop' and 'bishop of bishops[3]:' the subscriptions of some versions and late MSS. of the Pas-

[3] Clementin. *Recog.* I. 73 'Jacobus archiepiscopus' (so in later times, e.g. Conc. Ephes. c. 30 Ἰακώβου ἀποστόλου καὶ ἀρχιεπισκόπου): *Epist. Clem. ad Jacob.* inscr. Κλήμης Ἰακώβῳ τῷ κυρίῳ καὶ ἐπισκόπων ἐπισκόπῳ.

toral Epistles speak of Timothy and Titus as 'bishops' respectively of Ephesus and Crete[4]: but there is no early evidence of the use of these titles in this relation[5]: and on the other hand Irenaeus calls Polycarp indifferently 'bishop' and 'presbyter[6]:' and, what is even more significant, in a formal letter to the head of the Roman Church, in which, from the circumstances of the case, he would be least likely to omit any form of either right or courtesy, he speaks of his predecessors by name as 'presbyters[7].'

2. In the second place, there is clear proof of the existence of a theory of the nature of ecclesiastical organization which, from the fact of its persistent survival after a counter-theory had taken its place, may be supposed to have had a strong hold upon the communities among which it existed. To the writer

[4] The earliest MS. which does so is probably the *Codex Coislensis* of the sixth century: the version which does so is the Peschito: the statement which contains the word is omitted in the greater MSS. and in the early Latin versions.

[5] The earliest use of the word with a definite reference to an individual is the inscription of the letter of Ignatius to Polycarp: *Ἰγνάτιος, ὁ καὶ Θεοφόρος, Πολυκάρπῳ ἐπισκόπῳ ἐκκλησίας Σμυρναίων*: but the absence of the definite article, and the inscription of Polycarp's own letter, *Πολύκαρπος καὶ οἱ σὺν αὐτῷ πρεσβύτεροι*, are inconsistent with the hypothesis that the word was already specially appropriated to the head of the community. The next earliest use of the word is probably also in reference to Polycarp in the letter of Polycrates to Victor, ap. Euseb. *H. E.* 5. 24. It is worthy of note, i. that these earliest uses are in reference to officers of the Asiatic Churches, i.e. in the neighbourhood of communities in which *ἐπίσκοπος* was already a title of certain secular officers (see Lecture II, notes 26, 28): ii. that Hegesippus does not give any title to the heads of the Roman church.

[6] S. Iren. *Epist. ad Florin.* ap. Euseb. *H. E.* 5. 20. 7, *ὁ μακάριος καὶ ἀποστολικὸς πρεσβύτερος*: *adv. Haeres.* 3. 3. 4 *ὑπὸ τῶν ἀποστόλων κατασταθεὶς . . . ἐπίσκοπος.*

[7] S. Iren. *Epist. ad Victor.* ap. Euseb. *H. E.* 5. 24. 14 *οἱ πρὸ Σωτῆρος πρεσβύτεροι οἱ προστάντες τῆς ἐκκλησίας ἧς σὺ νῦν ἀφηγῇ, Ἀνίκητον λέγομεν καὶ Πίον κ.τ.λ.* So late as the third century, the extant epitaphs of Roman bishops do not give the title *episcopus*: De Rossi, *Bulletino di Archeologia Christ.* ann. ii. 1864, p. 50.

of the Ignatian Epistles each organized community of Christians is a perfect reflex of the whole Church of God. It is a pure theocracy. In our Lord's own lifetime He Himself had been the visible head of that Kingdom of Heaven which He preached: His Apostles had stood round Him as His ministers—the twelve heads and patriarchs of the tribes of the new Israel: the rest of the disciples—the new people of God—had listened and obeyed. So it was still: the bishop sat in the Lord's place: the presbyters were what the Apostles had been: it was for the rest of the community to listen and to obey [8]. Upon this theory of ecclesiastical organization the existence of a president was a necessity: and the theory seems to go back to the very beginnings of the Christian societies. For in those beginnings the Kingdom of God was realized in a concrete sense as the Kingdom of David. In the infant community at Jerusalem after the Lord had been 'taken up,' James, as being His kinsman and the next earthly representative of the royal house, presided in His stead [9]: on the death of James another 'brother' was appointed to succeed him [10]: other kinsmen of the Lord, as being His kinsmen, presided in other Churches [11]: and so the idea that the new Kingdom of David should have at its head one of David's line, until the Messiah should return to reign, remained as a fun-

[8] S. Ignat. *ad Magn.* 6. 1.

[9] Hegesipp. ap. Euseb. *H. E.* 2. 23. 4: Clem. Alex. *ibid.* 2. 1. 3.

[10] Hegesipp. ap. Euseb. *H. E.* 3. 32 (of Symeon), 'as being a descendant of David and a Christian': id. ap. Euseb. *H. E.* 4. 22 'Symeon the son of Clopas is appointed bishop, whom all proposed as being the next cousin of the Lord:' so *ibid.* 3. 11.

[11] Hegesipp. ap. Euseb. *H. E.* 3. 20. 32.

damental idea of Judaeo-Christian organization, until the long-delayed Parousia seemed almost to vanish in the far horizon of the unrealized future, and the desolation of the royal city began to turn men's thoughts from Jerusalem to Rome[12].

These facts, and these general considerations of probability, seem adequate to account for the fact that the Christian communities were borne along with the general drift of contemporary organizations, and that the council of presbyters had a permanent president[13]. They also seem to account for the fact that the functions of that council of presbyters, as described by Clement and Polycarp, are the same in kind as the functions of the bishop as described in the Ignatian Epistles. But they are all compatible with the view

[12] The importance to the Christian Church of the fall of Jerusalem (for the completeness of which see especially Aristo ap. Euseb. *H. E.* 4. 6. 3, S. Hieron. *Comm. in Sophon.* c. 1. 15, vol. vi. p. 692, ed. Vall., S. Greg. Nazianz. *Orat.* 6, c. 18, vol. i. p. 191, ed. Ben.) was to some extent recognized by Jerome (*Epist.* 120 *ad Hedib.* c. 8, vol. i. p. 27), and has frequently been pointed out by modern writers, e.g. Gfrörer, *Allgemeine Kirchengeschichte*, Bd. i. p. 253, Rothe, *Vorlesungen über Kirchengeschichte*, ed. Weingarten, Bd. i. pp. 75 sqq.

[13] It is not meant to be implied that, at least after the episcopal system had become firmly established, the bishop was himself always a presbyter: it is clear not only that there was an absence of the later rule which required a bishop to be elected from the body of presbyters, or to be formally admitted to the presbyterate before being invested with the episcopate, but also that a man might be appointed bishop at an earlier age than was allowable for a presbyter: this is the point of Jerome's argument against John of Jerusalem (*Epist.* 82 (62), vol. i. p. 516, ed. Vall.): and there is probably a reference to it in the disputed phrase νεωτέραν τάξιν of S. Ignat. *ad Magn.* 3. 1 (cf. Zahn's philological arguments in his *Ignatius von Antiochien*, pp. 305 sqq.). The distinction between administrative officers and the members of a deliberative assembly was familiar to the Roman world: in the municipal councils the administrative officers not only had a seat but presided: but they were only *ex officio* members of those councils, and at the next revision of the roll, after the expiration of their term of office, they might be excluded (cf. Marquardt, *Römische Staatsverwaltung*, Bd. i. pp. 503 sqq.).

that the early bishop stood to his presbyters in the relation of a dean to the canons of a cathedral, or of the chairman to the ordinary members of a committee. They do not account for the fact that the bishops of the third and subsequent centuries claimed for themselves exceptional powers, and that the relation of primacy ultimately changed into a relation of supremacy.

The causes of that important change seem to lie in a wholly different set of facts, into which it is necessary to enter at somewhat greater length.

Before the close of the Apostolic age Christianity had come into contact with various large tendencies of contemporary thought. Its first contact was with the great school of fantastic syncretism which had grown up within Judaism itself, and which has left a considerable monument in the works of Philo. To that school all facts past and present were an allegory. Nothing was what it seemed to be, but was the symbol of the unapparent. The history of the Old Testament was sublimated into a history of the emancipation of reason from passion. If Abel was described as a keeper of sheep, the meaning was that moral wisdom keeps the irrational impulses under control [14]. If Israel was described as warring against Amalek, the meaning was that when reason lifts itself up away from earth, as Moses lifted up his hands, it is strengthened by the vision of God [15]. If Abraham was described as migrating from Chaldaea to Canaan, the meaning was that wisdom

[14] Philo, i. p. 170, ed. Mang.

[15] *ibid.* p. 124.

leaves the prejudices and crude ideas of its original state, and seeks a new home among the realities of abstract thought[16]. To those who thought thus, the records of the Gospels were so much new matter for allegorical interpretation. To the lower intelligence, to the eye of sense, Christ was a Person who had lived and died and ascended: and the Christian communities were the visible assemblies of His followers: and the Christian virtues were certain habits of mind which showed themselves in deeds. But to the spiritual mind, to the eye of reason, all these things were like the phantasmagoria of the mysteries. The recorded deeds of Christ were the clash and play of mighty spiritual forces: the Christian Church was an emanation from God: the Christian virtues were phases of intellectual enlightenment which had but slender, if any, links with deeds done in the flesh. Before long the circle widened in which Christian ideas were rationalized. Christianity found itself in contact not merely with mysteries but with metaphysics. But they were the metaphysics of 'wonderland.' Abstract conceptions seemed to take bodily shape, and to form strange marriages, and to pass in and out of one another like the dissolving scenery of a dream. There grew up a new mythology, in which Zeus and Aphrodite, Isis and Osiris, were replaced by Depth and Silence, Wisdom and Power. Christianity ceased to be a religion and became a theosophy. It ceased to be a doctrine and became a Platonic poem. It ceased to be a rule of life and became a system of the universe. It was transferred

[16] Philo, i. pp. 436, 437, ed. Mang.

from the world of human action in which it had seemed to have its birth into a supersensuous world of unimaginable vastness, and its truths were no longer fixed facts of faith and life, but the gorgeous, and shifting, and unsubstantial pageantry of the clouds of an autumn sky [17].

The transfer seems to us as paradoxical as the attempt of some philosophers of our own day to construct a Church Catholic, with a priesthood and a ritual, upon the basis of a negation of the religious idea. But it was an age of paradoxes: and for a time the paradox seemed likely to triumph. The contact of Christianity with philosophy raised, in short, a problem which was not less fundamental in its bearing upon Christian organization than it was in its bearing upon Christian teaching. It was admitted on all sides that Christianity had its starting-point in certain facts and certain sayings: but if any and every interpre-

[17] The evidence for the opinions of the various schools of Gnostics has mostly to be gathered from the quotations of their writings by their opponents, especially Irenaeus and Hippolytus: the only complete Gnostic treatise which has come down to modern times is a late Valentinian work entitled Πίστις Σοφία, of which the Coptic text, with a Latin translation, was published by Schwartz and Petermann in 1851. The modern literature of the subject is extensive: the first clear view was given by Baur, *Die christliche Gnosis*, and *Geschichte der christlichen Kirche*, Bd. i. (Eng. Trans. published in the Theological Translation Fund Library, 1878 pp. 184 sqq.): the best general view is that of Lipsius in Ersch and Gruber's *Allgem. Encyclopädie*, s.v. Gnosticismus, vol. lxxi. pp. 230 sqq. (since printed separately), and the most accurate of shorter summaries, with valuable bibliographical references, that of Ueberweg, *Grundriss der Geschichte der Philosophie* (Eng. Trans. in the Theological and Philosophical Library, vol. i. pp. 280–290). English readers will also find some valuable information in Dean Mansel's posthumous work, *The Gnostic heresies of the first and second centuries*, London, 1875, and in Dr. Salmon's articles in the *Dictionary of Christian Biography*, especially s.v. Gnosticism: Mr. King's *The Gnostics and their remains*, London, 1864, is useful for the information which it collects as to the Eastern affinities, and possible sources, of Gnosticism.

tation of those facts and those sayings was possible, if any system of philosophy might be taught into which the words which expressed them could be woven, it is clear that there could be but little cohesion between the members of its communities. It was practically impossible to form, at least on any considerable scale, an association which should have for its intellectual basis free speculation about the unknowable, and for its moral basis a creed which should embrace all possible varieties from the extreme of asceticism to absolute indifference[18]. The problem arose and pressed for an answer—What should be the basis of Christian union? But the problem was for a time insoluble. For there was no standard and no court of appeal. It was useless to argue from the Scriptures that this or that system of philosophy was inconsistent with them, because one of the chief questions to be determined was whether the Scriptures did or did not admit of allegorical or philosophical interpretation. In our own day, it is true, the answer to such a question seems easy: but in those days the temper of many men was towards allegorizing, and mysticism was a prevailing attitude of mind. If Homer could furnish texts and proofs for Platonic lectures, the Gospels could furnish texts and proofs for Gnostic sermons. So hopeless was this kind of

[18] Gnostic morality, like the morality of all systems which press to an extreme the antithesis between the material and the spiritual elements of human nature, necessarily took a double direction: on the one hand it tended to repress the material element and so became ascetic (an extreme which is found in the *Encratitae*), on the other it tended to regard the material element as indifferent and so became antinomian (an extreme which is found in the *Antitactae*).

controversy that Tertullian deprecates it: 'incerta est victoria aut par incertae[19].' It was equally useless to appeal to a rule of faith—to the rudimentary form of creed which entered into the ritual of baptism: for those who admitted a rule of faith claimed the same liberty in its interpretation which they claimed in the interpretation of the Scriptures: Carpocrates, Basilides, and Valentinus all traced back their opinions to an esoteric and transmitted teaching, which was both more valuable than any written formula, and more authoritative[20].

The crisis was one the gravity of which it would be difficult to overestimate. There have been crises since in the history of Christianity, but there is none which equals in importance this upon the issue of which it depended, for all time to come, whether

[19] Tertull. *De praescr. haeret.* 19.

[20] There were three main points at issue: i. the determination of the canon of the Christian Scriptures: Basilides (Origen, *Hom.* 1 *in Luc.* vol. iii. p. 933, ed. De La Rue: Apelles (S. Hieron. *Prolog. in Matt.* vol. vii. p. 3, ed. Vall.): Valentinus S. Iren. 3. 11. 9): Marcion (Tertul *adv. Marcion.*, passim), all admitted some Gospel or other, but not, at least in their integrity, our canonical Gospels: ii. the determination of the terms of the 'regula fidei:' Marcion (Tertull. *adv. Marcion,* 1. 1), and other Gnostics (S. Iren. 3. 11. 3) had their 'regulae fidei' (that of Apelles is preserved by Hippolytus, 7. 9), which differed not only from the orthodox rule but from one another (S. Iren. 1. 21. 5, Tert. *De praesc. haeret.* 42): iii. the determination of the true and the false tradition of Apostolic teaching: Carpocrates (S. Iren. 1. 25. 5): Basilides (S. Clem. Alex. *Strom.* 7. 17, p. 900, ed. Pott.): the Valentinians (Ptolemaeus, *Epist. ad Floram,* ap. S. Epiphan. *Haeres.* 33. 7), and others (S. Iren. 3. 2. 1: Anon. ap. Euseb. *H. E.* 5. 28. 3: Justin M. *c. Tryph.* 48: Tertull. *adv. Prax.* 3: see especially Πίστις Σοφία, p. 1, which makes great account of the teaching of Christ after His resurrection), maintained that what they taught had been transmitted to them from the Apostles. The difficulty of this latter controversy was even greater than that of the other two, because the principle of an esoteric and therefore unverifiable γνῶσις was admitted by some orthodox writers, especially by Clement of Alexandria (cf. e.g. Dahne, *De γνώσει Clementis Alexandrini,* Leipsig, 1831).

Christianity should be regarded as a body of revealed doctrine, or the *caput mortuum* of a hundred philosophies—whether the basis of Christian organization should be a definite and definitely interpreted creed, or a chaos of speculations. But great crises give birth to great conceptions. There is a kind of unconscious logic in the minds of masses of men, when great questions are abroad, which some one thinker throws into form. The form which the 'common sense,' so to speak, of Christendom took upon this great question is one which is so familiar to us that we find it difficult to go back to a time when it was not yet in being. Its first elaboration and setting forth was due to one man's genius. With great rhetorical force and dialectical subtlety, Irenaeus, the bishop of the chief Christian Church in Gaul, maintained that the standard of Christian teaching was the teaching of the Churches which the Apostles had founded,—which teaching he held to be on all essential points the same [21]. He maintained the existence, and he asserted the authority, of a *fides catholica*—the general belief of the Christian Churches—which was also the *fides apostolica*—the belief which the Apostles had taught [22]. To that *fides catholica et apostolica* all individual opinions and interpretations were to be referred: such as were in

[21] The argument runs through the whole of the treatise: reference may be made especially to Bk. 3. 2 : 4. 26.

[22] The phrases 'fides catholica' and 'fides apostolica' are probably later than Irenaeus: but they came to be adopted as the technical expressions for that for which he contended. The former of the two phrases seems to be first used in the martyrologies: 'catholica fides et religio,' *Mart. Pion.* 18, ap. Ruinart, p. 137: 'fides catholica,' *Mart. Epipod. et Alex.* 3, ap. Ruinart, p. 149: cf. Görres in the *Zeitschrift f. wissenschaftl. Theologie*, 1879, Bd. xxii. p. 74 sqq.

conformity with it were to be received as Christian, such as differed from it were αἱρετικαὶ—not the general or traditional belief of the Christian Churches, but the belief of only a sect or party. In this view, which was already in the air, the Christian world gradually acquiesced: henceforth there was a standard of appeal: henceforth there was a definite basis of union.

Thus were the Christian communities saved from disintegration. Upon the basis of a Catholic and Apostolic faith was built the sublime superstructure of a Catholic and Apostolic Church [23]. But in the building of that superstructure there arose a concurrent and not less important question,—how was the teaching of the Churches to be known, and who were its conservators? Already in the Rabbinical schools stress had been laid upon the fact that there had been a succession of Rabbis from Moses downwards, who had handed on from generation to generation the sacred deposit of divine truth [24]. It might reasonably be supposed that in the Christian Churches there had been a similar tradition from one generation of officers to another: that, in other words, the Apostles had definitely taught those whom they had appointed, or recognized, as officers, and what had been so taught had been preserved by

[23] The phrase ἡ καθολικὴ ἐκκλησία occurs first in S. Ignat. *ad Smyrn.* 8. 2, though probably in a different sense from that which it afterwards acquired: it is also found in *Mart. Polyc.* 19. 2, and in the Muratorian Fragment, lines 61, 66. It is not found in Irenaeus, though equivalent phrases are frequent, but is found in both Tertullian and Clement of Alexandria: see Harnack on the *Symbolum Ecclesiae Romanae* in Gebhardt and H.'s *Patrum Apost. Op.* ed. ii. part i. fasc. 2, p. 141: and Keim, *Aus dem Urchristenthum*, p. 115.

[24] *Pirqe Aboth*, e.g. I. I (ed. Taylor, cf. Excursus, ii. p. 124).

those who had succeeded those officers. But those officers were in all, or if not in all at least in a great majority of Churches, more than one in number: and it is evident, from the nature of the case, that there was an element of danger in thus entrusting the sacred deposit of Apostolic teaching in each community to a plurality of persons, and that as the number of officers multiplied in a community the danger would be proportionately greater. The necessity for unity was supreme: and the unity in each community must be absolute. But such an absolute unity could only be secured when the teacher was a single person. That single person was naturally the president of the community. Consequently in the Clementines, for the first time, the president of the community is regarded in the light of the custodian of the rule of faith—in express distinction from the presbyters who are entrusted only with that which is relative to their main functions—the teaching of the maxims of Christian morality[25]. The point was not at once universally conceded; but in the course of the third century it seems to have won its way to general recognition. The supremacy of the bishop and unity of doctrine were conceived as going hand in hand: the bishop was conceived as having what Irenaeus calls the 'charisma veritatis[26];' the bishop's seat was conceived as being, what St. Augustine calls it, the 'cathedra unitatis[27];'

[25] Clementin. *Recog.* 3. 65.

[26] S. Iren. 4. 26. 2.

[27] S. August. *Epist.* 105 (166) c. 5, Op. ed. Migne, vol. ii. 403: 'neque enim sua sunt quae dicunt sed Dei qui in cathedra unitatis doctrinam posuit veritatis' so in the Clementines Peter entrusts to Clement τὴν ἐμὴν τῶν λόγων καθέδραν, and afterwards speaks of him as τὸν ἀληθείας προκαθεζόμενον, *Epist. Clem. ad Jacob.* c. 2.

and round the episcopal office revolved the whole vast system, not only of Christian administration and Christian organization, but also of Christian doctrine.

If I may now recall your attention to the problem which was originally proposed, I venture to think that adequate causes have been found not only for the existence of a president, but also for his supremacy, without resorting to what is not a known fact, but only a counter-hypothesis—the hypothesis of a special institution. The episcopate grew by the force of circumstances, in the order of Providence, to satisfy a felt need. It is pertinent to add that this view as to the chief cause which operated to produce it has not the merit or demerit of novelty. Although the view must rest upon its own inherent probability as a complete explanation of the known facts of the case, it has the support of the earliest and greatest of ecclesiastical antiquaries. St. Jerome, arguing against the growing tendency to exalt the diaconate at the expense of the presbyterate, maintains that the Churches were originally governed by a plurality of presbyters, but that in course of time one was elected to preside over the rest as a remedy against division, lest different presbyters, having different views of doctrine, should, by each of them drawing a portion of the community to himself, cause divisions in it[28].

The supremacy of a single officer which was thus

[28] S. Hieron. *Epist.* 146 (85) ad Evang. vol. i. p. 1082, ed. Vall.: so also *Dial. c. Lucif.* c. 9, vol. ii. p. 181, 'Ecclesiae salus in summi sacerdotis dignitate pendet, cui si non exsors quaedam et ab omnibus detur potestas, tot in ecclesiis efficientur schismata quot sacerdotes:' cf. *Comm. in Ep ad Tit.* c. i. vol. vii. p. 694.

forced upon the Churches by the necessity for unity of doctrine, was consolidated by the necessity for unity of discipline.

Early in the third century rose the question of readmission to membership of those who had fallen into grievous sin, or who had shrunk from martyrdom. For many years there had been comparative peace. In those years the gates of the Church had been opened wider than before. The sterner discipline had been relaxed. Christianity was not illegal, and was tending to become fashionable. On a sudden the flames of persecution shot fiercely forth again. The professors of Christian philosophy defended the policy of submission on the theological ground that Christ did not call on all men to be partakers of His sufferings in the flesh [29]. The fashionable church-goers accepted the easy terms which the state offered to those who were willing to acknowledge the state religion. Those who did not actually offer incense on heathen altars made friends with the police, purchased false certificates of having complied with the law, or bribed the officers of the courts to strike their names out of the cause-list [30]. When the persecution was over, many of the 'lapsed,'

[29] The Gnostic schools, with the exception of the Marcionites (Euseb. *H. E.* 4. 15. 46: 5. 16. 21: 7. 12: *De Mart. Pal.* 10. 2) discouraged martyrdom on both the ground mentioned above and other grounds: see e.g. Heracleon ap. Clem. Al. *Strom.* 4. 9. p. 595, ed. Pott.: Origen, *Hom. in Ezech.* 3. vol. iii. p. 366: S. Iren. 1. 24. 6: 3. 18. 5: Tertull. *Scorpiace* passim.

[30] Tertull. *De Fuga in Persec.* 12, 'Tu autem pro eo pacisceris cum delatore vel milite vel furunculo aliquo praeside': *ibid.* 13 'nescio dolendum an erubescendum sit cum in matricibus beneficiariorum [i.e. court officers] et curiosiorum [i.e. detective police] inter tabernarios et lenios et fures balneorum et aleones et lenones, Christiani quoque vectigales continentur.' For the 'libelli,' or false certificates, cf. e.g. S. Cyprian, *Epist.* 30 (31), c. 3, p. 550: *De Lapsis*, 27. p. 256.

as they were called, wished to come back again. The path had become easy: for martyrdom was a new beatitude [31]. The baptism of blood seemed to have vicarious merit: and even those who stood upon the lower steps of that sure stairway into heaven seemed entitled to claim some remission of the sins of a weaker brother [32]. The privilege, like the 'indulgences' of the Roman Church in later times, was singularly abused. Some of those who had undergone the bare minimum of imprisonment which entitled them to be ranked as confessors gave 'libelli,' or certificates of exemption, by wholesale. At one time, as we learn from Cyprian, the confessors in a body gave them to the whole body of the lapsed [33]. The scandal of the practice was increased by an innovation upon the mode of readmission. In earlier days each separate case came for judgment before the whole Church. The certificate of a confessor was of the nature of an appeal which the Church might upon occasion reject [34]. But persecution sometimes ren-

[31] Cf. e.g. Origen's *Exhortatio ad Martyrium*, Op. ed. De La Rue, i. 274 sqq.: the treatise *De Laude Martyrii* sometimes, erroneously, ascribed to Cyprian and printed with his works (ed. Hartel, Appendix, pp. 26 sqq.): and the expressions of martyrs themselves in e.g. St. Cyprian, *Epist.* 31 (26), c. 3, p. 559. It was regarded as cleansing a man from sin (e.g. Clem. Alex. *Strom.* 4. 9, p. 597); it was the true 'cup of salvation' (Origen, *Exhort. ad Mart.* 28), and as opening heaven ('sanguini nostro patet coelum . . . et inter omnium gloriam pulchrior sanguinis titulus est et integrior corona signatur,' Auct. *De Laude Mart.* 9).

[32] Cf. Origen's *Exhort. ad Mart.* 30 vol. 1. p. 293; 50 vol. 1. p. 309, where the sufferings of martyrs are represented as having, though in a less degree, the same kind of efficacy as the sufferings of Christ: Tertull. *De Pudic.* 22. represents 'moechi' and 'fornicatores' as going to one who has been recently imprisoned, 'ex consensione (*al.* confessione) vincula induit adhuc mollia,' to obtain his intercession.

[33] S. Cyprian, *Epist.* 23 (16), p. 536: so *Epist.* 20 (14), p. 528, 'thousands of certificates were given every day.'

[34] This is implied in S. Cyprian, *Epist.* 36 (30), p. 574: 15 (10), p. 513: 17 (11), p. 521: 43 (40), p. 592: but the form of the appeal which Celerinus makes

dered it impossible for the Church to be gathered together. The Church-officers took it upon themselves to act for the general body. They readmitted the lapsed without consulting the assembly[35]. That which had begun in a time of emergency tended to become a rule in a time of peace. The sterner sort looked on with dismay. The pure spouse of Christ was in peril of her virginity. The Churches for which some of them had sacrificed all they had were beginning to be filled with the weak brethren who had preferred dishonour to death. They were like Noah's ark, into which unclean as well as clean had entered[36]. There was a long and determined controversy. The extreme party maintained that under no circumstances was one who had lapsed to be readmitted[37]. At one time this view tended to prevail: but, as in almost all controversies, that which did prevail was the spirit of compromise. It was agreed on all sides that readmissions must not be indiscriminate: if the earlier usage of submitting each case to the tribunal of the whole assembly were impossible, at any rate individual presbyters and deacons must not act without the knowledge and approval of the president[38]. The rule was in many

to Lucianus, *ibid.* 21 (20), p. 532, implies that there was also a tendency to treat the martyrs' certificate as a final remission.

[35] This is shown by the strong remonstrances of Cyprian against the practice: e.g. *Epist.* 15 (10), p. 514: 16 (9), p. 517: 17 (11), p. 522: 41 (38), p. 588: 59 (55), p. 682: 61 (58), p. 730.

[36] S. Hippol. *Refut. omn. haeres.* 9. 12. p. 460, ed. Dunck. et Schneid.

[37] There was at first the compromise that although one who had 'lapsed' should be excluded from communion during his active lifetime, he might be readmitted at the point of death: but at last the party at Rome, of which Novatian was the head, refused even this concession (S. Cyprian, *Epist.* 55 (56), 57 (54): Euseb. *H. E.* 6. 43).

[38] Not only a uniform tradition of doctrine, but also a uniform tradition of

cases resisted: it frequently required formal reenactment[39]: but it ultimately became so general that the bishops came to claim the right of readmitting penitents, not in their capacity as presidents of the community, but as an inherent function of the episcopate.

In this way it was that the supremacy of the bishops, which had been founded on the necessity for unity of doctrine, was consolidated by the necessity for unity of discipline.

It was a natural effect of the same causes, and it forms an additional proof of their existence, that a rule should grow up that there should be only one bishop in a community. The rule was not firmly established until the third century. Its general recognition was the outcome of the dispute between Cyprian and Novatian. That dispute was one of the collateral results of the controversy, of which I have just now been speaking, in reference to the readmission of the lapsed. Novatian was the head of the puritan party in Rome. He was a theologian whose orthodoxy is expressly admitted by Cyprian himself, and who had done good service[40]. When, after a vacancy of some

discipline, was better preserved by a single person than by a plurality of persons. The bishop was the depositary of the traditionary rules of discipline: and it is on this fact that the Clementines base his special relation to it: Clementin. *Epist. ad Jacob.* 2 δήσει ὃ δεῖ δεθῆναι καὶ λύσει ὃ δεῖ λυθῆναι ὡς τῆς ἐκκλησίας εἰδὼς κανόνα: so *ibid.* 4 ὡς διοίκησιν ἐκκλεσίας παρ' ἐμοῦ μεμαθηκώς.

[39] e.g. in the Spanish Councils of Elvira, c. 32, 2 Seville, c. 9, the Gallican Councils of Orange, c. 1, 2 Arles, c. 26, the African Councils, 2 Carth. c. 3, 4, 3 Carth. c. 32: but the Greek rule, according to the *Poenitentiale Theodori*, 2. 3. 8, ed. Haddan and Stubbs' *Councils and Ecclesiastical Documents*, vol. iii. p. 188, allowed a presbyter to act without a bishop.

[40] He had been the organ of the Roman Church in writing to Cyprian the letter which is printed among those of Cyprian, *Epist.* 30 (31), p. 549: his *Liber de*

duration in the Roman episcopate, a bishop was elected who belonged to the anti-puritan party, and who formally accepted the principle that in the Church there must be a mingling of good and bad, the puritan party resolved to have a bishop of their own, and elected Novatian. All the elements of a valid election were present. Under ordinary circumstances, or in a newly organized community, the election would have been unchallenged. There was only one point in which it was exceptional. That exceptional point was that Rome already possessed a complete organization. The question arose whether it was competent, under any circumstances, for a new organization to be established side by side with an existing organization in the same city. The question does not seem to have been raised before: and in Asia Minor, in Syria, and in Africa Novatian's election was for a time held to be valid [41]. But, with the far-sightedness of a great politician, Cyprian saw the bearings of the question on Christian organization. He used the whole weight of his influence, and the whole force of his vehement rhetoric, to maintain that, the election of Cornelius having been valid, the election of Novatian was null. The controversy was keen, but in the end Cyprian prevailed.

Trinitate is printed in Gallandi, vol. iv. and Migne P. L. vol. iii: his orthodoxy is admitted in detail by Cyprian, *Epist.* 69 (76), c. 7, p. 756.

[41] Novatian seems to have written an encyclical letter announcing both his election and his policy on the question of the readmission of the lapsed (Socrat. *H. E.* 4. 28). In Asia Minor some churches sided with him strongly and permanently (Socrat. *ibid.*: Sozom. *H. E.* 6. 24). In Syria he would probably have been formally recognized by a council at Antioch, but for the death of Fabius (this is implied by Euseb. *H. E.* 6. 46): that he was not without adherents in Africa is shown, e.g. by Cyprian's letter to Antonianus, *Epist.* 55 (52), p. 625.

The necessity for unity outweighed all other considerations. Henceforth, whoever in any city claimed to be a member of the Christian Church must belong to the established organization of that city. The seamless coat of Christ must not be rent. As there was one God, and one Christ, and one Holy Spirit, so there could be but one bishop [42]. The attempt to form two communities side by side put its authors outside the pale of the Church Catholic: *σχίσμα*, like *αἵρεσις*, was a word of bad repute: the keystone of Christian organization was fitted firmly into its place: the free right of association existed no longer.

One other result flowed from this conception of the bishop as the embodiment of unity of doctrine and unity of discipline, which also helps to confirm the view that the prevalence of that conception was the main cause of his supremacy.

The earliest theory of the relation of the bishop to the community was, as we have already seen [43], that the bishop stood in the place of the unseen Lord, entrusted with the oversight of his Master's household until He should return from that far country into which He had gone. This view is found in the Ignatian Epistles, in the Clementines, and in the Apostolical Constitutions [44]. In none of these cases is there any ambiguity of expression. The bishop is in

[42] *Epist. Cornelii*, ap. S. Cypr. *Epist.* 46 (49), p. 611.

[43] See above, p. 87.

[44] Clementin. 3. 60 *ἐπὶ τῆς Χριστοῦ καθέδρας καθεσθείς*: 3. 70 *θρόνον οὖν Χριστοῦ τιμήσετε*: Const. Apost. 2. 26 *ὁ γὰρ ἐπίσκοπος προκαθεζέσθω ὑμῶν ὡς Θεοῦ ἀξίᾳ τετιμημενος*: Dionys. Areop. *Eccles. Hierarch.* uses *οἱ θεοειδεῖς ἱεροτελεσταί, ὁ θεοειδὴς ἱεράρχης*, passim, of bishops. S. Cyprian, *Epist.* 59 (55), c. 5, p. 672 'unus in ecclesia ad tempus sacerdos et ad tempus judex vice Christi.'

the place of God, or of Christ: the presbyters are in the place of the Apostles. But gradually another theory interweaves itself with this and ultimately takes its place. It was a not unnatural inference from the belief that the bishop was the custodian and conservator of Apostolic teaching that he, rather than the presbyters, took the Apostles' place. The bishops had succeeded the Apostles in the presidency of the several Churches by what Firmilian calls an *ordinatio vicaria*[45]—one officer being appointed in another's place, as governor succeeded governor in a Roman province, or as chancellor succeeds chancellor in our own University[46]. When discipline as well as doctrine found its centre in the bishops, it began to be argued that they had succeeded not only to the seats which the Apostles had filled, but also to the powers which the Apostles possessed[47]. It began to be urged that

[45] Epist. Firmilian, ap. S. Cyprian, *Ep.* 75, c. 16, p. 821.

[46] There is neither proof nor presumption that the word διαδοχή, which is ordinarily used, e.g. by Eusebius, *H. E.* 1. 1 and *passim,* to designate the succession of bishops, is to be taken in any other than the sense which it ordinarily bore. It is used not only by civil historians to designate the succession of civil officers, but also of the succession, i. of the heads of philosophical schools, e.g. Diog. Laert. *proem.*: ii. of Jewish high priests, Joseph, *B. J.* 4. 3. 6: iii. of heretical teachers, e.g. S. Hippol. *Haeres.* 9. 7, p. 440: Ptolem. *Epist. ad Floram,* ap. S. Epiph. *Haeres.* 33. 7: and of Marcionite bishops, Adamant. *Dial. de recta in Deum fide,* i. ap. Append. ad Origen. Op. vol. i. p. 810, ed. De la Rue.

[47] The view that bishops, and not presbyters, are the successors of the Apostles, appears first by implication in the claim of Zephyrinus and Callistus, during the Montanist controversy, to have the power of absolving penitents from sin (Tertull. *De Pudic.* 1: S. Hippol. *Haeres.* 9. 12. p. 458), which appears to have been based on the assumption of their succession to S. Peter (Tertull. *De Pudic.* 21, where Zephyrinus is addressed as 'apostolice,' and where, after quoting S. Matt. 16. 18, 19, Tertullian proceeds 'idcirco tu praesumis et ad te derivasse solvendi et alligandi potestatem, id est ad omnem ecclesiam Petri propinquam qualis es evertens atque commutans manifestam Domini intentionem personaliter hoc Petro conferentem.') Probably the earliest express statement of it as applicable to all bishops is by an

the powers, especially the power of 'binding and loosing,' which our Lord had conferred on the Apostles, were given to them not personally or as constituting the Church of the time, but in a representative capacity as the first members of a long line of Church officers[48]. Against an early assertion of this view Tertullian raised a vigorous protest: nor did the view win its way to general acceptance until the time of the great Latin theologians of the fifth century. It was a still later development of this view to maintain that the bishops had also succeeded to the power of the Apostles in the conferring of spiritual gifts, and that through them, and through them exclusively, did it please the Holy Spirit to enter into the souls either of individual Christians in baptism, or of

African bishop in the course of the controversy on rebaptism: 'manifesta est sententia Domini nostri Jesu Christi apostolos suos mittentis et ipsis solis potestatem a patre sibi datam permittentis, quibus nos successimus eadem potestate ecclesiam Domini gubernantes et credentium fidem baptizantes' (Clarus a Mascula in the *Sententiae Episcoporum*, 79, ap. S. Cyprian. Op. p. 459, ed. Hartel: printed as Concilium Carthag. vii. in Routh, *Reliquiae Sacrae*, vol. iii. p. 130): it is also stated about the same time, though less expressly, by Cyprian himself, *Epist.* 3 (65) p. 471, and by Firmilian of Caesarea, ap. S. Cyprian. *Epist.* 75, c. 16, p. 821. A compromise between the two theories of Apostolical succession was sometimes adopted in later times: the metropolitan was regarded as being in the place of Christ and his suffragans sat round him like the Apostles: S. Symeon. Thessal. *De sacris Ordinationibus*, c. 6.

[48] The contention of Tertullian (as a Montanist) was that the 'power of the keys' was personal to S. Peter (*De Pudic.* 21, quoted in preceding note). The view of Augustine was that it was given to the Church (S. Aug. *De Catech. Rud.* c. 31, Op. ed. Migne, vol. vi. 308: *c. advers. Legis*, 1. 17. vol. viii. 624: *Tract.* 50 *in S. Joann. Evang.* c. 12, vol. iii. 1763: *De baptismo c. Donat.* 7. 43, vol. ix. 237, from which it appears that what afterwards became the current view was held by the Donatists). But in Jerome the earlier Roman view reappears, and, as before, in express antithesis to Montanism (S. Hieron. *Epist.* 41 (54), vol. i. p. 189 'apud nos Apostolorum locum episcopi tenent'): and it was afterwards strengthened by the supposition that our Lord, before His Ascension, formally ordained the Apostles to the episcopate by imposition of hands (*Quaestiones ex Novo Testamento* in the Appendix ad S. August. Op. vol. iii. 2296 ed. Migne).

Church officers at ordination[49]. This latest development, which has frequently been confounded with the earlier view, is found in its completest form on the threshold of the middle ages: it was received as a doctrine by the Council of Paris in A.D. 829[50]; it forms the basis of several arguments in the pseudo-Isidorian decretals; it passed at length into the ordinals; and it still survives.

The further developments of the supremacy of bishops over presbyters fall for the most part outside the limits of these lectures. Between the primitive ἐπίσκοπος and the mediaeval bishop there is so wide an interval that those who are familiar with the picture of the latter may find it difficult to recognize the portrait of the former: at the same time, that interval is not the chasm of an impassable gulf; it is a space of historical ground every step of which can be traced.

And it is important to point out that the original conception of the relation of bishops to presbyters never wholly passed away.

The Church writers of the fourth and fifth cen-

[49] The 'last of the Greek Fathers,' John of Damascus, maintained that although in the first instance 'only the high-priests (i.e. bishops) had the power of binding and loosing in succession from the divine Apostles, yet that as time went on and the high-priests became degenerate, the power descended to the elect people of God, I mean, the monks' (S. Joann. Damasc. *Epist. de Confessione*, 11. Op. ed. Le Quien, vol. i. p. 606).

[50] Conc. Paris. lib. 1. c. 27, ap. Mansi, *Concilia*, vol. xiv. 556: which was incorporated by the author of the pseudo-Isidorian decretals as furnishing a strong argument in favour of one of the main contentions of those decretals, viz. that 'Chorepiscopi' were not bishops but presbyters, and that consequently they had not the power of conferring spiritual gifts (*Decreta Damasi papae de corepiscopis*, ap. Hinschius, *Decretales pseudo-Isidorianae*, p. 513: *Decreta Joannis III Papae, ibid.* p. 715).

turies, Chrysostom, Epiphanius, Jerome, Hilary the Deacon, expressly state that bishops and presbyters are equal save in the one respect that the former only have the right of appointing persons to church office [51]. It is maintainable upon the evidence that, even in this one respect, the writers in question write only of the usage of their own times, and that in earlier times the interposition of a bishop was not always required [52]. What the bishop was conceived as having was not peculiarity of function, but priority of rank. His office was designated by terms indicative of such priority —*προστασία, προεδρία* [53]. The presbyters were spoken of

[51] S. Chrysost. *Hom.* xi. *in Epist.* 1 *ad Timoth.*, Op. ed. Migne, vol. xi. 553: S. Epiphan. *Haeres.* 74. 4, p. 906 (who expresses the difference by saying that the order of bishops begets fathers for the Church, i.e. by ordaining officers, that of presbyters begets sons, i.e. by baptizing). S. Hieron. *Epist.* 146 (85) *ad Evangelum*, 'Quid enim facit excepta ordinatione episcopus quod presbyter non faciat?' cf. id. *Comm. in Epist. ad Tit.* c. 1): Ambrosiast. *Comm. in Epist.* 1, *ad Timoth.* c. 3, 7, ap. S. Ambros. Op. vol. ii. 295.

[52] The clearest instance of ordination by a presbyter without the intervention of a bishop is probably that which is recorded by Cassian, *Collat.* 4. 1, ap. Migne, *Patrol. Lat.* vol. xlix. 585: a monk named Daniel 'a beato Paphnutio, solitudinis ejusdem *presbytero*, ad diaconii praelatus est officium:' and afterwards Paphnutius, wishing to leave a worthy successor, 'eum presbyterii honore provexit.' Two centuries earlier than the time of Cassian, Novatus the African presbyter had appointed Felicissimus as deacon: and it is to be noted that Cyprian does not question the validity of the appointment, although he strongly objects to its having been made without his knowledge: 'Felicissimum satellitem suum diaconum nec permittente me nec sciente, sua factione et ambitione constituit,' S. Cyprian, *Epist.* 52 (49), p. 618: there is nothing in the context to support the supposition that Cyprian here uses 'constituit' in the unusual sense of 'procured the appointment.'

[53] *προστασία*, of a bishop, e.g. Euseb. *H. E.* 6. 35 (so the state of being without a bishop is *ἀπροστασία*, S. Basil. *Epist.* 102, p. 197): *προεδρία*, e.g. Euseb. *H. E.* 2. 17. 23. (The use of these and similar terms of a bishop must be distinguished from their earlier use of the whole council of governing officers: e.g. Origen, *Comm. in Matt.* tom. xvi. 22, vol. iii. p. 753, ed. De la Rue, *οἱ δὲ τὰς πρωτοκαθεδρίας πεπιστευμένοι τοῦ λαοῦ ἐπίσκοποι καὶ πρεσβύτεροι*; so probably Herm. *Vis.* 3. 10. 7: and as late as the end of the fourth century S. Greg. Naz. *Orat.* 26 (28) *in seipsum*, vol. i. p. 483.)

by terms which were in use for all councils whether civil or religious, for the assessors of a civil magistrate, for the committee of a charitable association—*συνέδριον*, *βουλή*, concilium. The bishop and his council were so far regarded as forming a unity that one of the chief collections of statutes lays down the rule that the judicial action of a bishop without his council was invalid: 'irrita erit sententia episcopi nisi clericorum praesentia confirmetur [54].' The early churches were constructed, as the Jewish synagogues had been constructed, in accordance with this theory of the nature of the governing body. The great division was not between clergy and laity, but between baptized and unbaptized: the place of the baptized was subdivided by a step or dais: on the dais the deacons stood: in the middle of it was the 'holy table:' at the end was a semicircle of seats for the council, with the seat of the bishop slightly raised above the rest [55].

To the dreamy eyes of the mystics of the early centuries these visible churches, dark and small as they were in comparison with the majestic temples of the pagan gods, seemed to be full of a divine light, and expanded to the spiritual sense until they were wide as heaven itself. The order of the Church below typified

[54] *Statuta Ecclesiae Antiqua* (sometimes known as the fourth Council of Carthage), c. 23.

[55] The *θρόνος* or *cathedra* of the bishop was the special symbol of his presidency: e.g. S. Cyprian, *Epist.* 3 (65), p. 469, 'pro episcopatus vigore et cathedrae auctoritate:' so *ibid.* 17 (11), p. 522: Euseb. *H. E.* 2. 23. 1: 3. 5. 2: 4. 23. 1, whereas the presbyters were *οἱ ἐκ τοῦ δευτέρου θρόνου*, id. 10. 5. 23. The epitaphs of bishops sometimes describe their tenure of office by 'sedit,' e.g. the epitaphs of the bishops of Capua, Mommsen, *Inscr. Regni Neapolitani*, Nos. 3894, 3897.

and realized the order of the Church above. The bishop was like the Eternal Father Himself upon His throne: the presbyters were like the 'four and twenty elders:' the deacons were transfigured into white-winged angels passing to and fro upon the ministry of God[56].

The vision was worthy of poets and of saints. To some of us, in these later days, it seems to belong to that vast cavern of the past which is tenanted by the ghost of many a noble poetry and many an ancient faith. And yet, as we emerge, with the sad eyes of vain regret, from that dim world of shadows into the light of this present noon—though we see around us no galaxy of white-winged angels, but rather what some think to be the ruins of a creed—there is given to us, if only we would know it, a not less divine order and a not less sacred work.

[56] Clem. Alex. *Strom.* 4. 8, p. 593 *εἰκὼν δὲ τῆς οὐρανίου ἐκκλησίας ἡ ἐπίγειος*: id. 6. 13, p. 793, the 'elders' of the Apocalypse are the heavenly figures of the elders of the church below (this is also implied in the difficult passage of the Διαταγαὶ Κλήμεντος, c. 18, where Hilgenfeld's reading seems almost certain). So in Gregory Nazianzen's dream of the church Anastasia at Constantinople the bishop is *ὑπέρθρονος*, the presbyters sit on each side of him, the deacons stand 'in shining garments, likenesses of angelic brightness' (S. Greg. Naz. *Carm.* lib. 2. 1. 16, p. 844). But in later times the vision of Isaiah or of Ezekiel rather than that of the Apocalypse seems to have presented itself as the heavenly counterpart of the church on earth: the presbyters are conceived as the Cherubim, S. Sophron. Hierosol. *Comment. Liturg.* c. 6, ed. Migne, *Patrol. Graec.* vol. lxxxvii. 3986: *Excerpt. e Const. Apost.* ap. Pitra, *Juris Eccles. Graec. Mon.* vol. i. p. 97.

LECTURE V.

CLERGY AND LAITY.

If we gather together all the words which, during the first two centuries, are used as collective terms for the officers of the Christian communities, we find that they agree in connoting primarily the idea of presidency or leadership [1].

If we further gather together the abstract terms which are used, during the same period, for ecclesiastical office, we find that—with the exception of διακονία—they exhibit the same phenomenon [2].

If we further gather together all the passages which speak of the relations of ordinary members of the communities to the officers, we find that they uniformly imply the correlative idea of subjection, and urge the duty of submission, to constituted authority [3].

If therefore the primitive Christian communities

[1] The words are *οἱ ἡγούμενοι*, Heb. 13. 7, 17, 24: 1 Clem. Rom. 1. 3: *οἱ προηγούμενοι*, 1 Clem. Rom. 21. 6: Herm. *Vis.* 2. 2. 6: 3. 9. 7: *οἱ προϊστάμενοι, οἱ προεστῶτες*, 1 Thess. 5. 12: 1 Tim. 5. 17: Herm. *Vis.* 2. 4. 3: Iren. 1. 10. 2: id. ap. Euseb. *H. E.* 5. 24. 14.

[2] The words are *πρωτοκαθεδρία*, Herm. *Mand.* 11. 12: Clem. Alex. *Strom.* 6. 13, p. 793: *πρωτεῖα*, Herm. *Sim.* 8. 7. 4: principalis concessio, S. Iren. 4. 26. 3: Magisterii locus, id. 3. 3. 1: ordo, Tertull. *De Exhort. Castit.* 7, *De Monogam.* 11, *De Idol.* 7.

[3] The passages are Heb. 13. 17: 1 Pet. 5. 5: 1 Clem. Rom. 1. 3: 57. 1: 63. 1: 2 Clem. Rom. 17. 5: S. Ignat. *ad Ephes.* 2. 2: 4. 1: 20. 2: *ad Magnes.* 13. 2: *ad Trall.* 2. 1, 2: 13. 2: *ad Philad.* 7. 1.

were institutions which had entirely passed away, and we were examining their constitution as a piece of ancient history, in the same manner as we examine the constitution of Athens or of Sparta, we should be led to the conclusion that the relation between the officers and the rest of the community was primarily a relation of priority of order.

If we extend the sphere of our induction, and look at not only the collective but also the particular terms for Church officers in the light of their contemporary use, we further find that none of them were peculiar to the Christian communities, but that they were all common to them with contemporary organizations. Some of them were in use in the imperial administration, some of them in the municipal corporations, some of them in the voluntary associations [4]. The most common, *ordo*, was in use in all three relations.

If, therefore, we could exclude all ideas except those which appear simply upon the evidence, and deal with the facts of Christian organization as we should deal with the facts of any other organization, we should undoubtedly be led to the conclusion that not only was the relation between Church officers and the rest of the community that of presidency or leadership, but that also the presidency or leadership was the same in kind as that of contemporary non-Christian societies.

But, even if this conclusion were admitted, it would not immediately follow that there were not other re-

[4] For ἐπίσκοπος see Lecture II. notes 26, 27: for πρεσβύτερος, Lecture III. notes 16, 27: for διάκονος, Lecture II. note 56.

lations between the officers and the ordinary members of the Christian communities, which though less apparent were not less important. It might undoubtedly be maintained, at least as a matter of *a priori* argument, that all this was the shell which enclosed a sacred kernel and kept it safe from profanation, and that underneath the conception of civil government, or side by side with it, there was another conception of the nature of ecclesiastical office which more closely resembled the prevalent conception of later times. It is therefore necessary to look not merely at the facts of language, but at the whole available evidence as to the prevailing conception of the nature of Christian organization, and to consider whether upon that evidence the argument which must be allowed to be possible *a priori* is defensible in fact.

The question is one of such supreme importance in relation to the Christian ministry not only of the period under investigation but also of later times, as to require more than ordinary care. It is, moreover, one which has been so frequently discussed, and upon which the different shades of possible opinion have been maintained with so much zeal, as to demand a more than ordinary effort on the part of those who approach it to rid themselves of preconceived opinions, and to deal with the facts in the temper not of advocates maintaining a thesis, but of judges reviewing evidence and weighing probabilities in an even balance of judgment.

The question before us may be thus stated :—A presumption having been raised by the terms which were in use for Church office that the conception of such office was one of presidency or leadership, does the existing evidence warrant an inference that Church officers were regarded as possessing other powers than those which naturally attach to presidents and leaders of a community?

It will be convenient to take in detail the several functions which in later times have been regarded as the special and peculiar functions of Church officers, and to enquire how far they were regarded as special and peculiar functions in the first two centuries.

1. In regard to the function of teaching or preaching, it is clear from both the Acts of the Apostles and St. Paul's Epistles that 'liberty of prophesying' prevailed in the Apostolic age[5]. It is equally clear that liberty of prophesying existed after the Apostolic age. In the first place, one of the most interesting monuments of the second century consists of a sermon or homily which was preached, probably by a layman at Rome, a fragment of which has long been known as the Second Epistle of Clement, and the remainder of which has come to light in two forms—a Greek MS. and a Syriac translation—within the last five years[6].

[5] Acts 8. 4: 11. 19–21: 13. 1: 1 Cor 14. passim: implied also in James 3. 1.

[6] That it is a homily and not a letter is an inference from its tone and manner of address: e.g. c. 19. 1, 'So then, my brethren and sisters, after the God of Truth I am reading to you an entreaty to pay heed to what has been written:' c. 20. 2, 'so then, my brethren and sisters, let us believe.' That it was written by a layman is an inference from the antithesis which he makes between himself and his hearers on the one hand, and the presbyters on the other, c. 17. 3. 5. That it was preached at Rome is an inference from the general similarity of its doctrine to that of the Shepherd of Hermas. The mention of it as a *letter* rather than a homily dates from

In the second place, the Apostolical Constitutions, which are of even later date, expressly contemplate the existence of preaching by laymen: 'Even if a teacher be a layman, still if he be skilled in the word and reverent in habit, let him teach: for the Scripture says, "They shall be all taught of God [7]."'

2. In regard to baptism, there is no positive evidence, but there is the argument *a fortiori* which arises from the fact that even in later times, when the tendency had become strong to restrict the performance of ecclesiastical functions to Church officers, baptism by an ordinary member of the Church was held to be valid, although if an officer might have been found it was held to be contrary to Church order [8].

a treatise of the fifth century, the *Quaestiones et responsiones ad orthodoxos*, c. 74 (printed in the works of Justin Martyr, vol. ii. p. 104, ed. Otto): the reference to *a* second letter of Clement in Euseb. 3. 38. 4 is vague, nor is there anything in the reference to connect that second letter with the work in question. The complete text was first found by Bryennius in the library of the patriarch of Jerusalem, and published by him at Constantinople in 1875: (since reprinted in the second edition of Gebhardt and Harnack's *Patres Apostolici*, part 1, fasc. 1, Leipsic, 1876, and by Bp. Lightfoot, *The Epistles of Clement of Rome*, London, 1876): and in 1876 a Syriac version of the complete text was discovered by Mr. Bensley, and is now in the University Library at Cambridge.

[7] Const. Apost. 8. 31: cf. Ambrosiast. *in Ephes.* 4. 11, 12, ap. S. Ambros. Op. vol. ii. p. 241, who says that in early times 'omnes docebant et omnes baptizabant,' but that afterwards 'coepit alio ordine et providentia gubernari ecclesia, quia si omnes omnia possent, irrationabile esset et vulgaris res et vilissima videretur.' This is, no doubt, only secondary evidence: but it is confirmed, i. by the fact that the exhortations of S. Ignatius against the performance by laymen of other official functions do not extend to preaching: ii. by the fact that in later times the gravamen against Origen was not that he had preached as a layman, but that he had done so in the presence of bishops and consequently in violation of church order (Euseb. *H. E.* 6. 19): iii. by the fact that, even when ecclesiastical regime was of the strictest, monks, who might be laymen, could preach. The earliest positive prohibitions seem to have been made, expressly in the interest of ecclesiastical order, by Leo the Great, *Epist.* 119 (92) *ad Maximum*, c. 6, 120 (93) *ad Theodoret.* c. 6, ed. Ballerin. pp. 1217, 1227.

[8] The earliest authorities for the validity of lay baptism are Tertullian (see below,

3. In regard to the Eucharist, the only explicit evidence is that of the Ignatian Epistles. The literary questions to which those Epistles have given rise do not affect their value in regard to the question before us. Their evidence remains practically the same whether Ignatius or some one else was their author, and whether the Syriac or the shorter Greek represents the original form. It is clear from them that the Christians of the cities to which they were addressed had held other meetings besides those at which the officers were present: and that in those meetings the bread had been broken and the Eucharist celebrated. The practice is reproved, but the reproof is a gentle one:—'Break one bread [9];' 'be careful to have only one Eucharist [10];' 'let that be the valid Eucharist which is celebrated in the presence of the bishop or of some one commissioned by him [11].' It appears from this that the celebration of the Eucharist without the presence of a Church officer was not of itself invalid. It is inconceivable that any one who held the view, which has been ordinarily held in later times, that the pre-

note 22), the Council of Elvira in A.D. 305, c. 38, Jerome, *Dial. c. Lucif.* c. 9: all of which admit, what is sufficient for the question in hand, that there were certain circumstances under which laymen might lawfully baptize.

[9] S. Ignat. *ad Ephes.* 20. 2, *οἱ κατ' ἄνδρα κοινῇ πάντες ἐν χάριτι ἐξ ὀνόματος συνέρχεσθε ἐν μιᾷ πίστει καὶ ἐν Ἰησοῦ Χριστῷ . . . . ἕνα ἄρτον κλῶντες.*

[10] id. *ad Philad.* 4, *σπουδάζετε οὖν μιᾷ εὐχαριστίᾳ χρῆσθαι.*

[11] id. *ad Smyrn.* 8. 1, *ἐκείνη βεβαία εὐχαριστία ἡγείσθω ἡ ὑπὸ τὸν ἐπίσκοπον οὖσα ἢ ᾧ ἂν αὐτὸς ἐπιτρέψῃ.* The form of expression *ἡ ὑπὸ τὸν ἐ. οὖσα* confirms the inference which is drawn from other evidence that the celebration of the Eucharist was regarded as the act of the whole community, assembled as a corporate whole and expressing itself by the voice of its head: cf. 1 Clem. Rom. 41. 1, *ἕκαστος ἡμῶν, ἀδελφοί, ἐν τῷ ἰδίῳ τάγματι εὐχαριστείτω Θεῷ ἐν ἀγαθῇ συνειδήσει ὑπάρχων, μὴ παρεκβαίνων τὸν ὡρισμένον τῆς λειτουργίας αὐτοῦ κανόνα, ἐν σεμνότητι.*

sence and action of a Church officer are essential to the valid celebration of the Eucharist, would have used the language of mild remonstrance, or would have brought arguments to urge the expediency of submission in this, as in other respects, to constituted authority.

4. In regard to the exercise of discipline, the earliest evidence is that of the First Epistle to the Corinthians: in it St. Paul addresses the whole community, and urges them to meet together and exercise the power of expulsion in the case of one who was guilty of open sin[12]. The other evidence consists in the Epistles of Clement and of Polycarp. A leading point in the Epistle of Clement is that the officers of the community should be obeyed, and that they should not be lightly removed. In writing it, he, like St. Paul, addresses the whole community. He does not question the right of the community to remove its officers, if it thinks fit; but he urges that it would not be a proper exercise of that right to remove those who have filled the office worthily[13]. The Epistle of Polycarp is complementary of that of Clement: as the latter urges that worthy officers should not be removed, the former urges that a presbyter who had been removed should be restored[14].

[12] 1 Cor. 5.

[13] 1 Clem. Rom. 44: cf. *ibid.* 54 where one whose presence in the Church had been a cause of dissension is supposed to say *ἄπειμι οὗ ἐὰν βούλησθε καὶ ποιῶ τὰ ὑποτάσσομενα ὑπὸ τοῦ πλήθους.*

[14] S. Polycarp. *ad Philipp.* 11: that cases of discipline were judged by the whole community, assembled under the presidency of its officers, so late as the time of Cyprian is clear from the letter of the Roman Church to him (S. Cyprian. *Epist.* 30 (31), p. 533) 'conlatione consiliorum cum episcopis, presbyteris, diaconis, confessoribus, pariter ac stantibus [i.e. those who had not 'lapsed'] laicis facta

Polycarp, like Clement, and like St. Paul, addresses the community at large: in doing so he implies that it was with the community that the power of restoration lay.

Whether therefore we look at preaching, at baptism, at the Eucharist, or at discipline, it seems probable that the officers were not conceived as having, as such, exclusive powers. In other words, the existing evidence in regard to the functions of Church officers, so far from establishing, tends to disprove the existence of any conception of the nature of their office, other than that which is gathered from the terms which were in use to designate such office. It supports the hypothesis that they existed in the Christian societies, as those who bore the same names existed in secular societies, for the general superintendence of the community and the general control of its affairs, that all things might be done 'decently and in order.'

Such a conclusion may appear strange when viewed by the light of later times, but it is not strange if it is viewed in relation to the circumstances of the first two centuries. In those early days—before the doors of admission were thrown wide open, before children were ordinarily baptized and men grew up from their earliest years as members of a Christian society, before Christianity had become a fashionable religion and

lapsorum tractare;' cf. also *Epist.* 31 (26), p. 562, 34 (28), p. 570. This is in harmony with the general analogy of the Christian communities to the contemporary secular communities, in which all matters of importance were decided 'conventu pleno:' see, for the Greek associations, Foucart, *Les Associations religieuses, &c.* p. 15, and for the Latin associations, Duruy, *Histoire des Romains*, vol. v. p. 155.

gathered into its net fish 'of every kind' both good and bad—the mere membership of a Christian Church was in itself a strong presumption of the possession of high spiritual qualifications. The Christian was in a sense which has often since been rather a satire than a metaphor, a 'member of Christ,' a 'king and priest unto God.' The whole body of Christians was upon a level: 'all ye are brethren[15].' The distinctions which St. Paul makes between Christians are based not upon office, but upon varieties of spiritual power. They are caused by the diversity of the operations of the Holy Spirit. They are consequently personal and individual. They do not mark off class from class, but one Christian from another. Some of these spiritual powers are distinguished from others by a greater visible and outward effect: but they are all the same in kind. The gift of ruling is not different in kind from the gift of healing. The expression 'he that ruleth' is coordinate with 'he that exhorteth,' 'he that giveth,' 'he that sheweth mercy[16].' Of one or other of these gifts every Christian was a partaker. There was a vivid sense, which in later times was necessarily weakened, that every form of the manifestation of the religious life is a gift of God—a χάρισμα, or direct operation of the Divine Spirit upon the soul. Now while this sense of the diffusion of spiritual gifts was so vivid, it was impossible that there should be the same sense of distinction between officers and non-officers which afterwards came to exist. Organization

[15] S. Matt. 23. 8. [16] Rom. 12. 6, 8.

was a less important fact than it afterwards became. That which gave organization its importance was the increase in the size of the communities. The need of order thereby became more imperative: the work of administration had to be systematized and centralized: the officers who had the control of order and administration came inevitably to have a higher relative status than they had had before. There were not only disputes, as we learn from Clement of Rome[17], about the appointment of officers, but also an exaggeration of the place of order in the Christian economy. The gift of ruling, like Aaron's rod, seemed to swallow up the other gifts.

Then came a profound reaction. Against the growing tendency towards that state of things which afterwards firmly established itself, and which ever since has been the normal state of almost all Christian Churches, some communities, first of Asia Minor, then of Africa, then of Italy, raised a vigorous and, for a time, a successful protest. They reasserted the place of spiritual gifts as contrasted with official rule[18]. They maintained that the revelation of Christ through the Spirit was not a temporary phenomenon of Apostolic days, but a constant fact of Christian life. They combined with this the preaching of a higher morality than that which was tending to become current. They were

[17] 1 Clem. Rom. 44. 1.

[18] The literature which bears upon Montanism is extensive: most earlier writers (including Schwegler, *Der Montanismus*, Tübingen, 1841) overlooked its special character as a protest of the 'ecclesia spiritus' against the 'ecclesia episcoporum' (Tertull. *De Pudic.* 21): the first enunciation of this special character is due to Ritschl, *Die altkatholische Kirche*, pp. 513 sqq., whose view is even more clearly expressed by Rothe, *Vorlesungen, &c.* ed. Weingarten, pp. 166 sqq.

supported in all this by the greatest theologian of his time, and it is to the writings of that theologian rather than to the vituperative statements of later writers that we must look for a true idea of their purpose. The fact of their having been supported by that theologian is of extreme significance. For Tertullian had done incalculable service alike in his defence of Christianity against the as yet unconverted world without, and in his refutation of heresies within [19]. To him, almost as much as to Irenaeus, were the Churches indebted for the dominance of the fundamental theory that Christian doctrine must be determined by Apostolic tradition. So far from being a heretic, he was the champion of the Church against heresy [20] : so far from disfavouring Catholicity, he was its chief living preacher: so far from holding that office was unimportant, he reproaches heretics with their insufficient recognition of its importance [21]. But the view which he took of the nature of office in the Church was that it does not, as such, confer any powers upon its holders which are not possessed by the other members of the community. As an ordinary rule, he maintains, the president, and he only, has the function of admitting new members into the community: but if there be emergency, the power descends to other Church officers and laymen [22]. As an ordinary rule,

[19] For a good account of Tertullian's services to the Church see Hauck, *Tertullians Leben und Schriften,* Erlangen, 1877, especially c. iii. and iv.

[20] His attitude towards heresy may be gathered from a treatise which he wrote when he was himself a Montanist: 'ad officium hereticos compelli, non illici, dignum est: duritia vincenda est non suadenda' (*Scorp.* 1).

[21] Tertull. *De Praescript.* 41.

[22] *De Baptismo,* 17, 'Dandi [sc. baptismum] quidem habet jus summus sacerdos

'it is only,' he says, 'from the hands of our presidents that we receive the Eucharist:' but if there be an emergency, a layman may celebrate as well as a bishop[23]. 'That which has constituted the difference between the governing body and the ordinary members is the authority of the Church:' but 'where three Christians are, though they be laymen, there is a Church[24].' These statements of a great theologian, in support of a great movement which was all but victorious, cannot be lightly set aside. In theological as in other wars the tendency is to cry 'Vae victis!' and to assume that the defeated are always in the wrong. But a careful survey of the evidence leads to the conclusion that the Montanism, as it was called, which Tertullian defended, was theoretically in the right, though its theory had become in practice impossible. It did not make sufficient allowance for changed and changing circumstances. It was a beating of the wings of pietism against the iron bars of organization. It was the first, though not the last, rebellion of the religious sentiment against official religion.

But the exigencies of organization of necessity prevailed: for in ecclesiastical as in other human affairs the ideal yields to the practicable. At the same time,

qui est episcopus: dehinc presbyteri et diaconi, non tamen sine episcopi auctoritate propter ecclesiae honorem. Quo salvo pax est. Alioquin etiam laicis jus est.'

[23] *De Corona*, 4.

[24] *De Exhort. Castit.* 6, 'Differentiam inter ordinem et plebem constituit ecclesiae auctoritas et honor per ordinis consessum sanctificatus. Adeo ubi ecclesiastici ordinis non est consessus, et offers et tinguis et sacerdos es tibi solus. Sed ubi tres, ecclesiae est, licet laici.'

the fact of the existence of Montanism, and of its considerable success, strongly confirms the general inferences which are drawn from other evidence, that Church officers were originally regarded as existing for the good government of the community and for the general management of its affairs: that the difference between Church officers and other baptized persons was one of status and degree: that, *quoad* the spiritual life, the two classes were on the same footing: and that the functions which the officers performed were such as, apart from the question of order, might be performed by any member of the community.

The metaphor which seems best to express the relation of the two classes is one which was frequently used, and which has survived until our own times. It is that which is implied in the word 'Pastor.' It came originally from the shepherd life of Eastern and Southern Palestine, where a shepherd wandered with his flocks of almost innumerable sheep over almost boundless tracts of undulating moorland. It passed naturally into Hebrew poetry: and three of the great Hebrew prophets, Jeremiah, Ezekiel, and Zechariah, use it constantly for both the ecclesiastical and the civil rulers of the people. It is found in the New Testament: and it is found in almost all early Christian literature [25]. Its fundamental idea is that of ruling [26]:

[25] ποιμὴν and its correlatives ποίμνη and ποίμνιον are found, e.g. (not including passages in which the reference is to the relation between the Church and Christ) 1 Pet. 5. 2, 3: Herm. *Sim.* 6. 1: S. Ignat. *ad Philad.* 2. 1: *ad Rom.* 9. 1: S. Iren. 4. 33. 1: Clem. Alex. *Paed.* 1. 6, p. 120: Const. Apost. 2. 6, 10, 15, 20. In Latin 'pastor,' e.g. S. Cypr. *Epist.* 8. (2), p. 486: 17 (11), p. 522.

[26] Cf. Jeremy Taylor, *Episcopacy asserted*, Sect. 1. 6 'In Scripture and other

and the Apostolical Constitutions, following chiefly Ezekiel's address to the rulers of his time, show how it was understood in regard to all the various functions of the Christian ministry: the bishop, as a good shepherd, guards the strong, *i.e.* those who are sound in the faith, heals those who are weak, *i.e.* those whose faith is wavering, binds up the wounded, *i.e.* restores to the flock those whom the sense of sin has smitten with contrition, seeks for those who have gone astray, *i.e.* brings back to the flock those whom the sense of sin has driven away in despair[27].

But although the original conception of ecclesiastical office ultimately passed away, it passed away only by slow degrees. Little by little those members of the Christian Churches who did not hold office were excluded from the performance of almost all ecclesiastical functions. At first a layman might not preach if a bishop were present: and then not if any Church officer was present: and finally not at all[28]. At

writers *to feed* and *to govern* is all one when the office is either political or economical or ecclesiastical:' the assertion is capable of being proved by abundant evidence, e.g. Philo, 1. 196, ed. Mang. *οἱ δὲ ποιμαίνοντες ἀρχόντων καὶ ἡγεμόνων ἔχοντες δύναμιν*: Clem. Alex. *Strom.* 1. 26, p. 421: S. Greg. Nazianz. *Orat.* 32, c. 10, p. 586, *τάξις κἂν ἐκκλησίαις τὸ μὲν εἶναί τι ποίμνιον τὸ δὲ ποιμένας διώρισε· καὶ τὸ μὲν ἄρχειν τὸ δὲ ἄρχεσθαι.*

[27] Const. Apost. 2. 20: so S. Cyprian. *Epist.* 8 (2), p. 486, (we shall be called negligent shepherds because) 'perditum non requisivimus et errantem non correximus et claudum non colligavimus et lactem eorum edebamus et lanis eorum operiebamur.'

[28] The 'gravamen' of Demetrius against Origen was not so much that he had preached, but that he had done so in the presence of bishops (*τὸ παρόντων ἐπισκόπων λαϊκοὺς ὁμιλεῖν*, Euseb. *H. E.* 6. 19. 17): and the Western canon, which was ultimately superseded by the letters of Leo the Great (see above, note 7), concedes the point for which the friends of Origen contended: 'laicus praesentibus clericis *nisi ipsis jubentibus*, docere non audeat' (Stat. Eccles. Antiq., = 4 Conc. Carth. c. 98).

first a layman brought his own gifts to the altar and communicated there[29]: and then he could only—unless he were an Emperor—stand outside the dais upon which the officers sat or stood: and finally, in the East, he might not even see the celebration of the 'mysteries[30].' At first the vote of laymen as well as of officers was taken in cases of discipline, and so late as the fifth century the existence of the disciplinary rights of laymen is shown by the enactment of an African council that a parish must not excommunicate its clergyman[31]: but finally laymen had no place whatever in the ecclesiastical tribunals. By the force of changing circumstances, and by the growth of new conceptions, the original difference of rank and order became a difference of spiritual power: and a mediaeval theologian, writing of the same officer whom Justin Martyr describes simply as a president, offering prayers and thanksgivings in which the congregation take their part by the utterance of the solemn Amen!, says that

[29] For the practice of laymen going to the altar, see e.g. S. Dionys. Alexandr. *Epist. ad Chrys.* ap. Euseb. *H. E.* 7. 9. 4: *Epist. ad Basilid.* ap. Pitra, *Jur. Eccl. Gr. Mon.* vol. i. p. 544: Routh, *Rel. Sacr.* vol. iii. p. 230: S. Ambros. *De Sacram.* 5. 2, 3, vol. ii. p. 374: S. Augustin. *Epist.* 111 (122), *ad Victorian.* Op. ed. Migne, vol. ii. 426. The practice seems to have survived longest at Milan where until comparatively late times the laity went to the altar to make their offerings, retired during the prayer of consecration, and returned to partake of the consecrated elements (Bona, *De Rebus Liturgicis*, vol. i. p. 184): it is also found in Gaul in the sixth century (S. Greg. Turon. *H. F.* 9. 3: 10. 8).

[30] The earliest prohibition was a local one, that of the council of Laodicea, c. 19, 44: the first general prohibition was that of the Trullan council, c. 69, which excepts kings. The custom of erecting a close screen (εἰκονόστασις) so as completely to shut out the laity from seeing the altar, probably belongs to a still later period (see Canon Venables in the *Dictionary of Christian Antiquities*, s. v. Iconostasis).

[31] Conc. Septimunicense ap. Ferrand. *Breviatio Canonum*, c. 139, 'Ut non liceat clericum a populo excommunicari sive praesente sive absente episcopo.'

'the orders of the heavenly host, although they enjoy beatitude and want nothing to the sum of felicity, still revere the glory of a priest, wonder at his dignity, yield to him in privilege, honour his power[32].'

The question will naturally arise, If the early conception of ecclesiastical office was that to which the evidence points, and which Tertullian states, what was the nature and significance of ordination?

The answer which, upon the evidence, must be given to this question strongly confirms the conclusion to which the evidence leads upon the question which has been already considered. The evidence is extensive and various, and can only be briefly recapitulated here.

1. In the first place, all the words which are in use to express appointment to ecclesiastical office connote either simple appointment or accession to rank[33].

2. In the second place, all these words were in use to express appointment to civil office. When other ideas than those of civil appointment came beyond question to attach themselves to ecclesiastical appointment other words were used[34]. The absence of such words in the earlier period of itself affords a strong

[32] S. Bernard. *Instructio Sacerdotis*, c. 9, vol. iii. p. 532.

[33] The words in use in the first three centuries are *χειροτονεῖν*, *καθιστάνειν*, *κληροῦσθαι*, cônstituere, ordinare. For instances of their use see my article in the *Dictionary of Christian Antiquities*, s. v. Ordination.

[34] After the first three centuries there were not only other words of the same kind as those mentioned in the preceding note, e.g. *προελθεῖν*, *προάγεσθαι*, promoveri, praeferri, but also *χειροθετεῖσθαι*, *ἱερᾶσθαι*, consecrari, benedici; for instances of which, and also for instances of the use of the words in relation to civil appointments, see *ibid.*

presumption of the absence of the ideas which are relative to them.

3. In the third place, all the elements of appointment to ecclesiastical office were also the elements of appointment to civil office. Those elements were nomination, election, approval, and the declaration of election by a competent officer. The conditions of ordinary appointment to civil office in the Roman municipalities are known to us from many and unimpeachable sources[35]. Those sources show that, though election prevailed, it did not of itself constitute an office, that any one who was so elected had to pass a preliminary examination as to his possession of the required qualifications, that the presiding officer might decline to take account of any one who did not possess those qualifications, and that, according to the constitutional fiction which we find in Rome itself, especially during the Republican period, the person appointed is said to be appointed, not by the people who elected, but by the officer who presided at the election[36]. These

[35] In addition to earlier sources, which are best given by Zumpt, *Commentationes Epigraphicae*, vol. i. p. 4 sqq., we have an almost complete account of the municipal laws of the early Empire relative to elections in the bronze tablets containing the laws of two Spanish towns, Salpensa and Malaga, which were discovered in 1851. They will be found in the *Corpus Inscr. Lat.* vol. ii. Nos. 1963, 1964, in Haenel, *Corpus Legum ante Justinianum latarum*, p. 63: and with an important commentary by Mommsen in his essay, *Die Stadtrechte der lateinischen Gemeinden Salpensa und Malaca*, printed in the *Abhandlungen der königl. sachs. Gesellschaft der Wissenschaft*, Bd. iii (the doubts which were at one time raised as to their genuineness have been disposed of by Giraud, *Les Tables de Salpensa et de Malaga*, Paris, 1856, and *La Lex Malacitana*, Paris, 1868). For clear summaries of the existing evidence in relation to municipal elections see Duruy, *Histoire des Romains*, vol. v. pp. 107 sqq.: Marquardt, *Römische Staatsverwaltung*, Bd. i. pp. 472 sqq.

[36] 'Creare' (consulem, praetorem) is strictly used of the action of the presiding officer: the people are said 'jubere,' i.e. to direct the appointment to be made: cf. Mommsen, *Römisches Staatsrecht*, Bd. i. pp. 157 sqq.

same conditions were ordinarily necessary at the appointment of all but the lowest grades of ecclesiastical officers: there was a nomination, an election, an examination into the fitness of the candidate, and the action of a presiding officer[37].

4. In the fourth place, the modes in which these elements of election were combined varied in the Church concomitantly with their variation in the State. In the State, first at Rome, and afterwards, though much later, in the municipalities, election by the people, subject only to the veto of the presiding officer, passed into election by the senate, subject only to a formal approval on the part of the people[38]. In the Church it came to pass that the officers nominated and the people approved: and ultimately, by steps which can be definitely traced, the part of the people was limited to the right of objecting to unsuitable candidates[39].

5. In the fifth place, all the modes of *admission* to ecclesiastical office were, with one exception, analogous to the modes of admission to civil office. A Roman *consul designatus* dressed himself in his official dress, went in state to the Capitol, took his seat on the curule chair, and held a formal meeting of the senate: by doing this he became consul *de facto*. A Roman *praetor designatus* went to the ordinary court-house, took his seat on the tribunal, heard and decided a

[37] For the evidence see the *Dictionary of Christian Antiquities*, s.v. Ordination, vol. ii. pp. 1504 sqq.

[38] For the evidence see e.g. Mommsen, *Röm. Staatsrecht*, Bd. ii. 860 sqq.: Marquardt, *Röm. Staatsverwaltung*, Bd. i. 474.

[39] See the *Dictionary of Christian Antiquities, ut supra.*

fictitious case, and became thereby praetor *de facto*[40]. There was no formal act of admission: what took place was a *usurpatio juris*; a person duly elected simply entered upon his office and was in full possession of it as soon as he had discharged, without let or hindrance, one of its ordinary duties. If we take the earliest form of what in later times would have been called the ritual of 'ordination' or 'consecration,' that which is given in the eighth book of the Apostolical Constitutions, it is clear that the same theory of admission to office prevailed in the Church. On the morning after his election the bishop is escorted to his chair by the other bishops who took part in the election, and at once enters on the active duties of a bishop by preaching a sermon and celebrating the Eucharist[41]. That a similar practice prevailed in regard to other Church officers must be inferred from the fact that in some instances it still survives. 'In the chief Western rituals the newly ordained deacon performs the deacon's function of reading the Gospel: in the Roman ritual the presbyter not only takes his place in the presbytery but is "concelebrant" with the bishop, *i.e.* he is associated with him in the celebration of the Eucharist: in the Greek ritual the reader performs his proper function of reading, and the subdeacon—who in early times was a kind of under-servant—washes the bishop's hands[42].'

All this, as far as analogy can guide us, is precisely

[40] See Mommsen, *Röm. Staatsrecht*, Bd. i. pp. 502 sqq.

[41] Const. Apost. 8. 4–14.

[42] *Dictionary of Christian Antiquities*, s.v. Ordination, vol. ii. pp. 1507.

what would have happened if the community, instead of being ecclesiastical, had been civil. The conception of ordination, so far as we can gather either from the words which were used to designate it, or from the elements which entered into it, was that simply of appointment and admission to office.

But there is one element, which was not present in admissions to civil office, and to which in later times great importance has been attached—the rite of the imposition of hands. It is therefore necessary to consider how far the existence of this rite indicates the existence of a different theory.

Two points have to be considered: first the existence of the rite, and secondly its significance.

In regard to the first of these points, there is the remarkable fact that the passage of the Apostolical Constitutions which describes with elaborate minuteness the other ceremonies with which a bishop was admitted to office, says nothing of this. It is mentioned that during a prayer after the election the deacons hold the open Gospels over the newly-appointed bishop's head: but of imposition of hands the passage makes no mention whatever [43]. Nor is the rite mentioned in the enumeration which Cyprian gives of the elements which had combined to make the election of Cornelius valid: it was of importance to show that no e sential particular had been omitted, but he enumerates only the votes of the people, the testimony of the clergy, the consent of the bishops [44]. In entire harmony with this

[43] Const. Apost. 8. 4.

[44] S. Cyprian. *Epist.* 55 (52), p. 629: *Factus est* autem Cornelius *episcopus* de

is the account which Jerome gives of the admission to office of the bishop of Alexandria: after the election the presbyters conduct the elected bishop to his chair: he is thereupon bishop *de facto*[45].

It follows from this that the rite was not universal: it is impossible that, if it was not universal, it can have been regarded as essential.

In regard to the second point, there are two kinds of evidence: that of other applications of the rite, and that of existing statements about it. The rite was Jewish: it was in use among the Jews on various occasions: chiefly in the appointment of members of the local courts, in admitting a scholar to study, and in giving him authority to teach—in the ceremony, in other words, which corresponds to our graduation[46]. It was in use in the Christian Church not only in admission to office, but also in the admission of an

'Dei et Christi ejus judicio, de clericorum paene omnium testimonio, de plebis quae tunc adfuit suffragio, et de sacerdotum antiquorum et bonorum virorum collegio, cum nemo ante se factus esset, cum Fabiana locus, id est, locus Petri et gradus cathedrae sacerdotalis vacaret.'

[45] S. Hieron. *Epist.* 146 (85), *ad Evangel.* vol. i. p. 1082 ed. Vall.: 'Alexandriae a Marco evangelista usque ad Heraclam et Dionysium episcopos presbyteri semper unum ex se electum in excelsiore gradu collocatum episcopum nominabant, quomodo si exercitus imperatorem faciat aut diaconi eligant de se quem industrium noverint et archidiaconum vocent.' (There is a later, but apparently independent, authority to the same effect, Eutychii Patriarch. Alexand. *Annales* interp. Pocock. ed. Oxon. 1658, i. p. 331: and Jerome's account is adopted as giving the normal mode of the ordination of a bishop by Flaccus Albinus (pseudo-Alcuin), *De Divinis officiis*, c. 37, vol. ii. p. 493, ed. Froben.). The account is corroborated by the fact that Synesius, *Epist.* 67, p. 210, appears to consider the phrase *ἀποδεῖξαι τε καὶ ἐπὶ τοῦ θρόνου καθίσαι* as expressing the constitutive elements of the ordination of a bishop.

[46] See the rabbinical references in Buxtorf, *Lexicon Chaldaicum, Talmudicum et Rabbinicum*, p. 1498, ed. 1639: Morin, *De Sacris ordinationibus*, pars iii. c. 14, p. 141, ed. 1655: Seerup. *Dissert. de titulo Rabbi* in Ugolini's *Thesaurus*, vol. xxi. p. 1091.

ordinary member, and in the readmission of a penitent. It was in all cases when used in the Christian Church accompanied with prayer. St. Augustine resolves it into a prayer. 'Quid aliud est manuum impositio quam oratio super hominem[47].' The eighth book of the Apostolical Constitutions makes the word which is ordinarily rendered 'imposition of hands' (χειροθεσία) a synonym for morning and evening prayer[48]. St. Jerome gives as the reason for its use in ordination simply that if a man were ordained by simple declaration of appointment, without any ceremony, he might sometimes be ordained clandestinely without his knowledge—'ne scilicet, ut in quibusdam risimus, vocis imprecatio clandestina clericos ordinet nescientes[49].'

It can hardly be maintained upon this evidence that the ceremony of imposition of hands establishes a presumption, which is clearly not established by the other elements of ordination, that ordination was conceived in early, as it undoubtedly was conceived in later, times as conferring special and exclusive spiritual powers.

It may be urged, though this is of course different from maintaining that such a presumption is established, that there is nothing in all this which is inconsistent with such a presumption.

But in a judicial review of evidence it is necessary to consider not only the abstract possibility of a

[47] S. Augustin. *De Baptism. c. Donatist.* 3. 16. Op. ed. Migne, vol. ix. p. 149.

[48] Const. Apost. 8. 36, 38. This use of the word probably refers to the bishop's attitude in praying.

[49] S. Hieron. *Comm. in Isai.* lib. xvi. c. 58, v. 10, vol. iv. p. 694.

hypothesis which may be advanced, but also the difficulties in the way of accepting it. It is therefore necessary to point to two sets of facts which appear to exclude the presumption in question.

1. The first is the fact of silence. The belief in the possession of exceptional spiritual powers is so important a fact that it must needs assert itself. When in later times that belief was undoubtedly entertained it shows itself in a great variety of forms: it is frequently stated: it is invariably implied. The fact that the writers of the first two centuries neither state nor imply it seems inexplicable, except upon the supposition that they did not hold it[50].

2. The second fact is the facility with which ordinations were made and unmade. When, in later times, the belief prevailed that ordination conferred exceptional spiritual powers, it was recognized as a necessary corollary of such a belief that the grace of ordination, even if irregularly conferred, was inalienable[51]. The non-existence of a belief

[50] Stress has sometimes been laid on the fact that in 1 Tim. 4. 14 the imposition of hands is mentioned as the means by which Timothy received a χάρισμα: but at the same time the wide latitude in which that word was used has been sometimes forgotten. It was used of every faculty and privilege which a Christian possessed: to be a Christian was itself a χάρισμα; to be orthodox was a χάρισμα; and in the same way to hold office in the Church was a χάρισμα (Const. Apost. 8. 2). Its nearest modern equivalent is probably the word 'talent.'

[51] This idea first appears in the course of the Donatist controversy: S. Augustine considered ordination to be in this respect analogous to baptism, *De Baptism. c. Donatist.* 1. 1. vol. ix. p. 109: *Contra Ep. Parmen.* 2. 28, vol. ix. p. 70: cf. especially *De Bono Conjugali,* 24, vol. vi. p. 394, 'quemadmodum si fiat ordinatio cleri ad plebem congregandam, etiamsi plebis congregatio non subsequitur, manet tamen in illis ordinatis sacramentum ordinationis: et si aliqua culpa quisquam ab officio removeatur sacramento Domini semel imposito non carebit, quamvis ad judicium permanente.'

in the inalienability of orders affords a strong presumption that they were not conceived to confer the powers which in later times were believed to attach to them. Besides this, the trifling nature of some of the causes which were regarded as rendering an ordination invalid *ab initio*, while wholly consistent with the hypothesis that appointment to ecclesiastical office was of the same kind as appointment to civil office, cannot be reconciled with the hypothesis that it was regarded as conferring exceptional and inalienable powers. If the person whom a bishop ordained belonged to another church [52], or if the person ordained were not designated to some particular church [53], or if the ordainer and ordained stood in the relation of father and son [54], the ordination was invalid. These regulations reach a climax in a Gallican council of the fifth century, which enacts that all irregular ordinations are invalid *except by arrangement* [55]. It is improbable, except upon an extreme theory of the close correspondence between the 'terrestrial and celestial hierarchies,' that the grace of the Holy Spirit should so closely follow the details of ecclesiastical organization as to flow or not to flow, according as a bishop stood just within or just without the geographical limits of his jurisdiction: it is inconceivable, even upon such an extreme theory, that the same mysterious grace should have been supposed to come or

[52] Conc. Nicaen. c. 16, ἄκυρος ἔσται ἡ χειροτονία: so Conc. Antioch. c. 22, Conc. Sardic. c. 15, 1 Conc. Arelat. c. 13.

[53] Conc. Chalcedon. c. 6.

[54] Can. Apost. 76.

[55] 1 Conc. Turon. A.D. 461, c. 10, 'Ordinationes vero illicitas in irritum devocamus nisi satisfactione quae ad pacem pertinent componantur.'

go, to remain or to vanish away, according as a person ordained in violation of some local rule did or did not succeed in making his peace with his superiors. The difficulty which these facts present is so obvious that later canonists were compelled to invent a distinction between 'sacramental' and 'canonical' validity: but even those who uphold that distinction admit that there is no trace of its existence in early times[56].

The existing evidence as to the conception which was entertained of the nature of ordination thus confirms the inference which follows from the consideration of office in itself. The conception of office was that of order: by virtue of their appointment the officers of the Christian communities were entitled to perform functions which in themselves were the functions of the whole Church or of individual Christians. Ecclesiastical office existed, no doubt, by divine appointment, but by divine appointment only 'for the edifying and well-governing' of the community. Of the existence of the idea that ecclesiastical office in itself, and not as a matter of ecclesiastical regulation and arrangement, conferred special and exceptional powers, there is neither proof nor reasonable presumption.

Upon this earlier conception there supervened—in the order of Providence and in the slow course of years—a most significant change. Into the history of that change it is beyond the plan of these Lectures to enter: but since it has its beginnings even in the period which

[56] e.g. Hefele, *Conciliengeschichte* (Eng. Trans.) vol. ii. p. 359.

we are considering, it is necessary briefly to indicate its main causes.

1. The first of these causes was the wide extension of the limits of Church membership which was caused by the prevalence of infant baptism. In the earliest times the rules of morality which were binding on Church officers were binding also on ordinary members: Tertullian, writing as a Montanist, and endeavouring to keep up the earlier standard, makes the fact that a particular rule as to marriage is binding on presbyters an argument for its being binding also on laymen [57]. But when infant baptism became general, and men grew up to be Christians as they grew up to be citizens, the maintenance of the earlier standard became impossible in the Church at large. Professing Christians adopted the current morality: they were content to be no worse than their neighbours. But the officers of all communities tend to be conservative, and conservatism was expected of them: that which had been the ideal standard of qualifications for baptism became the ideal standard of qualifications for ordination: and there grew up a distinction between clerical morality and lay morality which has never passed away.

2. The second cause was the intensity of the sentiment of order. The conception of civil order under the Imperial régime was very different from the conception of it in modern times, and in Teutonic societies. The tendency of our own society is to have the greatest

[57] Tertull. *De Exhort. Cast.* 7, 'vani erimus si putaverimus quod sacerdotibus non liceat laicis licere.'

amount of freedom that is compatible with order: the tendency of the Empire was to have the greatest amount of order that is compatible with freedom. Civil order was conceived to be almost as divine as physical order is conceived to be in our own day. In the State the head of the State seemed as such by virtue of his elevation to have some of the attributes of a divinity: and in the Church the same Apostolical Constitutions which give as the reason why a layman may not celebrate the Eucharist that he has not the necessary dignity (*ἀξία*), call the officer who has that dignity a "god upon earth[58]." When, in the decay of the Empire, the ecclesiastical organization was left as the only stable institution, it was almost inevitable that those who preserved the tradition of imperial rule should, by the mere fact of their status, seem to stand upon a platform which was inaccessible to ordinary men.

3. The third cause was the growth of an analogy between the Christian and the Mosaic dispensations. The existence of such an analogy in the earliest times was precluded by the vividness of the belief in the nearness of the Second Advent. The organization of the Christian churches was a provisional arrangement until 'the Lord should come.' There was a keen controversy whether Christianity was inside or outside Judaism: but there is no trace of a belief that the ancient organization was to be replaced, through

[58] Const. Apost. 3. 10 *ἀλλ' οὔτε λαϊκοῖς ἐπιτρέπομεν ποιεῖν τι τῶν ἱερατικῶν ἔργων. . . . . διὰ γὰρ τῆς ἐπιθέσεως τῶν χειρῶν τοῦ ἐπισκόπου δίδοται ἡ τοιαύτη ἀξία*: *ibid.* 2. 26 of the bishop, *οὗτος ὑμῶν ἐπίγειος θεὸς μετὰ θεόν.*

a long vista of centuries to come, by a corresponding organization of the Christian societies. But after the Temple had long been overthrown and its site desecrated—after the immediate return of the Messiah to a temporal reign in Judaea had passed from being a living faith to be a distant hope—after the Christian Churches had ceased to circle round Jerusalem and had begun to take the form of a new spiritual empire wide as the Roman empire itself, there grew up a conception that the new *Ecclesia Dei*, whose limits were the world, was the exact counterpart, though on a larger scale, of the old *Ecclesia Dei* whose limits had been Palestine. With an explanation in the one case—which shows that the conception is new, with a hesitating timidity in the other case—which shows that it had not yet established itself, Tertullian [59] and Origen [60], speak of Christian ministers as priests. It was a century and a half after the time of Tertullian and Origen before the analogy came to be generally accepted, or before the corollaries which flowed from it found general expression in literature: but, when once established, it became permanent, and in the course of those weary wastes of years which stretch between the ruins of the Empire and the foundation

[59] Tertull. *De Baptismo*, c. 17 'dandi (sc. baptismum) quidem habet jus summus sacerdos qui est episcopus:' the explanation of the meaning of 'summus sacerdos' was not needed a century later, e.g. in S. Ambros. *Expos. in Psalm. cxviii.* c. 23, vol. i. p. 989.

[60] Origen, *Comment. in Joann.* tom. 1. 3. vol. iv. p. 3, οἱ δὲ ἀνακείμενοι τῷ θείῳ λόγῳ καὶ πρὸς μόνῃ τῇ θεραπείᾳ τοῦ Θεοῦ γινόμενοι . . . . Λευῖται καὶ ἱερεῖς οὐκ ἀτόπως λεχθήσονται: cf. S. Augustin. *De Civit. Dei*, 20. 10, Op. ed. Migne, vii. 676, in reference to Rev. 20. 6, 'non utique de solis episcopis et presbyteris dictum est qui *proprie jam* vocantur in ecclesia sacerdotes.'

of the modern kingdoms of the West and North it became not only permanent but universal.

But in earlier times there was a grander faith. For the kingdom of God was a kingdom of priests. Not only the 'four and twenty elders[61]' before the throne, but the innumerable souls of the sanctified upon whom 'the second death had no power[62],' were 'kings and priests unto God.' Only in that high sense was priesthood predicable of Christian men. For the shadow had passed: the Reality had come: the one High Priest of Christianity was Christ.

[61] Rev. 5. 10. [62] Rev. 20. 6.

LECTURE VI.

THE CLERGY AS A SEPARATE CLASS.

THE fourth century of our era is not less remarkable in the history of Christian organization than it is in the history of Christian doctrine. At the beginning of that century Christianity was the religion of a persecuted sect: the prisons and the mines were thronged with Christian confessors: the executioner's sword was red with Christian blood [1]. In a few years it was tolerated and favoured: its adherents held high places in the Empire: its churches rivalled in splendour the temples of the pagan gods [2]. At the end of the century it was no longer merely tolerated but dominant: it was the religion of the State: and heresy was a political crime [3].

[1] The persecutions of the twelve years immediately preceding the formal toleration of Christianity, A.D. 300–312, were even more severe than those of earlier times: they are described in detail by Eusebius, *H. E.* Bks. viii. & ix. *passim*, and by Lactantius, *De mortibus Persecutorum*, 11–16, 21–22: for a good modern account see Mason, *The Persecution of Diocletian*, Cambridge, 1876.

[2] For the changes which were effected by Constantine in the external fortunes of the Christian churches see Euseb. *H. E.* 10. 1–6, *Vit. Constant.* Bks. 2–4: and, of modern writers, especially Keim, *Der Uebertritt Constantins der Grossen zum Christenthum*, Zürich, 1862.

[3] The following law of Gratian, Valentinian, and Theodosius, in A.D. 388, Cod. Theodos. 16. 5. 15, is one of many proofs that heresy was treated as an offence not only against the Church, but against the State: 'omnes diversarum perfidarumque sectarum quos in Deum miserae vesania conspirationis exercet nullum usquam

It was inevitable that so great a change in its external fortunes should be attended with a great change in its internal organization. The transition from a state of subordination to one of supremacy necessarily affects the conditions under which, in any society, officers hold their office. Their status is altered not only in relation to the world outside but also in relation to their members within. It was so in the Christian societies: at the beginning of the century, in spite of the development of the episcopate, the primitive type still survived: the government of the Churches was in the main a democracy: at the end of the century the primitive type had almost disappeared: the clergy were a separate and governing class.

I propose in the present lecture to analyse the complex and heterogeneous causes which operated to produce a change which, in the great mass of Christian communities, has been permanent from that time until now.

1. In the first place, the State conceded to the officers of the Christian Churches those immunities which were enjoyed by the heathen priesthood and by some of the liberal professions [4]. Hitherto Church officers had been

sinantur habere conventum, non inire tractatus, non coetus agere secretos, non nefariae praevaricationis altaria manus impiae officiis impudenter tollere, et mysteriorum simulationem ad injuriam verae religionis aptare. Quod ut congruum sortiatur effectum in specula sublimitas tua fidissimos quosque constituat, qui et cohibere hos possint et deprehensos offerre judiciis, severissimum secundum praeteritas sanctiones et Deo supplicium daturos et legibus.'

[4] The exempted classes were, with certain limitations as to numbers, chiefly priests, physicians, professors of literature, philosophy, rhetoric, and law: a full account is given by Kuhn, *Die städtische u. bürgerliche Verfassung des römischen Reichs*, erster Theil, pp. 83–123.

liable to the same public burdens as ordinary citizens. They might be called upon to hold office as municipal magistrates or senators, to act as trustees, to serve in the army. Nor is there any ground for assuming that the discharge of such duties, except where it involved the recognition of the State religion, was regarded as incongruous or derogatory. In some parts of the Empire the question in relation to civil office would rather be speculative than practical—the number of Christians who were rich enough to be eligible for office being comparatively few. But in the busy commercial towns of North Africa Christianity gained a hold at a comparatively early stage upon the wealthier as well as upon the poorer classes. The number of Church officers who were liable to public burdens was therefore proportionately larger: and at the same time their duties as Church officers were somewhat greater. It is in North Africa, therefore, that a feeling seems first to have arisen against combining civil with ecclesiastical functions [5]. The ground of objection was not that the two functions were inherently incompatible, but rather that the proper discharge of the duties of the one did not leave sufficient leisure for the proper discharge of the duties of the other. 'The ministers of the Church,' says Cyprian, 'ought to serve exclusively the altar and sacrifices, and to give their whole time to supplications and prayers.' Consequently, since one Geminius Victor had named a

[5] The first trace is in Tertull. *De praescript.* c. 41: and in a later treatise, *De Corona Militis*, 11, he raises the question 'an in totum Christianis militia conveniat.'

presbyter as his executor, he inflicts upon him, as a deterrent to others, the posthumous punishment of excluding his name from the list of those for the repose of whose souls the Church should pray [6]. And hardly had Christianity been put upon the footing of a recognized religion when Constantine addressed a letter to the proconsul of the African province requiring him to exempt all who were in the ranks of the Christian clergy from the ordinary public burdens [7]. The same exemption was soon granted to the Christians of other provinces [8]. But it was strongly resisted, and required frequent repetition [9]. The opposition to it is not surprising. In our own days, and under our own system of taxation, municipal magistracies and offices are in most instances a coveted honour. They entail upon those who hold them a certain amount of trouble, but not necessarily any considerable expense. But under the vicious system of the later Empire they were an almost intolerable burden. The magistrates were charged with the collection of the revenue, and, the quota of each municipality being fixed, they had

[6] S. Cyprian. *Epist.* 1 (66), p. 465.

[7] Constantin. *Epist. ad. Anulinum*, ap. Euseb, *H. E.* 10. 7: Sozom. 1. 9: incorporated in Cod. Theodos. 16. 2. 1. The report of Anulinus, to which Constantine's letter is an answer, is given by S. Augustin. *Epist.* 88 (68), Op. vol. ii. 302, ed Migne.

[8] Cod. Theodos. 16. 2. 2, A.D. 319.

[9] Laws of Constantine in Cod. Theodos. 16. 2. 7, A.D. 330 (= Letter quoted from a MS. of P. Pithou in Baronius ad ann. 316, n. 64): of Constantius, *ibid.* 16. 2. 8. A.D. 343 (= with the omission of the last clause Cod. Justin. 1. 3. 1, cf. Sozom. *H. E.* 3. 17): of Constantius and Constans, *ibid.* 16. 2. 10, A.D. 353 (probably = Auctor Vitae Spiridionis, ap. Hänel, *Corp. Leg. ante Justinian. lat.* p. 209), and *ibid.* 16. 2. 11, A.D. 354, *ibid.* 16. 2. 14, A.D. 357, *ibid.* 16. 2. 15, A.D. 360 (partly = Cod. Justin. 1. 3. 3): of Valentinian and Valens, *ibid.* 16. 2. 19, A.D. 370?: of Valens, Gratian, and Valentinian, *ibid.* 16. 2. 24, A.D. 377 (partly = Cod. Justin. 1. 3. 6).

to make up the deficit—in days in which deficits were chronic—out of their private resources[10]. The holding of office consequently involved in some cases an almost ruinous expenditure. It was a heavy and unequal tax upon property. An addition to the number of those who were exempt from it added to its oppressiveness and its inequality. It had also another result, it added to the number of claimants for admission to the privileged class. When the officers of Christian Churches were exempted, many persons whose fortunes were large enough to render them liable to the burden of municipal offices, sought and obtained admission to the ranks of the clergy, with the view of thereby escaping their liability. The exemption had barely been half-a-dozen years in operation before the Emperor found it necessary to guard it with important limitations[11]. These limitations were, for the most part, in the direction of prohibiting those who were liable to municipal burdens from being appointed to ecclesiastical office. As the Church grew in power the limitations were evaded, and several times in the course of the fourth century they had to be repeated[12]: but it is

[10] See e.g. Kuhn, *Verfassung* &c., erster Theil, p. 245: Walter, *Geschichte des römischen Rechts,* erster Theil, § 396: and especially Rüdiger, *De Curialibus Imperii Romani post Constantinum M.*, Wratislaw, 1838.

[11] The exemptions were first granted in A.D. 313: the first law restricting them is now lost, but it is quoted in a law of A.D. 320, Cod. Theodos. 16. 2. 3, 'cum constitutio emissa praecipiat nullum deinceps decurionem vel ex decurione progenitum idoneis facultatibus atque obeundis publicis muneribus opportunum *ad clericorum nomen obsequiumque confugere,* sed eos de cetero in defunctorum duntaxat clericorum loca surrogari qui fortuna tenues neque muneribus civilibus teneantur, obstricti . . . . :' there are similar restrictions in a law of A.D. 326, Cod. Theod. 16. 2. 6.

[12] Law of Constantius and Constans, A.D. 360, Cod. Theodos. 16. 2. 15: of Constantius and Julian, A.D. 361, Cod. Theodos. 8. 4. 7: of Valentinian, Theodosius.

important in relation to the point in hand to notice that, in spite of evident abuses, the exemptions themselves were never repealed: it is equally important to notice that, although no doubt the exemption was claimed in almost all cases in which it could be claimed, the right to exemption did not constitute ineligibility. It was not until the Council of Chalcedon that the holding of civil office by clerks became an offence against ecclesiastical law [13]: and it was not until eighty years after that Council that the appointment of a civil officer to ecclesiastical office became an offence against civil law [14].

2. In the second place, the State granted to the officers of the Christian Church an exemption from the ordinary jurisdiction of the civil courts. It so far recognized the validity of the consensual jurisdiction to which the members of Christian societies submitted themselves [15]. That consensual jurisdiction was to some extent recognized for all members. The civil law which recognized associations recognized also the right of such associations to frame and to enforce

and Arcadius, A.D. 398, Cod. Theodos. 16. 2. 32: Cod. Justin. 1. 3. 12: cf. Socrates, *H. E.* 6. 5: Sozomen. *H. E.* 8. 7.

[13] Conc. Chalced. A.D. 451, c. 7 *τοὺς ἅπαξ ἐν κλήρῳ κατειλεγμένους ἢ καὶ μονάσαντας ὡρίσαμεν μήτε ἐπὶ στρατείαν μήτε ἐπὶ ἀξίαν κοσμικὴν ἔρχεσθαι* under penalty of anathema.

[14] Law of Justinian, A.D. 532, Cod, Justin. 1. 3. 53 (52), *θεσπίζομεν μήτε βουλευτὴν μήτε ταξεώτην ἐπίσκοπον ἢ πρεσβύτερον τοῦ λοιποῦ γίνεσθαι*: so Novell. 123. 15, A.D. 546.

[15] Law of Valens, Gratian, and Valentinian in A.D. 376, Cod. Theodos. 16. 2. 23: 'Qui mos est causarum civilium idem in negotiis ecclesiasticis obtinendus est: ut si qua sunt ex quibusdam dissentionibus levibusque delictis ad religionis observantiam pertinentia, locis suis et a suae dioeceseos synodis audiantur: exceptis quae actio criminalis ab ordinariis extraordinariisque judicibus aut illustribus potestatibus audienda constituit.'

their own rules. In the Christian societies matters of religious dispute, or offences against religion, might be decided by the individual societies or by the representative assembly of a province. The limitation to such matters was, in the case of ordinary members, a strict one. The administration of justice would have come to an end if all those who came soon to constitute a preponderating majority of the citizens of the Empire had been exempted from its ordinary operation. But for Church officers the rule went far beyond this. At first the rule that all causes in which officers of the Churches were concerned should be decided by the Churches themselves was permissive[16]. But at last it became compulsory[17]. The right of appeal to the emperor was reserved on the part of the State[18], but fenced round with conditions on the part of the Churches: and so began that long struggle between civil and ecclesiastical jurisdiction over Church officers, which forms so important an element in mediaeval

[16] It is spoken of as a permission and not as an obligation: Sozom. *H. E.* I. 9, 15, *τῶν δὲ ἐπισκόπων ἐπικαλεῖσθαι τὴν κρίσιν ἐπέτρεψε τοῖς δικαζομένοις ἣν βούλωνται τοὺς πολιτικοὺς ἄρχοντας παραιτεῖσθαι.*

[17] Law of Honorius and Theodosius, A.D. 412, Cod. Theodos. 16. 2. 41, 'clericos nonnisi apud episcopos accusari convenit:' *ibid.* 16. 2. 47: but a law of Leo, A.D. 459, ap. Theodos. Lector. I. 14: Niceph. Callist. 15. 22 (Hänel, *Corpus Legum*, No. 1220, p. 259) makes clerks amenable only to *τῷ ἐπάρχῳ τῶν πραιτωρίων*.

[18] That the right of appeal existed is shown by the fact that the Council of Antioch, c. 11, 12, punished with ecclesiastical penalties a clerk who availed himself of it: and also by the fact, e.g. Athanasius (Socrat. *H. E.* I. 33), and Priscillian (Sulp. Sev. *Chron.* 49, p. 102, ed. Halm) did actually appeal. But, according to the ordinary law, such a right did not exist where the ecclesiastical judge was in the position of an arbitrator, accepted by both parties to a suit: cf. Hebenstreit, *Historia Jurisdictionis Ecclesiasticae ex legibus utriusque Codicis illustrata*, Diss. ii. § 26, iii. § 6, Lips. 1776: Bethmann-Hollweg, *Der römische Civilprozess*, Bd. 3. p. 114, Bonn, 1866.

history, and which has not altogether ceased in our own times [19].

The joint effect of these exemptions from public burdens, and from ordinary courts, was the creation of a class *civilly* distinct from the rest of the community. This is the first element in the change which we are investigating: the clergy came to have a distinct civil status.

From the same general causes flowed another result of not less importance.

The funds of the primitive communities had consisted entirely of voluntary offerings. Of these offerings those officers whose circumstances required it were entitled to a share. They received such a share only on the ground of their poverty. They were, so far, in the position of the widows and orphans and helpless poor. Like soldiers in the Roman army, or like slaves in a Roman household, they were entitled to a monthly allowance [20]. The amount of that allowance was variable. When the Montanists proposed to pay their clergy a fixed salary the proposal was condemned as a heretical innovation, alien to Catholic practice [21]. Those who could supplemented their allowances by farming or by trade. There was no sense of incongruity in their

[19] For an exact account of the legislation which served as the basis of the later Canon Law on the subject, see Dove, *De jurisdictionis Ecclesiasticae apud Germanos Gallosque progressu*, Berlin, 1855, and Sohm, *Die geistliche Gerichtsbarkeit im fränkischen Reich* in the *Zeitschrift für Kirchenrecht*, vol. ix. 1870, pp. 193 sqq.

[20] 'Divisio mensurna,' S. Cyprian. *Epist.* 34 (28), p. 570, 39 (34), p. 582.

[21] Euseb. *H. E.* 5. 18. 2: 5. 28. 10: this salary, like the allowances of the Catholic clergy, was to be paid monthly (μηνιαῖα δηνάρια ἑκατὸν πεντήκοντα), the point of objection being apparently that it was fixed, and not dependent on the freewill offerings of the people.

doing so. The Apostolical Constitutions repeat with emphasis the apostolical injunction, 'If any would not work, neither should he eat[22].' There is no early trace of the later idea that buying and selling, handicraft and farming, were in themselves inconsistent with the office of a Christian minister. The bishops and presbyters of those early days kept banks, practised medicine, wrought as silver-smiths, tended sheep, or sold their goods in open market[23]. They were like the second generation of non-juring bishops a century and a half ago, or like the early preachers of the Wesleyan Methodists. They were men of the world taking part in the ordinary business of life. The point about which the Christian communities were anxious was, not that their officers should cease to trade, but that, in this as in other respects, they should be ensamples to the flock. The chief existing enactments of early councils on the point are that bishops are not to huckster their goods from market to market, nor are

[22] Const. Apost. 2. 62.

[23] This is proved by the existence of both general regulations and particular instances: i. among the former are the enactment of the Civil Law exempting clerks from the trading-tax: 'si exiguis admodum mercimoniis tenuem sibi victum vestitumque conquirent' (Law of Constantius and Constans, A.D. 360, Cod. Theodos. 16. 2. 15), and the enactments of the *Statuta Ecclesiae Antiqua*, c. 51, 'clericus quantumlibet verbo Dei eruditus artificio victum quaerat:' c. 52, 'clericus victum et vestimentum sibi artificiolo vel agricultura absque officii sui detrimento paret:' ii. among the latter are the case of Spiridion who tended sheep in Cyprus, Socrates, *H. E.* 1. 12, of a bishop who was a weaver at Maiuma, Sozom. *H. E.* 7. 28, of one who was a shipbuilder in Campania, S. Greg. M. *Epist.* 13. 26, vol. ii. p. 1235, of one who practised in the law courts, *ibid.* 10. 10. vol. ii. p. 1048, of a presbyter who was a silversmith at Ancyra, *Corp. Inscr. Graec.* No. 9258: Basil, *Epist.* 198 (263), vol. iv. p. 290) speaks of the majority of his clergy as earning their livelihood by sedentary handicrafts (*τὰς ἑδραίας τῶν τεχνῶν*), and Epiphanius, *Haeres.* 80. 6, p. 1072, speaks of others doing it in order to earn money for the poor: so Gennad. *De Script. Eccles.* c. 69, of Hilary of Arles.

they to use their position to buy cheaper and sell dearer than other people [24].

Into this primitive state of things the State introduced a change.

1. It allowed the Churches to hold property [25]. And hardly had the holding of property become possible before the Church became a kind of universal legatee. The merit of bequeathing property to the Church was preached with so much success that restraining enactments became necessary. Just as the State did not abolish, though it found it necessary to limit, its concession of exemption to Church officers, so it pursued the policy of limiting rather than of abolishing

[24] Conc. Illib. c. 19, 'Episcopi, presbyteres, et diacones de locis suis negotiandi causa non discedant, nec circumeuntes provincias quaestuosas nundinas sectentur:' Conc. Tarracon. c. 2 'Quicumque in clero esse voluerit emendi vilius vel vendendi carius studio non utatur.'

[25] In several cases the Christian communities had held property before the time of Constantine: but they appear to have done so rather by concession than of right, and in time of persecution the property was liable to be seized. They had been formally permitted by Gallienus, Euseb. *H. E.* 7. 13. 3, to have common cemeteries: and De Rossi in the *Bulletino di Archeol. Christian.* Ann. iii. 1865, pp. 89 (also in the *Revue Archéologique*, vol. xiii. 1866, pp. 225 sqq.), maintains that the right existed in relation to cemeteries from the first. But on the other hand, the proceedings in the case of Paul of Samosata seem to show that, at least in some cases, the property was held personally by the bishop: since Paul's opponents, not being able to eject him by the ordinary processes of law, as they could have done if the property had belonged to the community, had to seek the extraordinary intervention of Aurelian (Euseb. *H. E.* 7. 30. 19). Lampridius mentions that in a special case Alexander Severus had allowed the Christians rather than the tavern-keepers to occupy a piece of once public land (Lamprid. *Vit. Alex. Sev.* 49): and, the year before the Edict of Milan, Maximinus (Euseb. *H. E.* 9. 10. 11) restored the churches and other property of which the Christians had been deprived: but it does not appear that until that Edict the right of holding property was ordinary and incontestable. Even then the right was probably limited to the occupation of churches, cemeteries, and other buildings used for worship or cognate purposes: the right of receiving property bequeathed by will for the purpose of endowment was not granted until A.D. 321, by a law which is preserved in Cod. Theodos. 16. 2. 4.

the right to acquire property [26]. 'I do not complain of the law,' says Jerome, writing on this point, 'but of the causes which have rendered the law necessary [27].'

2. The enthusiasm, or the policy, of Constantine went considerably beyond this. He ordered that not only the clergy but also the widows and orphans who were on the Church-roll should receive fixed annual allowances [28]: he endowed some Churches with fixed revenues chargeable upon the lands of the municipalities [29]: in some cases he gave to churches the rich revenues or the splendid buildings of heathen temples [30].

[26] The most stringent enactment was that of Valentinian and Valens in A.D. 370, Cod. Theodos. 16. 2. 20, to the effect that 'ecclesiastici' are not even to visit the houses of widows and wards.

[27] S. Hieron. *Epist.* 52 (2), *ad Nepotianum*, c. 6, 'Pudet dicere sacerdotes idolorum, mimi, et aurigae, et scorta, haereditates capiunt: solis clericis et monachis hac lege [i.e. the law referred to in the preceding note] prohibetur: et prohibetur non a persecutoribus sed a principibus christianis. Nec de lege conqueritur: sed doleo cur meruerimus hanc legem,' cf. S. Ambros. *Epist.* 18. 13: *Expos. Evang. sec. Luc.* 8. 79, vol. i. p. 1491.

[28] Theodoret. *H. E.* 1. 10: Incert. Auct. de Constant. ap. Hänel, *Corpus Legum*, p. 196, 'literas ad provinciarum praesides dedit quibus imperabat ut per singulas urbes virginibus et viduis et aliis qui divino ministerio erant consecrati, annuum frumentum suppeditaretur:' cf. Euseb. *H. E.* 10. 6. Julian not only withdrew the privilege, but also compelled widows and virgins to repay what they had received from the public funds, Sozom. *H. E.* 5. 5: but the privilege was restored by his successor, Theodoret. *H. E.* 4. 4.

[29] Euseb. *Vit. Const.* 4. 28: Sozom. *H. E.* 1. 8. 10: 5. 5. 3.

[30] Later writers sometimes represented the transfer of temples and their revenues to the Christian churches as having been made on a considerable scale: e.g. Theophanes, p. 42, ed. Class.: Niceph. Callist. 7. 46: Cedren. pp. 478, 498. But although instances of such a transfer can be found, e.g. that of the Temple of Mithra at Alexandria, Sozom. *H. E.* 5. 7, and that which is recorded in an extant inscription at Zorava in Trachonitis (*Θεοῦ γέγονεν οἶκος τὸ τῶν δαιμόνων καταγώγιον*, Le Bas et Waddington, No. 2498), yet on the other hand the confiscation of temples and their revenues did not become general until the time of Theodosius, and the funds so realized were applied not to Christian, but to imperial and secular purposes: this is shown by Cod. Theodos. 16. 10. 19 (law of A.D. 408 = Constit. Sirmond. 12, p. 466, ed. Hänel), 'templorum detrahantur annonae et rem annonariam juvent, expensis devotissimorum militum profuturae:' so *ibid.* 16. 10. 20.

This is the second element in the change: the clergy became not only independent, but in some cases wealthy. In an age of social decay and struggling poverty they had not only enough but to spare. They could afford to lend: and they lent. The frequent repetition in provincial councils of the rule that the clergy should not take interest upon their loans, while it shows that the practice was reprehended, shows also that it existed [31].

The effect of the recognition of Christianity by the State was thus not only to create a class civilly distinct from the rest of the community, but also to give that class social independence. In other words, the Christian clergy, in addition to their original prestige as office-bearers, had the privileges of a favoured class, and the power of a moneyed class.

In the meantime, cooperating with these causes, though wholly different from them, was another group of causes which operated in the same general direction.

The fourth century of our era saw not only the recognition of Christianity by the State as the religion of the State, but also the first great development within Christianity itself of those practices and tendencies which are covered by the general name of Monasticism. Those practices and tendencies consist in the main of two elements—asceticism and isolation from the world. Each of these elements has a separate history: the significance of monasticism lies in their combination.

[31] Councils of Elvira, c. 20: Arles, c. 12: Laodicea, c. 4: Nicaea, c. 17: 1 Tours, c. 13: Tarragon, c. 3: 3 Orleans, c. 27: Trull. c. 10: so also the Cod. Eccles. Afric. c. 16: Can. Apost. 44.

1. Asceticism belongs to almost the first beginnings of the Christian faith. The teaching of our Lord had been a teaching of self-abnegation: the preaching of more than one Apostle had gone beyond this and had been a preaching of self-mortification. The maxim of the Master had been, 'Sell all that thou hast and give to the poor[32]:' the maxim of the Apostle was, 'Mortify your members which are upon earth[33].' Those who had begun by giving a literal interpretation to the one—'having all things common[34],' proceeded to give a literal interpretation to the other—'crucifying the flesh[35].' In other words, the profound reaction against current morality which had already expressed itself in some of the philosophical sects expressed itself within the limits of Christianity. In our own days, in which the social system has become more settled, and in which the divine influence of the Christian faith has raised even the current standard, it is difficult to realize to ourselves the passionate intensity of that striving after the moral ideal. We know of men struggling for freedom: but in those days they struggled less for freedom than for purity. Such struggles admit of no compromise: for compromise, like diplomacy, finds no place in the mêlée of the battlefield. And this struggle for moral purity became a war *à outrance* against human nature. At first it was confined to a few: it rather hovered on the outskirts of Christianity than found a recognized place within: it was Judaeo-Christian or Gnostic rather than Catholic: it was rather dis-

[32] S. Matt. 19. 21.
[33] Col. 3. 5.
[34] Acts 2. 44.
[35] Gal. 5. 24.

couraged than inculcated—until, with the sudden rush of a great enthusiasm, it became a force which even the whole weight of the confederated Churches could not resist [36].

2. Side by side with it, but for the first three centuries confined to a still smaller number of persons [37], was the tendency to live in partial or total isolation from society.

This, like the ascetic tendency, was not confined to Christianity. It had already taken an important place in the religions of both Egypt and the East.

In Egypt there had been for several centuries a great monastery of those who were devoted to the worship of the deity whom the Greeks called Serapis. The monks, like Christian monks, lived in a vast common building, which they never left: they might retain a limited control over their property, but they were dead to the world [38].

[36] The tendency towards the laudation of virginity is found in e.g. Herm. *Sim.* 9. 10. 11: S. Justin M. *Apol.* 1. 15: Athenag. *Legat.* 32: Origen, *c. Cels.* 7. 48: Tertull. *De Veland. Virg.* 2, *De Exhort. Cast.* 21: S. Cyprian. *De habitu Virg.* c. 3, p. 189: *De Mortalitate*, 26, p. 314: *Epist.* 55 (52), c. 20, p. 638, 62 (60), c. 3, p. 699.

[37] There is the instance of Narcissus of Jerusalem, Euseb. *H. E.* 6. 9. 6, of the fugitives from the Decian persecution mentioned by Dionysius of Alexandria ap. Euseb. *H. E.* 6. 42. 2, of those with whom 'the great monk' Antony met before he himself founded the later system of Egyptian monachism, (pseudo-) Athanas. *Vit. S. Anton.* c. 3, Op. vol. i. p. 634. The fact that in the middle of the fourth century there was already a παράδοσις ἄγραφος (Sozom. 1. 13) of monastic rules is a further proof of the existence of monks before that time: on the other hand Tertullian's protest that the Christians were not 'Brachmanae, Gymnosophistae, silvicolae, exules vitae' (*Apol.* 42) shows that the tendency had not become general.

[38] The institution of monachism in Egypt goes back to remote times: a hieroglyphic inscription in the Louvre, No. 3465, speaks of an abbess of the nuns of Ammon (Revillout in the *Archives des Missions scientifiques et litteraires*, 3me Serie, vol. 4, p. 479): but our chief knowledge of it is derived from the papyri, which exist in considerable numbers, referring to the Serapeum at Memphis. The most

In the greatest of Oriental religions there had also been for many centuries a monastic system, which gained so firm a hold upon the professors of that religion that to the present day, in some countries where Buddhism prevails, every member of the population, whether he will or no, must at some period of his life adopt the monastic habit, and life, if only for a month or two, in retreat [39].

The fact that Christian monasticism first appears in Egypt [40], where the Serapeum was a familiar object to the inhabitants of Memphis [41], and also in those

important of them are published by Brunet de Presle, *Papyrus Grecs du Musée du Louvre et de la Bibliothèque Impériale*, in the *Notices et Extraits des MSS. de la Bibliothèque Impériale*, vol. xviii. pp. 261 sqq., who has also published an excellent *Mémoire sur le Sérapeum de Memphis* in the *Mémoires présentés par divers savans à l'Académie des Inscriptions et Belles-lettres*, 1re série, vol. ii. pp. 552 sqq. (see also Leemans, *Papyri Graeci Musei Ant. publ. Lugduni-Batavi*, pap. B, p. 9, and Mai, *Class. Auct.* vol. v. pp. 352, 601). The worship of Serapis was widely spread in both Greece and Italy (see e.g. Herzberg, *Die Geschichte Griechenlands unter der Herrschaft der Römer*, Bd. ii. p. 267: Preller in the *Berichte der königl. sächs. Gesellschaft d. Wissenschaft*, phil. hist. classe, Bd. vi. 1854, pp. 196 sqq.: Boissier, *La Religion Romaine*, vol. i. pp. 400 sqq.), and there were associations of Serapis-worshippers (e.g. at Athens, a decree of which is to be found in the *Corpus Inscr. Graec.* No. 120 = Hicks, *Greek Inscriptions in the British Museum*, part i. No. 21), but there are no traces of religious recluses out of Egypt.

39 R. S. Hardy, *Eastern Monachism*, p. 57.

40 The early appearance of Monasticism in Egypt is shown not only by the 'Eremitenroman' (Weingarten, p. 20), entitled *Vita S. Antonii*, and ascribed to S. Athanasius (Op. vol. i. pp. 630 sqq.), but also by the more important treatise *De Vita Contemplativa*, which is printed among the works of Philo (*Op.* vol. ii. pp. 471 sqq. ed. Mang.). The controversies which have for some time been carried on as to the probable authorship and date of this treatise (of which a short and convenient account will be found in Kuenen, *De Godsdienst van Israel*, Eng. Trans. vol. iii. pp. 217 sqq.) seem to have been set at rest by Lucius, *Die Therapeuten und ihre Stellung in der Geschichte der Askese*, Strassburg, 1879, who maintains that it is really an account, written not long before the time of Eusebius, of the communities of Christian ascetics which had already begun to exist in Egypt: (see Hilgenfeld's panegyric upon the work in his *Zeitschrift f. wissensch. Theologie*, Bd. xxiii. 1880, pp. 423 sqq.)

41 The remains of the Serapeum were first explored by Mariette, and have been described in his work entitled *Le Sérapeum de Memphis*, Paris, 1857.

extreme parts of Asia Minor which were locally nearest to the Buddhist populations [42], has led to the supposition that one or other or both of these external causes may account for its introduction into Christianity [43].

But great enthusiasms are never adequately explained by external causes. No torch would have kindled so great a conflagration if the fuel had not been already gathered together for the burning. The causes of the sudden outburst of monasticism in the fourth century must be sought, and can be found, within Christianity itself. They lie in the general conditions of the age. It was an age, in the first place, in which the artificial civilization of the Empire seemed to culminate. That civilization carried in its train a craving for artificial luxuries and artificial excitements. Such a craving is never satisfied. It begets a vague restlessness, which in its turn passes into *ennui*. There are men

[42] There are some, though not considerable, traces of monasticism in Armenia at the beginning of the fourth century, to which period the foundation of the monastery of Etchmiazin is traditionally ascribed: (see the life of St. Gregory the Illuminator by Agathangelos, translated in Langlois, *Historiens de l'Arménie*, Paris, 1867, vol. i. p. 181). There are also some, though not considerable, traces of Buddhism having spread as far as Parthia a century and a half earlier than the above-mentioned date (Max Müller, *Selected Essays*, vol. ii. p. 316). But there is no trace of actual contact between Buddhism and Christianity, nor is there anything in the form of early Armenian monasticism which shows a specially Buddhist impress.

[43] Käuffer in the *Zweite Denkschrift der hist.-theol. Gesellschaft zu Leipsig*, Leipsig, 1819: and Weingarten, in his valuable essay *Der Ursprung des Monchtums*, in the *Zeitschrift für Kirchengeschichte*, Bd. i. 1877, pp. 1 sqq. (since published separately) trace Christian monachism to Egyptian influences: Hilgenfeld, in his *Zeitschrift für wissenschaftliche Theologie*, Bd. xxi. 1878, pp. 147 sqq., lays great stress on Buddhist influences: the general view, which is given above, that both these influences were subordinate in their effects to causes which existed within Christianity itself, has been stated with great force by Keim, *Ursprung des Monchwesens* in his collection of essays entitled *Aus dem Urchristenthum*, pp. 204 sqq., Zurich, 1878.

who stand on the threshold of life who yet are weary of it. There are those who have passed through life and have found it vanity. There are social ambitions which have been disappointed, and political schemes which have been baffled, and moral reformations which have failed,—and which have resulted in an exodus of despair.

Again, it was an age of newly realized religious freedom, in which, after the lapse of half a century, men began to idealize the age which had preceded it. The age of martyrdoms had ceased, but the spirit of the martyrs began to live again. For martyrdom had been in many cases the choice of a sublime enthusiasm. There had been men and women who, so far from shrinking from it, had sought and welcomed the occasion of it[44]. They had 'counted it all joy to suffer for His name's sake.' All this had come to a sudden end. Persecution had ceased. But the idea of the merit of suffering had not ceased. There were those who, if they could not be martyrs in act, would at least be martyrs in will (μάρτυρες τῇ προαιρέσει)[45]. They sought lives of self-mortification. They would themselves torture the flesh which the lictors would no longer scourge. They would construct for themselves the prisons which no longer kept Christian confessors for the lions.

[44] For instances see Euseb. *De Martyr. Palaestinae*, 3. 3: *Acta Theodoti*, c. 22 in Ruinart, *Acta Martyrum sincera*, p. 346, Tertull. *Ad Scapulam*, 5: Le Blant, *Sur la preparation au Martyre dans les premieres siecles de l'Église*, in the *Memoires de l'Academie des Inscriptions*, vol. xxviii. 1 partie, pp. 54 sqq., speaks with both force and truth of 'cette immense soif de mort, cette indomptable passion de souffrir, ressentie par les ames ardentes;' cf. Euseb. *H. E.* 7. 12, of some martyrs at Caesarea, πόθου γλιχομένοις οὐρανίου.

[45] S. Basil. M. *Hom. in XL Martyres*, Op. ed. Garn. vol. ii. p. 149.

And again, it was an age in which the antithesis between mind and matter, between the unreal world of sense and the real world of spirit, expressed itself in more than one philosophy and more than one religion. It was the first and fullest bloom in the Western world of that love of haze upon the horizon which, however alien to the modern temper, has almost won its way to a permanent place among human tendencies, and which is known by the name of mysticism. There were men to whom philosophy had ceased to be philosophy, and had become an emotion. There were the pure and passionate souls to whom contact with sin was intolerable, and who fled from a world which they did not know to dream of a world which could be but a dream. There were those to whom life was thought, and thought was the contemplation of God, and the contemplation of God was the love of Him, and the love of Him was absorption in Him—as the morning mist floats upwards from some still mountain tarn, and rests for a while in embodied glory in the sunlight, and is lost in the pure infinity of noon.

To those who have studied the history of great social movements it will not be surprising that these various elements should have combined together, in the course of a single generation, to form an enthusiasm or a fanaticism. The movement began in the East, but it spread rapidly to the West: and wherever, in East or West, the stream of life ran strong, there were crowds of men and women who were ready to forsake all, and follow John the Baptist into the desert rather than Christ into the world.

Monasticism became henceforward a permanent factor in Christian society. Its first result was to give a new meaning to the antithesis between the Church and the world. That antithesis in its original form was an antithesis between the new chosen people and the Gentiles outside. But monasticism transferred the distinction to the Church itself, between those who stood within the sanctuary and followed 'counsels of perfection,' and those who were content with the average morality of Christian men[46]. The result of this upon ecclesiastical organization was practically to compel the clergy to live what was thought to be the higher—that is the more ascetic—life. This result was not effected without resistance. For asceticism had in some cases been the protest of heresy against catholicity[47]: but when the Arians set themselves to persecute monasticism, by a remarkable rebound of feeling, monasticism became a protest of catholicity against Arianism[48]. Henceforth there was for the clergy that

[46] 'Religion' came to mean the monastic life and rule: e.g. 1 Conc. Aurel. A.D. 511, c. 11; 5 Conc. Paris. A.D. 615, c. 13; 4 Conc. Tolet. A.D. 633, c. 55; 10 Conc. Tolet. A.D. 656, c. 6. 'Secular' came to mean whatever was outside the monastic life and rule: and 'conversion' was no longer the turning 'from the power of Satan unto God,' but the adoption of the monastic habit: e.g. Conc. Agath. A.D. 506, c. 16; 1 Conc. Aurel. A.D. 511, c. 21; 4 Conc. Arelat. A.D. 524, c. 2; 5 Conc. Aurel. A.D. 529, c. 9; 2 Conc. Arvern. A.D. 549, c. 9: also so 'poenitentia:' e.g. 2 Conc. Arelat. A.D. 451? c. 22.

[47] e.g. in the second century it had prevailed among the Marcionites, who admitted no married person to baptism unless he consented to a divorce, Tertull. *Adv. Marc.* 1. 29: 5. 7.

[48] The violence of the Arian reaction against the Catholic institution of perpetual virginity is shown by e.g. S. Athanas. *Epist. Encycl.* 3, vol. i. p. 90, ed. Ben.; Socrat. *H. E.* 2. 28: S. Hil. Pictav. *Ad Constant. Aug.* 1. 6: *Fragm. Hist.* 2. 3;

which is an infallible mark of an exceptional status, exceptional legislation.

That legislation affected chiefly marriage and social life. The legislation which affected marriage varied widely, not only from century to century, but between East and West. In the East the ascetic rule prevailed for bishops [49]: in the West it came ultimately to prevail for all the higher orders of clergy. At first they might not marry after ordination, and then 'they that had wives were to be as though they had none,' and lastly, though not until prevalent practice had rendered a law almost needless, they might not marry at all [50].

The legislation which affected social life began by excluding clergy from the amusements of life, and went on gradually to exclude them from its ordinary pursuits, and at last, though not for some centuries, clenched the distinction by requiring them to wear a special dress [51].

3. 9: S. Greg. Naz. *Orat. in laud. Basil. M.* c. 46, vol. i. p. 805, *Orat. c. Arian.* c. 3, vol. i. p. 605: so also against monks, S. Basil M. *Epist.* 256 (200), vol. iv. p. 390.

[49] Conc. Trull. c. 48.

[50] The evidence upon which the above paragraph is based is altogether too extensive and intricate to admit of being stated concisely: it will be found at length in the excellent work of J. A. and A. Theiner, *Die Einführung der erzwungenen Ehelosigkeit bei den christlichen Geistlichen und ihre Folgen*, Altenburg, 1828.

[51] There are many injunctions to the clergy in earlier centuries to use modest and becoming dress: but there is probably no direct enactment as to the form of dress which the clergy should wear in ordinary life earlier than the Capitulary of Karloman in 742, c. 7 (Pertz, *Legum*, vol. i. p. 17, = Conc. German. c. 7, Mansi, *Concilia*, vol. xii. p. 365), which prohibited clerks from wearing the 'sagum,' or short cloak, and required them to wear the 'casula' (for the meaning of which see the *Dictionary of Christian Antiquities, s. v.*), and the Capitulary of Pippin two years later (*Capit. Suession.* A.D. 744, c. 3, Pertz, *Legum*, p. 21) which enacts that 'omnes clerici fornicationem non faciant, et *habitu laicorum* non portent nec apud canes venationes non faciant nec acceptores non portent.' For the disputed questions when and whether church officers had a distinctive dress in church in early times, reference may be made to W. B. Marriott, *Vestiarium Christianum*, London,

If we add all these various causes together, we shall see that the isolation of the clergy as a separate class of the community became at length inevitable. They had a separate civil status, they had separate emoluments, they were subject to special rules of life. The shepherd bishop driving his cattle to their rude pasturage among the Cyprian hills, the merchant bishop of North Africa, the physician presbyter of Rome, were vanished types whose living examples could be found no more.

All this was intensified by the decay and fall of the Roman Empire. When the surging tides of barbarian invasion swept over Europe, the Christian organization was almost the only institution of the past which survived the flood. It remained as a visible monument of what had been, and, by so remaining, was of itself an antithesis to the present. The chief town of the Roman province, whatever its status under barbarian rule, was still the bishop's see. The limits of the old 'province,' though the boundary of a new kingdom might bisect them, were still the limits of his diocese. The bishop's tribunal was the only tribunal in which the laws of the Empire could be pleaded in their integrity. The bishop's dress was the ancient robe of a Roman magistrate. The ancient Roman language which was used in the Church services was a standing protest against the growing degeneracy of the 'vulgar tongue.' These survivals of the old world which was passing away gave to the Christian clergy a still more

1868, and for a contrary view Hefele, *Die liturgischen Gewänder* in his *Beiträge zur Kirchengeschichte, Archäologie u. Liturgik*, Bd. ii, Freiburg, 1864.

exceptional position when they went as missionaries into the villages which Roman civilization had hardly reached, or into the remote parts of the Empire where Roman organization had been to the masses of the population only what English rule is to the masses of the population of India. To the 'pagani' of Gaul and Spain, to the Celtic inhabitants of our own islands, and, in rather later times, to the Teutonic races of Central Europe, they were probably never known except as a special class, assuming a special status, living a special life, and invested with special powers.

There were two usages which, though they were not without significance even in the seats of the older civilization, became in the great mass of the nations of the West circumstances of great significance.

1. The first is one which might seem trivial, if we did not bear in mind that a dispute concerning it constituted a principal cause why the British Churches refused to combine with the organization which was introduced into the English kingdoms by Augustine[52].

Part of the protest which had been made by early preachers against the current effeminacy had been a protest against the elaborate fashion of dressing the hair[53]. The first book of the Apostolical Constitutions exhorts all Christians to trim their hair becomingly[54]: Clement of Alexandria lays down minute rules in this

[52] Bede, *H. E.* 4. 1; 5. 21; see Haddan and Stubbs, *Councils, &c.* vol. i. p. 154.

[53] Compare the address of Epictetus to the young rhetorician who came to him περιεργότερον ἠσκημένου τὴν κόμην, *Diss.* 3. 1. 1.

[54] Const. Apost. 1. 3.

respect for both men and women[55]; and Chrysostom repeatedly quotes the Apostolical injunction against 'broided hair' in his appeals to the court-ladies of Constantinople[56]. But, as in other cases, that which had been a primitive rule for all Christians became in time a special rule for the clergy. They must not either shave their heads like the priests of Isis[57], nor let their hair grow long like heathen philosophers. Then came a more exact and stringent rule: they must not only trim their hair but trim it in a particular way. The trimming of the hair in this particular way became one of the ceremonies of admission to ecclesiastical office: and, throughout both East and West, clerks became differentiated from laymen by the 'tonsure[58].'

2. The second usage is one which was partly primitive and partly monastic.

In the earliest times, the living of all those who shared in the Church offerings at a common table had probably been one of those simple economies by which the resources of the infant Churches had been husbanded[59]. When, long after this primitive practice had

[55] Clem. Alex. *Paedag.* 3. 11, p. 290, ed. Pott.

[56] S. Chrys. e.g. *Hom. ix. in Ep. ad Rom.* vol. ix. 742, *Hom. xxvi. in Ep. i. ad Corinth.* vol. x. 235, *Hom. viii. in Ep. i. ad Tim.* vol. xi. 590.

[57] S. Hieron. *Comm. in Ezech.* lib. 13, c. 44.

[58] The direction of the *Statuta Ecclesiae Antiqua*, c. 44 is simply 'clericus nec comam nutriat nec barbam:' and it is clear that for some time there was a diversity of usage. The earliest directions as to the manner of trimming the hair which have conciliar authority are probably those of the fourth Council of Toledo, A.D. 633, c. 41: 'omnes clerici vel lectores sicut levitae et sacerdotes detonso superius toto capite inferius solam circuli coronam relinquant.' This was known as the 'coronal tonsure:' its adoption seems to have been at least partly due to mystical reasons, as symbolizing the crown of thorns (ps.-Alcuin, *De Divinis officiis*, c. 35): but when once adopted it became a badge of orthodoxy, and as such became universal.

[59] Epist. ad Diognet. 5. 7 τράπεζαν κοινὴν παρατίθενται ἀλλ' οὐ κοινήν. The fourth

passed away, monasticism asserted its place in Christian life, a pious bishop of the West, Eusebius of Vercelli, began the practice of gathering together his clergy in a common building [60]. St. Augustine followed his example, and instituted in Africa what he calls by a kind of paronomasia, considering the antithesis between monks and clerks, a 'monasterium clericorum [61].' Hence grew the practice, to which I must refer again in a subsequent lecture [62], of the clergy living together—a practice which in the country districts of the West became as much a practical necessity as it is for the missionaries of our modern Churches to live by themselves in mission-stations. But the practice served still further to emphasize, especially in those districts, the difference between clergy and laity: for the former not only had a distinctive personal mark, but also lived an isolated life.

So grew the Christian clergy. They came to be what they were by the inevitable force of circumstances, that is to say, by the gradual evolution of that great scheme of God's government of the world which, though present eternally to His sight, is but slowly unfolded before ours. But of what they came to be it is difficult to speak with a calm judgment, because the incalculable good

Apostolical Canon directs those offerings which could not properly be placed upon the altar to be taken εἰς οἶκον for the use of the bishop and clergy. It is conceivable that this οἶκος was a kind of clergy-house, or at least a common refectory.

[60] S. Maxim. *Serm.* 23 ap. Muratori, *Anecdota Latina*, vol. 4; S. Ambros. *Epist.* 63, c. 66, 82, vol. ii. p. 1038.

[61] S. Augustin. *Serm.* 355 = *De divers.* 49, Op. ed. Migne, *Patr. Lat.* vol. v, p. 1570.

[62] See Lecture VIII.

which they have wrought in the midst of human society has been tempered with so much of failure and of sin. One point at least, however, seems evident, that that incalculable good has been achieved rather by the human influence which they have exercised than by the superhuman power which they have sometimes claimed. The place which they have filled in human history has been filled not by the wielding of the thunderbolts of heaven, but by the whispering of the still voice which tells the outcast and the sad of divine mercy and divine consolation. And if it be possible to draw from the past an augury of the future, they will have their place in the days that are to come, whether those days be a reign of chaos or a reign of peace, not by living in the isolation which the decay of the Empire forced upon the clergy of the middle ages, but by recurring to the earlier type, by being within society itself a leaven of knowledge and of purity, of temperance and of charity. In this way will their influence be as permanent as human need: in this way will they, and not others in their stead, be the channels and the exponents of those spiritual forces which underlie all faiths and all civilizations, which, whoever be their ministers, live in themselves an everlasting life, and of which, as of the deepest of human emotions, though the outward form perishes and the earthly voices die, the 'Echoes roll from soul to soul, And grow for ever and for ever.'

LECTURE VII.

COUNCILS AND THE UNITY OF THE CHURCH.

An important feature of the Roman imperial administration was the respect which it showed to local liberties. For many important purposes a *municipality* was independent: the reality, as well as the form, of republican government lingered in the towns long after it had become extinct at Rome[1]. For certain other purposes a *province* was independent: and the form which its independence assumed anticipated in a remarkable way those representative institutions which have sometimes been regarded as the special product of modern times. Every year deputies from the chief towns of a province met together in a deliberative assembly[2]. This assembly had to some extent a re-

[1] This is shown by the general regulations as to municipal administration in the *Lex Julia municipalis* (*Corp. Inscr. Lat.* vol. i. No. 206), and in the *Lex Malacitana* (*ibid.* vol. ii. Nos. 1963, 1964; see *supra*, Lect. V, note 35).

[2] For these provincial councils see Marquardt, *De Provinciarum Romanarum Conciliis et Sacerdotibus* in the *Ephemeris Epigraphica*, vol. i. pp. 200-214, and also his *Römische Staatsverwaltung*, Bd. i. pp. 365-377, where references will be found to almost all the existing literature on the subject. It is important to note that they are found in full activity during the imperial period in all the provinces in which Christian councils came to exist: viz. Greece, (see, in addition to Marquardt, Herzberg, *Geschichte Griechenlands*, Bd. ii. 465; Dittenberger, *Corpus Inscr. Att.* vol. iii. No. 18); Syria (coins of Trajan and Caracalla, Mionnet, vol. v. 110, 334);

ligious character. Its meeting-place was the altar of Augustus: its deliberations were preceded by a sacrifice: its president was named High Priest [3].

In the course of the second century the custom of meeting in representative assemblies began to prevail among the Christian communities. There were points of practice—for example, the time of keeping Easter—on which it was desirable to adopt a common line of action [4]: there were questions as to Christian teaching—for example, those which grew out of Montanism—on which individual Churches were divided, and on which they consequently desired to consult with their neighbours [5]: there were questions of discipline which affected more than one community—especially the question, which for a time assumed a great importance, as to the terms upon which those who had renounced Christianity under pressure of persecution should be received back again [6].

At first these assemblies were more or less informal. Some prominent and influential bishop invited a few neighbouring communities to confer with his own: the

Asia Minor (Kuhn, *Verfassung des röm. Reichs*, i. 107 sqq.); Africa (Hirschfeld, *Annali di instit. Archeol. Rom.* vol. xxxviii. 1866, p. 70); Spain (Hübner, *Corpus Inscr. Lat.* vol. ii. p. 540; *Hermes*, vol. i. p. 111); and Gaul (Boissieu, *Inscriptions Antiques de Lyon*, p. 84).

[3] For this title see the epigraphical evidence collected by Marquardt, *Ephem. Epigraph.* vol. i. pp. 207–214; *Röm. Staatsverw.* Bd. 1. p. 367.

[4] Councils were held on this point in Asia Minor before the close of the second century, Euseb. *H. E.* 5. 23. 2.

[5] Councils were held on this point in Asia Minor about A.D. 160–170, Euseb. *H. E.* 5. 16. 10.

[6] Councils on this point are frequently mentioned in Cyprian: cf. the *Sententiae Episcoporum de hereticis baptizandis* ap. S. Cyprian. Op. p. 435, ed. Hartel, and *Epist.* 17 (11), p. 523; 20 (14), p. 529; 32, p. 565; 43 (40), p. 592; 55 (52), p. 626; 56 (53), c. 3, p. 649; 70, p. 766; 71, c. 1, p. 771; 73, c. 1, p. 778.

result of the deliberations of such a conference was expressed sometimes in a resolution, sometimes in a letter addressed to other Churches [7]. It was the rule for such letters to be received with respect: for the sense of brotherhood was strong, and the causes of alienation were few. But so far from such letters having any binding force on other Churches, not even the resolutions of the conference were binding on a dissentient minority of its members. Cyprian, in whose days these conferences first became important, and who was at the same time the most vigorous of early preachers of catholic unity—both of which circumstances would have made him a supporter of their authoritative character if such authoritative character had existed—claims in emphatic and explicit terms an absolute independence for each community. Within the limits of his own community a bishop has no superior but God. 'To each shepherd,' he writes, 'a portion of the Lord's flock has been assigned, and his account must be rendered to his own Master.' The fact that some bishops refused to readmit to communion those who had committed adultery is no argument, he contends, for the practice of other bishops; nor is the fact that a number of bishops meeting in council had agreed to

[7] These had been preceded by letters written by one church to another, in its own name and without conference with other churches. That the First Epistle of Clement of Rome is an example of such a letter is shown, chiefly on the evidence afforded by the newly-discovered portion, by Harnack in Schürer's *Theol. Lit. Zeitung*, Bd. iv. 1876, p. 102, and in the prolegomena to the letter in his *Patrum Apost. Opera*, ed. alt. p. lxi. Of letters addressed by more than one church to another church or group of churches, examples will be found in the letters of the churches of Vienne and Lyons, Euseb. *H. E.* 5. 1. 2, and of the African to the Spanish churches, S. Cyprian. *Epist.* 67 (68), p. 736.

admit the lapsed a reason why a bishop who thought otherwise should admit them against his will [8].

But no sooner had Christianity been recognized by the State than such conferences tended to multiply, to become not occasional but ordinary, and to pass resolutions which were regarded as binding upon the Churches within the district from which representatives had come, and the acceptance of which was regarded as a condition of intercommunion with the Churches of other provinces. There were strong reasons of imperial policy for fostering this tendency. It was clearly advisable that the institutions to which a new status had been given should be homogeneous. It was clearly contrary to public policy that not only status but also funds should be given to a number of communities which had no other principle of cohesion than that of a more or less undefined unity of belief [9]. Consequently, when the vexed question of the ordination of Caecilian threatened to divide the African Churches, Constantine summoned all the bishops of Christendom—each with representative presbyters from his Church—to a conference or council at Arles [10]. It

[8] S. Cyprian. *Epist.* 59 (55), c. 14, p. 683, 'cum . . . singulis pastoribus portio gregis sit adscripta quam regat unusquisque et gubernet, rationem sui actus Domino redditurus:' id. *Epist.* 55 (52), c. 21, p. 639, 'non tamen a coepiscoporum suorum collegio recesserunt aut catholicae ecclesiae unitatem vel duritiae vel censurae suae obstinatione ruperunt, ut quia apud alios adulteris pax dabatur, qui non dabat de ecclesia separaretur: manente concordiae vinculo et perseverante catholicae ecclesiae individuo sacramento actum suum disponit et dirigit unusquisque episcopus rationem propositi sui Domino redditurus.'

[9] A law of Constantine in A.D. 326, Cod. Theodos. 16. 5. 1, confines the privileges and immunities which had been granted to Christians to '*catholicae* legis observatoribus.'

[10] The mandate of Constantine to the bishop of Syracuse is preserved, doubtless as a typical form, by Euseb. *H. E.* 10. 5. 21-24: it gives him the right to convey-

was an obvious condition of such a conference that its decisions should be binding on those who so far took part in it as to subscribe to its acts. And since those who did so take part in it were the most important bishops in Christendom, a *confederation* was thereby established, which placed dissentients at a great disadvantage. The main points of agreement which were arrived at in this conference have constituted the basis of the confederation of Christian Churches ever since. It was resolved that those who had been appointed to minister in any place should remain in that place and not wander from one place to another[11]; that a deacon should not offer the Eucharistic sacrifice[12]; that bishops should be appointed ordinarily by eight, but at the least by three bishops, and that one bishop should not have the right of appointing another by himself alone[13].

Henceforward there were two kinds of meetings or councils. For matters which affected the whole body of Christian Churches there were general assemblies of the bishops and other representative members of all the Churches of the world: for minor matters, such as a controversy between one Church and another, or

ance at the public cost (δημόσιον ὄχημα). Optatus, *De Schism. Donat.* p. 187, adds that those who were summoned had the right to provisions as well as to conveyance ('angarialem cum annonaria competentia').

[11] 1 Conc. Arelat. c. 21.

[12] *ibid.* c. 15, 'de diaconibus quos cognovimus multis locis offerre, placuit minime fieri debere': c. 18, 'de diaconibus urbicis ut non sibi tantum praesumant sed honore presbyteris reservent, ut sine conscientia ipsorum nihil tale faciat.' It may be inferred from the expression of the Council of Elvira, c. 67, 'diaconus regens plebem,' that up to this time a deacon might be the chief or sole officer of a parish, and hence both 'offer' (sc. the Eucharist) and baptize.

[13] *ibid.* c. 20.

between the majority of the members of a Church and one of its officers, there were provincial assemblies. These latter were held upon a strictly local basis: they followed the lines of the civil assemblies whose ordinary designation they appropriated. They followed them also in meeting in the metropolis of the province. The bishop of that metropolis was their ordinary president: in this respect there was a difference between the civil and the ecclesiastical assemblies, for in the former the president was elected from year to year. In this way the bishop of the metropolis came to have a preeminence over the other bishops of a province. By a natural process, just as the vote and sanction of a bishop had become necessary to the validity of the election of a presbyter, so the vote and sanction of a metropolitan became necessary to the validity of the election of a bishop[14]. In time a further advance was made. Just as civil provinces were grouped into dioceses, and the governors of a 'province' were subordinated to the governor of a 'diocese,' so a gradation was recognized between the bishop of the chief city of a province and the bishop of the chief city of a diocese. In both cases the civil names were retained: the former were called metropolitans, the latter exarchs or patriarchs[15].

It was by these gradual steps that the Christian

[14] Conc. Nicaen. c. 4, 6; Conc. Antioch. c. 19; Conc. Laod. c. 12.

[15] The equivalence of the title 'exarch' and 'patriarch' is shown by a comparison of Conc. Chalc. c. 9 with Justin. *Novell.* 123. c. 22, and also by the scholium upon the canon of Chalcedon which is printed in Pitra, *Jur. Eccles. Graec. Mon.* vol. ii. p. 645. For an account of the correspondence between the ecclesiastical and civil divisions see my articles in the *Dictionary of Christian Antiquities*, s.vv. Patriarch, Primate.

Churches passed from their original state of independence into a great confederation. It is important to observe not only the closeness with which that confederation followed the lines of the imperial government but also the wholly *voluntary* nature of the process by which it was formed. There was no attempt at coercion. The cause which operated to change its voluntary character is one which flows from the very nature of association, and which existed in the individual communities before confederation began. For it is of the essence of an association that it should have power to frame regulations, not only for the admission, but also for the exclusion, of its members. In the Christian as in the Jewish communities an offending member was liable to be expelled. But the utility of excommunication as a deterrent in the primitive Churches had been weakened by the fact that its operation did not necessarily extend beyond the particular Church of which a man had been a member. If he had been expelled for a moral offence, no doubt the causes which led to his expulsion by one community would prevent his reception into another. But where the ground of expulsion had been the holding of peculiar opinions, or the breach of a local by-law, it might be possible to find some other community which would ignore the one or condone the other. When the Churches of a province, and still more when the Churches of the greater part of the Empire, were linked together by the ties of a confederation, meeting in common assembly, and agreeing upon a common plan of action, exclusion by a single Church came to mean exclusion from all the confederated Churches[16]. This rule was recognised by the Council of Nicaea, which at the same time made provision against an arbitrary exercise of the power of excommunication[17]. But as no penalty was attached to a violation of the rule, it was probably disregarded, for the Council of Antioch, about twenty years later, found it necessary to enact that a church officer who admitted to communion one whom another church had excluded should himself be cut off from communion[18]. This later form of the enactment was repeated in the code which is known as the Apostolic Canons[19]: and ultimately became the standing rule in both East and West. The observance of the rule was fenced round by the further enactment that no one should be received into another Church without a letter from the bishop of the Church to which he belonged[20]. In primitive days a Christian who travelled, or who changed his residence from one town to another, was received into communion with but little question: but the interests of social order, no less than of faith, compelled a change. Henceforth any one who was formally expelled from his Church was cut off also from all the Churches of the association. Nor was he cut off only

16 The attempt to exclude a group of churches from the general association was first made, but without success, by Victor of Rome in reference to the churches of Asia Minor, on account of the tenacity with which they clung to the Quartodeciman theory (*τῆς 'Ασίας πάσης ἅμα ταῖς ὁμόροις ἐκκλησίαις τὰς παροικίας ἀποτέμνειν, ὡσὰν ἑτεροδοξούσας, τῆς κοινῆς ἑνώσεως πειρᾶται*, Euseb. *H. E.* 5. 24. 9; cf. Heinichen's *Meletema VIII*, in his edition of Eusebius, vol. iii. p. 676, ed. alt.). He succeeded only in that which was within his competence, viz. in excluding them from communion in his own church, Socrat. *H. E.* 5. 22.

17 Conc. Nicaen. c. 5.

18 Conc. Antioch. c. 2

19 Can. Apost. 10.

20 Conc. Antioch. c. 7; Can. Apost. 12. 33.

from public worship and from participation in the Church offerings. He was denied social intercourse with those who remained faithful: the rigorous command of the Apostle was applied to him, 'with such an one no not to eat [21].'

Now as long as Christians were in a great minority, a man might be cut off from social intercourse with them without sustaining any serious social loss. But when Christians began to be a majority in all the great centres of population, excommunication became a real deterrent, and consequently a powerful instrument in the hands of those who were desirous of tightening the bonds of association.

And yet it is doubtful whether it would have been a sufficiently powerful instrument to produce the uniformity which ultimately prevailed, if the State had not interfered. The associated Churches might have been strong enough to crush isolated individuals, but it may be questioned whether they could have held their ground, without State interference, against whole Churches or a combination of Churches. It might happen that not an individual but a whole community—bishops, presbyters, deacons, and people—declined to

[21] 2 Conc. Arelat. c. 49, which professes to be based upon earlier regulations, 'si quis a communione sacerdotali fuerit auctoritate suspensus, hunc non solum a clericorum sed etiam a totius populi colloquio atque convivio placuit excludi, donec resipiscens ad sanitatem redire festinet:' so 1 Conc. Tolet. c. 15. Under the close union of Church and State in the Frankish domain the law was both more explicit and more effective: 'et ut sciatis qualis sit modus istius excommunicationis, in ecclesiam non debet intrare, nec cum ullo Christiano cibum vel potum sumere, nec ejus munera quisquam accipere debet vel osculum porrigere, nec in oratione se jungere, nec salutare, antequam ab episcopo suo fuerit reconciliatus' (Pippin, *Capit. Vern. duplex*, A.D. 755, ap. Pertz, *Legum*, vol. i. p. 26 = Conc. Vern. ap. Mansi, vol. xii. p. 577; cp. *Capit. Ticin.* A.D. 801, c. 17, ap. Pertz, vol. i. p. 85).

accept the resolutions of a provincial council, and that they were consequently cut off from the association. There was nothing to prevent their continuing to be and to do what they had been and done before. Even before Christianity had been recognized by the State, when Paul of Samosata refused to give up possession of the Church-buildings at Antioch, and claimed still to be the bishop of the Church, there were no means of ejecting him except that of an appeal to the Emperor Aurelian[22]. A number of such Churches might join together and form a rival association. In one important case this was actually done. A number of Churches in Africa held that the associated Churches were too lax in their terms of communion. How far they were right in the particular points which they urged cannot now be told[23]. But the contention was for purity. The seceding Churches were rigorists. Their soundness in the faith was unquestionable[24]. They resolved to meet together

[22] See Lecture VI, note 25.

[23] The dispute was in the first instance mainly as to a matter of fact, viz. whether Felix of Aptunga was a 'traditor,' i.e. one who in a time of persecution had delivered up the sacred books to be burnt. The Donatists contended that he was so, and that consequently his ordination of Caecilian was invalid. Out of this arose the wider question, on which the controversy chiefly turned, whether 'the unworthiness of the minister hindered the effect of the sacrament?' For a clear, though partial, history of the controversy see F. Ribbeck, *Donatus und Augustinus*, Elberfeld, 1857.

[24] They probably did no more than continue the stricter African discipline, for which Cyprian had in his time strongly contended. There had been, in other words, for some time two parties in the African Church, and the dispute between them was brought to a crisis by the Diocletian persecution and a personal animosity towards Caecilian: (this is the view of Rieck, *Ueber Entstehung und Berechtigung des Donatismus im Hinblick auf verwandte Erscheinungen innerhalb der christlichen Kirche*, Friedland, 1877, Gymnas-Progr.). The strong contrast between the position of Cyprian, and that of those who, under different auspices or with less force of character, held his views in subsequent times, struck even early writers: 'Et, O mira rerum conversio, auctores ejusdem opinionis catholici, con-

as a separate confederation, the basis of which should be a greater purity of life; and but for the interference of the State they might have lasted as a separate confederation to the present day. The interference of the State was not so much a favour shown to the bishops who asked for it as a necessary continuation of the policy which Constantine had begun. For as, on the one hand, it was necessary to draw a strict line of demarcation round the persons by whom the privileges of Christians could be claimed, so, on the other hand, it was impossible for the State to assume the office of determining for itself what was and what was not Christian doctrine. It was enough for the State that a great confederation of Christian societies existed. With that confederation, and it alone, the State found it expedient to deal. The terms of membership of the confederation must be left to the confederation itself. Those who were within it, and those only, were Christians and entitled to the privileges of Christians.

The interposition of the State took three forms:

(1) The State recognized the decisions of Councils—i.e. the resolutions of the representative assemblies of the associated Churches [25].

sectatores vero haeretici judicantur: absolvuntur magistri, condemnantur discipuli: conscriptores librorum filii regni sunt, adsertores vero gehenna suscipiet.' (S. Vincent. Lirin. *Commonitorium*, c. 6).

[25] e.g. Constantine followed up the decision of the Council of Nicaea by decreeing that Arius and his followers should be 'infames,' and that his books should be burnt (Socr. *H. E.* 1. 9 gives the text of the decree). Theodosius punished with confiscation any one who impugned the decision of the Council of Ephesus (Cod. Theodos. 16. 5. 66). Valentinian and Marcian affixed penalties in varying degrees to those who refused to accept the decisions of the Council of Chalcedon (*Acta Conc. Chalc.* ap. Harduin, *Concilia*, vol. ii. pp. 659, 661: Zeno and Anastasius formally abrogated the decisions of this Council, but Justin restored

(2) The State recognized the validity of sentences of deposition from office, or exclusion from membership of a Church, by a person or body within the Church whose competence was admitted by the associated Churches [26].

(3) The State discouraged and ultimately prohibited the formation of new associations outside the general confederation. 'Let all heresies,' says a law of Gratian and Valentinian, 'for ever hold their peace: if any one entertains an opinion which the Church has condemned let him keep it to himself and not communicate it to another [27].'

their authority: Zonaras, 14. 2, 5; Victor Tunn. *Chron.* ap. Roncall. *Vet. Lat. Script. Chron.* pars ii. p. 353, Isidor. *Chron. ibid.* p. 458).

[26] Euseb. *Vit. Constant.* 4. 27 *καὶ τοὺς τῶν ἐπισκόπων ὅρους τοὺς ἐν συνόδοις ἀποφανθέντας ἐπεσφραγίζετο ὡς μὴ ἐξεῖναι τοῖς τῶν ἐθνῶν ἄρχουσι τὰ δόξαντα παραλύειν. παντὸς γὰρ εἶναι δικαστοῦ τοὺς ἱερεῖς τοῦ θεοῦ δοκιμωτέρους*: so Sozom. *H. E.* 1. 9, (in both authors *συνόδοις* probably includes the ordinary council of a bishop and his presbyters as well as provincial or other assembles: cf. Heinichen *ad Euseb.*, *l. c.*). A deposed clerk was forthwith made liable to the fiscal burdens from which, as a clerk, he had been exempt: (Cod. Theodos. 16. 2. 39.; Const. Sirmond. c. 6).

[27] The extent to which the State employed coercion to prevent the Christian societies from being disintegrated by heresy or schism will appear from the following summary of the penal enactments against various classes of heretics, and ultimately also of schismatics, during the latter part of the fourth, and the beginning of the fifth, century. It must be borne in mind that under the name of heresy was included the least deviation from the doctrine of the associated churches; 'haereticorum vocabulo continentur et latis adversus eos sanctionibus debent succumbere qui vel levi argumento a judicio catholicae religionis et tramite detecti fuerint deviare' (law of Arcadius and Honorius in A.D. 395, Cod. Theodos. 16. 5. 28). i. The churches and other buildings of heretics were to be confiscated: laws of Valentinian and Valens, A.D. 372, Cod. Theodos. 16. 5. 2. A.D. 376. Cod. Theodos. 16. 5. 4; of Gratian, Valentinian, and Theodosius, A.D. 381, Cod. Theodos. 16. 5. 8: A.D. 383, *ibid.* 16. 5. 12; of Arcadius and Honorius, A.D. 396, *ibid.* 16. 5. 30: A.D. 397, *ibid.* 16. 5. 33: A.D. 398, *ibid.* 16. 5. 34: of Honorius and Theodosius, A.D. 408, *ibid.* 16. 5. 45: A.D. 415, *ibid.* 16. 5. 58: in some cases their private property was also confiscated, law of Arcadius and Honorius, A.D. 408, Cod. Theodos. 16. 5. 40. ii. They were not allowed to assemble by laws of Valens, Gratian, and Valentinian, and their successors, in A.D. 376, Cod. Theodos. 16. 5. 4: A.D. 379, *ibid.* 16. 5. 5: A.D. 381, *ibid.* 16. 5. 6. (cf. Theodoret, 5. 16; Zonaras, 13. 19): A.D. 383, *ibid.* 16. 5. 10, 11, 12 (cf. Sozom.

In this way it was that, by the help of the State, the Christian Churches were consolidated into a great confederation. Whatever weakness there was in the bond of a common faith was compensated for by the strength of civil coercion. But that civil coercion was not long needed. For the Church outlived the power which had welded it together. As the forces of the Empire became less and less, the forces of the Church became more and more. The Churches preserved that which had been from the first the secret of Imperial strength. For underneath the Empire which changed and passed, beneath the shifting pageantry of Emperors who moved across the stage and were seen no more, was the abiding empire of law and administration,—which changed only as the deep sea changes beneath the wind-swept waves. That inner empire was continued in the Chris-

H. E. 7. 12): A.D. 388, *ibid.* 16. 5. 14, 15: A.D. 389, *ibid.* 16. 5. 19, 20: A.D. 394, *ibid.* 16. 5. 24: A.D. 395, *ibid.* 16. 5. 26: A.D. 396, *ibid.* 16. 5. 30: A.D. 410, *ibid.* 16. 5. 51, which first prescribed the penalty of proscription and death to those who ventured to assemble, so in A.D. 415, *ibid.* 16. 5. 56: A.D. 412, *ibid.* 16. 5. 53, which punished with 'deportatio' those who availed themselves of the permission which Jovian had given them to hold assemblies outside the walls of a city: A.D. 415, *ibid.* 16. 5. 57, 58. iii. They were made 'intestabiles,' incapable of bequeathing or receiving money by will, by a law of Gratian, Valentinian, and Theodosius in A.D. 381, Cod. Theodos. 16. 5. 7 (which is made retrospective), and in A.D. 382, *ibid.* 16. 5. 9, (which goes so far as to exempt informers from the ordinary penalties of 'delatio'): laws of Valentinian, Theodosius and Arcadius in A.D. 389, *ibid.* 16. 5. 17, 18: of Arcadius and Honorius in A.D. 395, *ibid.* 16. 5. 25, and in A.D. 407, *ibid.* 16. 5. 40, iv. They or their teachers were banished from cities by laws of Gratian, Valentinian, and Theodosius, and their successors in A.D. 381, Cod. Theodos. 16. 5. 6, 7 (cf. Sulp. Sever. *Chron.* 2. 47): A.D. 384, *ibid.* 16. 5. 13: A.D. 389, *ibid.* 16. 5. 19: A.D. 396, *ibid.* 16. 5. 30, 31, 32: A.D. 398, *ibid.* 16. 5. 34: A.D. 425, *ibid.* 16. 5. 62 (=Const. Sirmond. 6), 64. In addition to this they were sometimes branded as 'infames' (Cod. Theod. 16. 5. 54): they were liable to fines (*ibid.* 16. 5. 21, 65), they were excluded from the civil service of the State (*ibid.* 16. 5. 29, 42), their books were to be sought and burnt (*ibid.* 16. 5. 34, which makes concealment a capital offence), and provincial judges and governors were fined unless they carried out the above laws rigidly (*ibid.* 16. 5. 40, 46).

tian Churches. In the years of transition from the ancient to the modern world, when all civilized society seemed to be disintegrated, the confederation of the Christian Churches, by the very fact of its existence upon the old imperial lines, was not only the most powerful, but the *only* powerful organization in the civilized world. It was so vast, and so powerful, that it seemed to be, and there were few to question its being, the visible realization of that Kingdom of God which our Lord Himself had preached — of that 'Church' which He had purchased with His own blood. There seemed to loom out in all its grandeur before the eyes of men the vision of a vast empire, of which, as of the ancient kingdom of David or of Solomon, the boundaries could be told and the members enumerated. The metaphors in which the Jewish Rabbis had spoken of the ancient Israel, and the metaphors which had been consecrated by inspired writers to the service of the new Israel, were applied to it. This confederation, and no other, was the 'city of God;' this, and no other, was the 'body of Christ;' this, and no other, was the 'Holy Catholic Church.' In it were fulfilled the ancient types. It was the Paradise in which the regenerated souls of the new creation might walk, as Adam walked, and eat without the threatening of a curse the fruit of the tree of knowledge [28]. It was the ark of Noah, floating with its rescued multitude of holy souls over the moving waters of this world's troubled sea [29]. It was Solomon's

[28] E.g. S. August. *De Genesi*, lib. xi. c. 25, Op. ed. Migne, vol. iii. p. 442, *De Civit. Dei*, lib. xiii. c. 21, vol. vii. p. 395. Pseudo-Ambros. *In Apocal. Expos. de vis. tert.* c. 6, vol. ii. pars ii. p. 520.

[29] E.g. S. August. *In Joann. Tract.* 6, c. 1. 19, vol. iii. p. 1434, *Epist.* 187.

temple whose golden roofs glistened with a divine splendour through the dark world's mists and storms, and whose courts were thronged with the new priests and people of God holding sacred converse, and offering spiritual sacrifices upon its altars [30]. It was the new Jerusalem into which 'the sons of them that had afflicted her' came bending, and whose 'sun could no more go down [31].' It was the 'fenced garden' of Solomon's Song, and in its midst was a well of living water, of which all who drank were healed of sin [32]. It was like the widow of Sarepta, whose cruse of oil never failed [33]. It was like the Queen of Sheba, always gathering some new knowledge, and marvelling at some new wonder, among the treasures of the distant Lord [34]. There was hardly a hero of Hebrew story whose life did not seem to prefigure the fortunes and the oneness and the glory of this vast organized aggregate of believing souls [35].

(57), vol. ii. p. 847, *De Catechiz. Rud.* c. 32, vol. vi. p. 334: S. Hilar. Pictav. *Tract. in Ps. cxlvi.* c. 12, vol. i. p. 638, ed. Ben.: S. Maxim. Taurin. *Serm.* 114, p. 641: S. Greg. M. *Moral.* lib. 35, c. 8, vol. i. p. 1149, *Epist.* lib. ii. 46, vol. ii. p. 1133.

[30] E.g. S. Ambros. *Expos. Evang. sec. Luc.* lib. 2, c. 89, vol. i. p. 1311.

[31] E.g. S. August. *De Civit. Dei,* lib. 17, c. 16, vol. vii. p. 549: Prosper. Aquitan. *Expos. Psalm. cxxxi.* v. 13, p. 483: S. Hieron. *Comm. in Zach.* lib. 3, c. 14, vol. vi. p. 932.

[32] E.g. S. Optat. *De Schism. Donat.* 2. 13: S. August. *De baptism. c. Donat.* lib. 5. 27, vol. ix. p. 195, *Contra Crescon.* lib. 2. 13, vol. ix. p. 477, *ibid.* lib. 4. 63, vol. ix. p. 590: S. Maxim. Taurin. *Serm.* 15, p. 433.

[33] E.g. S. Ambros. *De Viduis,* c. 3, vol. ii. p. 190: Cæsar. Arelat. *Serm. de Elisaeo* in Append. ad. S. August. Op. vol. v. *Serm.* 42, p. 1828: S. Greg. M. *Hom. in Ezech.* lib. 1, hom. 4. 6, vol. i. p. 1194.

[34] E.g. S. Hilar. Pictav. *Tract. in Psalm. cxxi.* c. 9, Pseudo-August. *Serm.* 231 (253), in Append. ad S. August. Op. vol. v. p. 2172.

[35] E.g. The Church is compared to Eve, as being the 'mater vivorum,' S. August. *De Genesi,* 2. 24, vol. ii. p. 215, *Enarr. in Psalm. cxxvi.* c. 8, vol. iv. p. 1673: S. Maxim. Taurin. *Hom.* 55, p. 172, *Serm.* 34, p. 486: to Sarah, S. Ambros. *De Abraham,* lib. i. c. 4, vol. i. p. 294: to Rachel, 'diu sterilis, nunc vero fecunda'

It is impossible not to sympathize with the poetry and with the hope.

But if we look more closely at the assumption upon which all this is founded—the assumption that the metaphors in which the Church of Christ is described in Scripture are applicable only to this confederation which the State had recognized and consolidated, that whatever is predicated in the New Testament of the Church of Christ is predicated of it, and it only, that this confederation, and no other, is the Church of Christ in its visible and earthly form—we shall find that assumption attended with difficulties which do not readily admit of solution.

(1) In the first place, there is no proof that the confederation was ever complete in the sense of embracing all the communities to which by common consent the name Christian was in its fullest sense applicable. For the most part the Christian Churches associated themselves together upon the lines of the Roman Empire[36]:

S. Hilar. Pictav. *Comm. in Matt.* c. 1. 7, vol. i. p. 672: S. Greg. M. *Moral.* lib. xxx. c. 25, vol. i. p. 988: to Rebecca, S. Ambros. *De Jacob.* lib. 2, c. 2, vol. i. p. 461: S. August. *Enarr. in Psalm. cxxvi.* c. 8, vol. iv. p. 1673 ('quamdiu parturit ecclesia ipsi sunt intus et boni et mali,' as Esau and Jacob struggled in the womb of Rebecca), *Serm.* 4 (44), c. 11, vol. v. p. 39: S. Greg. M. *Moral.* lib. xxxv. c. 16, vol. i. p. 1160: to Jephthah's daughter, S. August. *Quaest. in Heptateuch.* lib. 7, c. 51: to Bathsheba, S. August. *In Faust. Manich.* 23. 87, vol. viii. p. 459, Cassiodor. *Expos. in Psalm. l.* ed. Garet, vol. ii. p. 169: to Esther, S. Hieron. *Epist.* 53 (103), c. 7, vol. i p. 279: to Judith, S. Hieron. *Epist.* 79 (9), vol. i. p. 508.

[36] It is important to notice, as corroborating this general view, that when the ecclesiastical organization passed outside the network of the imperial organization, it changed its character: in Ireland, for example, 'the spiritual jurisdiction of the bishops was coextensive with the temporal sway of the chieftain' (Reeves, *Ecclesiastical Antiquities of Down, Connor, and Dromore*, Append. p. 303): the limits of both the one and the other were continually shifting, and dioceses in the ordinary sense did not exist until the Synod of Rath Breasail in A.D. 1141 (*ibid.* pp. 135, 139).

and, so far, just as there were gradations of dioceses, provinces, and municipalities in the one, so were there gradations of exarchs or patriarchs, metropolitans, and bishops in the other. But some churches remained independent. They were not subordinate to any other church. Their bishops had no superior. They were what the *Notitiae*, or lists of orthodox Churches, call *αὐτοκέφαλοι*[37]. They were in the position which Cyprian had in earlier times asserted to be the true position of all bishops: their responsibility was to God alone.

(2) In the second place, there is no proof that the terms of confederation were ever settled. The fact that the State did not tolerate any Churches which were not recognized by the confederation is not pertinent to the purely ecclesiastical question. There is no proof that it was not possible for any Church to refuse to admit to communion the members of other Churches, with as little formality as it had accepted them. There is no proof that intercommunion ever changed its original character of a voluntary contract—a corollary of the goodwill and amity which one Christian community should have towards another—so as to become an indissoluble bond. It would be a strong assertion to say that God is always on the side of the majority: and

[37] Nilus Doxapatrius, *Notitia patriarchatuum*, ed. Parthey p. 284, *εἰσὶ δὲ ἐπαρχίαι τινὲς αἳ οὐ τελοῦσι ὑπὸ τῶν μεγίστων θρόνων ὥσπερ καὶ ἡ νῆσος* Κύπρος *ἣ ἔμεινεν αὐτοκέφαλος παντελῶς καὶ μηδενὶ θρόνῳ τῶν μεγίστων ὑποκειμένη ἀλλ' αὐτεξούσιος οὖσα διὰ τὸ εὑρεθῆναι ἐν αὐτῇ τὸν ἀπόστολον* Βαρνάβαν *ἔχοντα ἐπιστήθιον τὸ κατὰ* Μάρκον *ἅγιον* Εὐαγγέλιον: so also of Cyprus in the *Notitia* compiled by the authority of the Emperor Leo Sapiens, ed. Parthey, p. 93: and of Armenia, *ibid.* p. 90. In the same way, though the fact is not recognised in the *Notitiae*, there is no proof whatever either that the early British Churches were subordinate as a whole to any other church, or that their bishops recognised any gradation of rank among themselves.

that, when the confederation was once formed, whatever the majority of its members resolved upon was binding *de jure divino* upon the minority. But this is the only tenable position if it be asserted, as it sometimes is asserted, that individual Churches which at any one time sent deputies to the general council of the confederation, or admitted an appeal to such an assembly, or admitted the other constituent members of such an assembly to Church privileges, thereby forfeited for all time to come their original right to independent action.

(3) In the third place, there is no proof that the words of Holy Scripture in which the unity of the Church is expressed or implied refer exclusively, or at all, to unity of organization. There is, on the other hand, clear proof that they were in early times applied to another kind of unity.

There have been in fact three forms which the conception of unity has taken.

In the earliest period the basis of Christian fellowship was a changed life—'repentance toward God and faith toward our Lord Jesus Christ [38].' It was the unity of a common relation to a common ideal and a common hope. The contention of those who looked upon Christians as a whole was that they were 'not under the law but under grace'—that they were, as one of the earliest Christian writings phrases it, a *τρίτον γένος*—neither Jews nor Gentiles, but a class apart [39]. The word

[38] Acts 20. 21.

[39] Κήρυγμα Πέτρου ap. Clem. Alex. *Strom.* 6. 5, p. 650; Hilgenfeld, *Novum Testamentum extra canonem receptum* Fasc. iv. p. 58: so Tertull. *Scorpiace* 10, 'usque quo genus tertium.' This separate existence of Christianity is strongly asserted by S. Ignatius, e.g. *Ad Magnes.* 9. 10, *Ad Philad.* 6. 8.

'Church' is used for the aggregate of Christians, 'the general assembly of the firstborn,' but the hypothesis of its use for that aggregate conceived as a mass of organizations seems to be excluded by its having been said to have existed before the world, and to have been 'manifested in the body of Christ [40].'

In the second period, the idea of definite belief as a basis of union dominated over that of a holy life [41]. The meshes of the net were found to be too wide. The simple creed of primitive days tended to evaporate into the mists of a speculative theology. It became necessary to define more closely the circle of admissible beliefs. The contention of those who looked upon Christians as a whole was that they were held together by their possession of a true and the only true tradition of Christian teaching. 'There is one body of Christ,'

[40] 2 Clem. Rom. 14, 'So then, brethren, if we do the will of God our Father, we shall be of the first, the spiritual, Church, which was created before the sun and moon: but if we do not the will of the Lord, we shall fall under the Scripture which says "My house became a den of robbers." So then let us choose to be of the Church of Life, that we may be saved. But I think that ye are not ignorant that the living Church is the Body of Christ: (for the Scripture says, "God made man male and female:" the male is Christ, the female is the Church), and that the Scriptures and the Apostles tell us not only that the Church exists but that it is from above (ἄνωθεν). For it was spiritual, as also was our Jesus, and was manifested in the last days to save us. Now the Church, being spiritual, was manifested in the flesh of Christ, showing us that if any of us keep it in the flesh and corrupt it not, he will receive it in the Holy Spirit.' Similarly, Herm. *Vis.* 2. 4. 1 says that the Church 'was created first of all things, and for her sake the world was framed.'

[41] The phrase ἡ ἕνωσις τῆς ἐκκλησίας first appears in Hegesippus: but he uses it in antithesis to αἱρέσεις, and evidently implies that kind of unity which consisted in adherence to the Catholic tradition of Apostolic teaching: ἀπὸ τούτων [i.e. the heresiarchs whom he had just mentioned] ψευδόχριστοι, ψευδοπροφῆται, ψευδαπόστολοι, οἵτινες ἐμέρισαν τὴν ἕνωσιν τῆς ἐκκλησίας φθοριμαίοις λόγοις κατὰ τοῦ Θεοῦ καὶ κατὰ τοῦ Χριστοῦ αὐτοῦ (Hegesipp. ap. Euseb. *H. E.* 4. 22. 5). In the following chapter Eusebius describes the letter of Dionysius of Corinth to the Lacedaemonians as ὀρθοδοξίας κατηχητική, εἰρήνης τε καὶ ἑνώσεως ὑποθετική.

says Origen, 'but it has many members: and those members are individual believers [42].' Not until the dispute between Cyprian and Novatian does the question appear to have been raised whether those who held the Catholic faith were bound to be members of particular associations, or whether they had the right to form associations for themselves [43].

In the third period, insistence on Catholic faith had led to the insistence on Catholic order—for without order dogma had no guarantee of permanence. Consequently the idea of unity of organization was superimposed upon that of unity of belief. It was held not to be enough for a man to be living a good life, and to hold the Catholic faith and to belong to a Christian association: that association must be part of a larger confederation, and the sum of such confederations constituted the Catholic Church [44].

This last is the form which the conception of unity

[42] Origen, c. Cels. 6. 48.

[43] See above Lecture IV, pp. 102–104.

[44] This view is clearly expressed by the great Latin Fathers: e.g. S. August. *De Baptism. c. Donat.* lib. 4, c. 18, vol. ix. p. 270 'Constituamus ergo aliquem castum, continentem, non avarum, non idolis servientem, hospitalem indigentibus ministrantem, non cujusquam inimicum, non contentiosum, patientem, quietum, nullum aemulantem, nulli invidentem, sobrium, frugalem, sed haereticum: nulli utique dubium est propter hoc solum quod haereticus est regnum Dei non possessurum:' id. *Serm. ad Caesar. Eccles. plebem.* c. 6, vol. ix. p. 695, 'extra ecclesiam catholicam totum potest haberi praeter salutem. Potest habere honorem, potest habere sacramentum, potest cantare Alleluia, potest respondere Amen, potest evangelium tenere, potest in nomine Patris et Filii et Spiritus Sancti fidem et habere et praedicare: sed nusquam nisi in ecclesia catholica salutem potest invenire.' S. Leon. M. *Serm.* 79 (77), c. 2, vol. i. p. 317, 'extra ecclesiam catholicam nihil est integrum, nihil castum, dicente Apostolo 'omne quod non est ex fide peccatum est:' cum divisis ab unitate corporis Christi nulla similitudine comparamur, nulla communione miscemur.' S. Greg. M. *Moral.* lib. 14, c. 5. 5, vol. i. p. 457, 'Sancta autem universalis ecclesia praedicat Deum veraciter nisi, intra se coli non posse, asserens quod omnes qui extra ipsam sunt minime salvabuntur.'

took in the fourth century, and which to a great extent has been permanent ever since.

But both in the fourth century, and afterwards, it did not gain its position of dominance without a struggle. The same difficulty presented itself in early times which has presented itself again and again in modern times. How can an organization be said to be identical with the Church of Christ when some of both its members and its officers are in reality living unholy lives? The difficulty first took form in the time of Cyprian, when the puritan party in the Church of Rome declined to recognize the election of Cornelius. It was renewed with a longer and more important struggle in the fourth century by the great section of the African Churches of which I have already spoken, and who were known as Donatists. 'Above all other things,' said the Donatists, 'the Church of Christ should be pure, and we defend its purity[45].' Their opponents, chiefly St. Augustine, pointed to the parable of the wheat and the tares. 'The field is the world,' they said, 'and the good and the bad grow together until the harvest.' 'The field is the *world*,' replied the Donatists, 'and not the Church: it is in the world and not in the Church that the good and the bad are to grow together[46].' '*Your* Catholic Church,' they said to their opponents, 'is a geographical expression: it means the union of so many societies in so many provinces or in so many nations: *our* Catholic Church is the union of all those who are Christians in

[45] *Gesta Collationis Carthag.* iii. c. 258. Ed. Dupin, p. 313.

[46] *Ibid.* p. 314.

deed as well as in word: it depends not upon intercommunion, but upon the observance of all the divine commands and Sacraments: it is perfect, and it is immaculate [47].'

The Donatists were crushed: but they were crushed by the State. They had resisted State interference: *Quid Imperatori cum ecclesia?* they asked [48]. But the Catholic party had already begun its invocation of the secular power: and the secular power made ecclesiastical puritanism a capital crime [49].

The fame of the great theologian who, with somewhat less of Christian charity than might have been expected from so good a man, opposed the Donatists, and the fact that as a matter of history they ultimately passed out of existence, have caused the name of schism which was given by their opponents to their movement to be

[47] Gaudentius, a Donatist Bishop, says in the *Gesta Collat. Carthag.* iii. c. 102, 'Catholicum nomen putant [sc. Catholici] ad provincias vel ad gentes referendum, cum hoc sit catholicum nomen quod sacramentis plenum est, quod perfectum, quod immaculatum, non ad gentes,' cf. S. Augustin. *Epist.* 93 (48), Op. ed. Migne, vol. ii. 333, 'Acutum autem aliquid tibi videris dicere cum Catholicae nomen non ex totius orbis communione interpretaris sed ex observatione praeceptorum omnium divinorum atque omnium sacramentorum.' At the same time, although the accounts which their opponents have transmitted to us may be exaggerated, there can be little doubt that the Donatists counted among their followers many who were far from realizing the ideal purity of their leaders.

[48] The expression is that of the Donatist bishops at the Council of Carthage in A.D. 348 (*Monumenta Vetera ad Donatistarum historiam pertinentia*, Migne, Patrol. Lat. vol. viii. 776.

[49] After the conference between the Catholic and Donatist bishops in A.D. 411, Marcellinus, the imperial tribune who presided, pronounced his sentence in which he ordered all persons to join in putting down the Donatist assemblies, and the Donatists themselves to hand over their buildings to the Catholics (*Sententia Cognitoris* in the *Append. ad Opp. S. Optati*, ed. Dupin, p. 325): as this did not prove to be sufficient it was enacted three years later that the Donatists should lose the privileges of Christians (Cod. Theodos. 16. 5. 54), and in the following year that they should be punished with death (Cod. Theodos. 16. 5. 56).

unquestioned by most historians. But though they were crushed the question which they raised was not thereby solved—At what point did voluntary intercommunion become an indissoluble bond? In other words, assuming that, in the opinion of a Church or group of Churches, the dominant majority of an association to which that Church or group of Churches has hitherto been attached are lax in discipline or unsound in faith, do the dissentients cease to be Catholic, or cease to be Christian, when they decline any longer to be bound by the resolutions of the association?

And there are some no doubt who will think that even this is but part of a larger question, and that the real point at issue is not so much the terms of association as its necessity. There are some who will look back with lingering eyes at that earlier time in which there was no formal association of Churches, but only what Tertullian calls the 'communication of peace, the appellation of brotherhood, the token of hospitality, and the tradition of a single creed [50].' There are some who will think that the effect of the enormous power which the Roman Empire in the first instance, and the fall of the Roman Empire in the second instance, gave to the association has been to exaggerate its importance, and to make men forget that there is a deeper unity than that of external form.

For the true communion of Christian men—the 'communion of saints' upon which all Churches are built—is not the common performance of external acts,

[50] Tertull. *De Praescr. Haeret.* 20.

but a communion of soul with soul and of the soul with Christ. It is a consequence of the nature which God has given us that an external organization should help our communion with one another: it is a consequence both of our twofold nature, and of Christ's appointment that external acts should help our communion with Him. But subtler, deeper, diviner, than anything of which external things can be either the symbol or the bond is that inner reality and essence of union—that interpenetrating community of thought and character—which St. Paul speaks of as the 'unity of the Spirit,' and which in the sublimest of sublime books, in the most sacred of sacred words, is likened to the oneness of the Son with the Father and of the Father with the Son[51].

[51] S. John 17. 11, 21.

LECTURE VIII.

THE PARISH AND THE CATHEDRAL.

In preceding Lectures I have endeavoured to trace the successive steps by which the simple communities of Apostolic times resulted in the vast and complex confederation which we find in existence at the fall of the Western Empire. How that confederation developed into the still more complex system which we find in the Middle Ages, is a problem so intricate, so interesting, and in many respects so important, as to deserve more attention than it has hitherto received from those who make historical problems their study. And although the complete solution of that problem is beyond alike my province and my powers, and although in the short compass of a single Lecture I cannot do more than draw the rough outlines of a great picture, yet I cannot so far leave the general subject incomplete as to refrain from pointing out the chief links which connect the organization of the early Churches with the organization of mediaeval, and thereby virtually of modern, times.

The two chief links are the Parish, and the Cathedral.

The Parish, as we see it in Western Christendom, owes its origin to several causes, and is the final result of several earlier forms. The *παροικία* of early days was neither a parish nor a diocese, but the community of Christians living within a city or a district, regarded in relation to the non-Christian population which surrounded it [1]. Every such community seems to have had a complete organization, and there is no trace of the dependence of any one community upon any other. But, as time went on, there were several groups of circumstances which modified in various ways this original completeness and autonomy.

(1) The first of these circumstances were those of the great cities, in which a single building was not large enough to contain the whole assembly of the faithful. In them the tradition of unity, the analogy of the municipal corporations, and possibly also the personal predominance of the bishop, seem to have prevented the multiplication of organizations. The most important instance is that of Rome, which in this, as in some other respects, preserved for many centuries an exceptional simplicity. For eleemosynary and disciplinary purposes that city was divided into districts ('regiones'), each of which was entrusted to a deacon, who reported to the bishop the temporal wants, or the moral delinquencies, of those Christians who resided in them [2]. For purposes of worship congregations seem

[1] See Lecture III. note 15, and my article 'Parish' in the *Dictionary of Christian Antiquities*, vol. ii. p. 1554.

[2] Liber Pontificalis, *Vit. Caii* p. 29: *Ordo Romanus* I, p. 3, ap. Mabillon, *Mus. Ital.* vol. ii. Cf. *ibid. Comm. praev. in Ord. Rom.* p. xvii. See also Gregorovius, *Geschichte der Stadt Rom.* Bd. i. p. 78, 2[te] Aufl.: Nardini, *Roma Antica*, ed. Nibby, vol. i. p. 124 sqq.: De Rossi, *Roma sotteranea,* vol. iii. p. 515.

to have been gathered together wherever convenience suggested or the law allowed—in public buildings, in private houses, and in the catacombs[3]. When the altered relations of Christianity to the State permitted the same congregation to meet regularly in the same place, one or more presbyters seem to have been temporarily or permanently detached from the bishop's council to preside over it: but the theory that the church of the city was one, though locally divided, was preserved by a practice of which there is no clear trace elsewhere. There continued to be, as there had probably been in the infant community of Apostolic days, only one consecration of the Eucharistic elements. The bishop and his clergy consecrated in one of the churches enough bread and wine for all the faithful in the city, and sent the consecrated elements round by the hands of messengers to the several presbyters and congregations[4]. In this way they were all literally 'partakers of that one bread,' and so realized with a vividness which later usage weakened that they were 'one body.'

(2) Another group of circumstances was that of suburban or rural districts and their outlying hamlets. In the civil government two systems prevailed in such

[3] Cf. De Rossi, *Roma sotteranea*, vol. i. pp. 199 sqq., vol. ii. pp. 478 sqq.

[4] S. Innocent I. *Epist. ad Decent.* c. 5 'De fermento [sc. the consecrated elements] vero quod die dominico per titulos [sc. the parishes within the city] mittimus superflue nos consulere voluistis quod omnes ecclesiae vestrae intra civitatem sint constitutae. Quarum presbyteri quia die ipso propter plebem sibi creditam nobiscum convenire non possunt, idcirco fermentum a nobis confectum per acolythos accipiunt ut se a nostra communione maxime illa die non judicent separatos:' (He goes on to disallow the practice in the case of cemeteries and outlying parishes on the ground that 'non longe portanda sunt sacramenta'). See also Liber Pontif, *Vit. Melchiad.* p. 33, *Vit. Siric.* p. 55: Mabillon, *comm. praev. in Ord. Rom.* p. xxxviii. in *Mus. Ital.* vol. ii: Bona, *De Rebus liturgicis* vol. ii. p. 205.

cases: sometimes such districts were within the jurisdiction of the magistrates of a neighbouring city[5], and sometimes they had magistrates of their own[6]. There were, similarly, two systems of ecclesiastical government. In Syria and some parts of Asia Minor the suburban and rural communities seem to have had a complete organization: but the bishop of such a community was held not to be of the same rank as the bishop of a city, and had a special name—*ἐπίσκοπος τῶν ἀγρῶν*, or *χωρεπίσκοπος*[7]. This system gradually fell into disuse, though not complete disuse, in the East, and does not appear to have existed in early times in the West[8]. In the eighth century, however, when there was one of those antiquarian revivals which have taken place from time to time in the history of the Church, it was

[5] The name for the district to which a city formed the centre of administration was 'regio' (Siculus Flaccus, ed. Lachmann *Gromatici*, p. 135), 'territorium' (Digest. 50. 16. 239. 8), διοίκησις (Cic. *ad Fam.* 13. 53). The two latter names came to be used for the same districts in their ecclesiastical relations to the bishop of the city church: ('territorium' is so used: e.g. 2. Conc. Arelat. c. 23, 1 Conc. Aurel. c. 17, 3 Conc. Aurel. c. 18): 'dioecesis' was sometimes also used for the district entrusted to a single presbyter—the modern 'parish,' 'paroecia (parochia),' being used in the wider sense of the bishop's district; ultimately, however, though not until far on in the middle ages, 'diocese' came to be generally used in the wider, 'parish' in the narrower sense: for some instances of the variations in the use of the terms see *Dictionary of Christian Antiquities* s. v. 'Parish,' vol. ii. p. 1554).

[6] For the details of organization of country districts which were not within the 'territorium' of a city, see Marquardt, *Römische Staatsverwaltung*, Bd. i. pp. 7–17.

[7] First mentioned in Conc. Ancyr. A.D. 314 c. 13, Conc. Neocaes. A.D. 314, c. 14, Conc. Nicaen. c. 8, Conc. Antioch. c. 10. For an important indication of the relation of chorepiscopi to city bishops, see Basil's letter to his Chorepiscopi (*Epist.* 54 (181), op. ed. Ben. vol. iv. p. 148).

[8] Denzinger, *Ritus Orientalium,* vol. i. p. 121, following J. S. Assemann, *Bibl. Oriental.* vol. iii. pars ii. p. 829, says that the Maronites have two kinds of chorepiscopi, one being a survival of the ancient rural bishops, the other being equivalent to the city archpresbyters of the Western organization. Among the Nestorians (Denzinger, vol. i. p. 126) the chorepiscopi survive as rural officers, but with the rank and functions only of the rural archpresbyters of the West.

instituted in the Frankish domain: but some inconveniences soon arose: the pseudo-Isidorian Decretals made the system a principal object of attack: and in the tenth century it had almost altogether passed away [9]. Of the other system the chief early traces are found in the suburbs of the greater cities, especially Rome and Alexandria. At Alexandria, for example, the Christians who lived in the outlying suburbs, and in the adjacent district of Mareotis, were regarded as members of the bishop's church, and, though the several congregations met in separate buildings, they had no separate constitution, but a presbyter was detached from the bishop's church to preside over each of them [10]. They were analogous to the 'chapels of ease' of our own organization. The presbyter who presided was apparently competent, *quoad sacra*, to perform the

[9] The only mention of chorepiscopi in Western canons before the ninth century is in Conc. Regens. A.D. 439, c. 3, which treats an irregularly ordained bishop as the Council of Nicaea had resolved to treat Novatian bishops: *i.e.* it gives him the inferior rank of chorepiscopus. But in the eighth century, when, as is evident from the translation of early Eastern canons and their repeated incorporation in the Capitularies, there was a determined effort on the part of some Frankish bishops to revive the early Eastern usages, the office of chorepiscopus was revived. In the following century a strong reaction set in, the chief reason for which was probably the fact that the civil power used the chorepiscopi as a foil against the bishops. Hence the pseudo-Isidore (e.g. Damasi *De vana corepiscoporum superstitione vitanda*, ed. Hinschius, *Decret. pseudo-Isidor.* p. 509) set himself to show in vehement language that the chorepiscopi, in spite of their name, were properly not bishops but presbyters, and therefore incompetent to discharge episcopal functions: on the other hand, Hrabanus Maurus defended their episcopal character (*De Chorepiscopis*, Opusc. ii. Op. ed. Migne, *Patr. Lat.* vol. cx. p. 1195). For the details of the controversy, especially in relation to the Decretals, see Weiszäcker, *Der Kampf gegen dem Chorepiscopat des fränkischen Reichs in neunten Jahrhundert*, Tubingen 1859: also an article by the same writer in von Sybel's *Historische Zeitschrift* for 1860, pp. 42 sqq., and by van Noorden in the same journal for 1862. pp. 311 sqq.

[10] S. Epiphan. *Adv. Haeres.* 68. 4: 69. 1: Socrat. *H. E.* I. 27: Sozom. *H. E.* I, 15: S. Athanas. *Apol. c. Arian.* cc. 63, 85, vol. i. pp. 143, 158.

functions which in the central church were performed by the bishop: but the high dignity of the bishop of Alexandria, who reflected and rivalled the dignity and jurisdiction of the civil prefect, and for whom no higher title than that of bishop had as yet been found, enforced a subordination which in a smaller city might have been abnormal, and made the district of which Alexandria was the centre the earliest example of a modern 'diocese.'

(3) Another group of circumstances was that of the small scattered villages of the East, which were neither in the neighbourhood of a great city nor in themselves sufficiently large to furnish the elements of a complete organization. In them two of the residents seem to have been appointed as presbyters, and two others as deacons [11], but the bishop was itinerant (περιοδευτής), travelling from one community to another [12]. When the later diocesan system came to prevail, the itinerant bishop preserved his designation but lost his functions: the name still lingers in some Eastern Churches, but the functions are only those of a Western 'rural dean [13].'

[11] This is an inference from an existing inscription of A.D. 354 at Eitha (El-hît) in Batanea (Le Bas et Waddington, *Inscriptions Grecques et Latines*, vol. iii. No. 2124, = *Corpus Inscr. Graec.* No. 8819), where the clergy consist of two presbyters, one of whom was also archimandrite of the local monastery, and two deacons, one of whom was also *οἰκονόμος* or 'bursar.'

[12] Περιοδευταὶ are mentioned in Conc. Laod. c. 57, which forbids the appointment of any other class of bishops in villages and country districts: in the encyclical letter of Gennadius of Constantinople, A.D. 459, ap. Mansi, *Concilia*, vol. vii. 911, and in Cod. Justin. I. 3. 42 (41), § 9: also in inscriptions, in the Haurân, Le Bas et Waddington, No. 2011, in Palmyrene, *ibid.* No. 2633, and in Phrygia, *Corpus Inscr. Graec.* No. 8822.

[13] They remain among the Jacobite Syrians, the Maronites, and the Nestorians: Denzinger, *Ritus Orientalium*, vol. i. pp. 118, 121, 126.

(4) Another group of circumstances was that of the great estates, upon which many Christians were resident, but which probably lay outside the jurisdiction of the municipal magistrates[14]. The fact that the owner was supreme, and that all others who lived on an estate were either serfs or slaves, probably prevented the free growth of that kind of organization which had come to exist elsewhere. The owner seems to have appointed church officers as he would have appointed farm-bailiffs. He could do so of his own mere motion, without regard to the ecclesiastical organization of any other place, because there was no one whose rights were thereby touched. Dioceses in the later sense of the term did not yet exist, and the system of subordinating one community to another had hardly begun. But the system led to abuses, especially when Arian and other non-Catholic opinions were abroad. Some owners appointed to office on their estates persons whose opinions were heretical[15]: a limitation of the rights of owners in this respect became necessary in the interests of orthodoxy: and the imperial legislation, with its usual support of the Catholic party, enacted that any presbyter who was appointed to minister on an estate

[14] For the internal economy of these great estates, which survived the fall of the Empire and formed the most important element in the economical history of Europe during many succeeding centuries, see Savigny, *Ueber den römischen Colonat* in his *Vermischte Schriften*, Bd. ii, and Kuhn, *Die städtische und bürgerliche Verfassung des römischen Reichs*, 1 Theil, pp. 257 sqq.

[15] This is clear from the repeated provisions of the Civil Law for cases in which heretics were allowed or appointed to minister on estates: viz. laws of Valentinian, Theodosius, and Arcadius in A.D. 392, Cod. Theodos. 16. 5. 21: of Arcadius and Honorius in A.D. 398, *ibid.* 16. 5. 34, in A.D. 399, *ibid.* 16. 5. 36, in A.D. 407, *ibid.* 16. 5. 40: of Honorius and Theodosius in A.D. 414, *ibid.* 16. 5. 54, § 6.

should first be approved by the bishop of the neighbouring city[16]. This enactment seems to have been evaded by ceasing to appoint presbyters. The imperial legislation consequently interfered again, and prohibited laymen from meeting for public worship without the presence of an authorized officer[17]. But, subject to this limitation, the right of an owner to appoint his own church officers remained, and probably constituted the principal source from which has flowed the modern system of patronage[18].

(5) The circumstances out of which the modern Parish was more directly produced were those of Gaul and Spain. The original Christians of those great provinces of the West seem to have consisted almost entirely of inhabitants of the Roman towns. These towns were the civilized centres of semi-civilized districts, and they were seldom situated off the lines of the great military roads. Each of them had a

[16] Justin. *Novell.* 57, c. 2, A.D. 537.

[17] Justin. *Novell.* 123, c. 32: 131, c. 8, A.D. 545.

[18] It is clear from the repeated enactments on the subject in the Carolingian capitularies that, in spite of both civil and canon law, laymen frequently appointed and dismissed clerks without reference to a bishop: but the legislation of the Frankish kings, though sometimes at variance with their own practice, was decisive in favour of the rights of bishops, and at the same time guarded that right with the provision that a bishop should not reject a clerk who was presented for approval, except in case of evident scandal: (Karoli M. *Edictum pro Episcopis*, A.D. 800, ap. Pertz, *M. H. G. Legum* vol. i. p. 81: *Capit. General. Aquens.* A.D. 802, c. 13, *ibid.* p. 106: *Capit. de Presbyter.* A.D. 809, c. 2, *ibid.* p. 161: *Excerpt. Can.* A.D. 813, c. 2, *ibid.* p. 189: Hludowic. *Capit. Aquisgran.* A.D. 817, c. 9, *ibid.* p. 207: *Constit. Wormat.* A.D. 829, c. 15, *ibid.* p. 337: *Constit. Wormat. Petit.* c. 12, *ibid.* p. 340: *Capit. Wormat.* c. 1, *ibid*, p. 350: *Convent. Ticin.* I. c. 18, A.D. 850, *ibid.* p. 399: *Convent. Ticin.* II. A.D. 855, *ibid.* p. 431: Karoli II. *Edict. Pistens.* c. 2, A.D. 861, *ibid.* p. 489). For a sketch of the history of patronage see my article 'Patron' in the *Dictionary of Christian Antiquities*, vol. ii. p. 1575: and for a more complete account Hinschius, *Das Kirchenrecht der Katholiken und Protestanten in Deutschland*, 3er Bd. Berlin, 1880.

municipal organization, and each of them had also its place in the perfect framework of the provincial system. So closely did the ecclesiastical organization follow the civil organization, and so firm was its hold upon society, that in the France of the present day, with hardly an exception, there is a bishop wherever there was a Roman municipality, and an archbishop wherever there was a provincial metropolis [19]. As the municipal organization became weak the ecclesiastical organization became strong: Christianity was so enormous a factor in contemporary society, that the bishops gradually took the place of the Roman magistrate and exercised some of the civil jurisdiction which had belonged to him. Consequently when the native Celts or the newly-settled Teutons began to be converted in large numbers to Christianity, the 'castellum' or 'pagus' in which they lived, instead of receiving a separate organization with a bishop at its head, was regarded as being under the control of the bishop of the chief town of the civil district within which it was situated. The church officers of such a 'castellum' or 'pagus' were properly officers of the bishop's church, temporarily detached,

[19] E.g. in the province of Lugdunensis Senonia (=quarta), Sens, the ancient metropolis is still an archbishopric, and of the other municipalities which are mentioned in the *Notitia Provinciarum et civitatum* (of the fourth century A.D.: see Desjardins, *Geographie de la Gaule d'apres la Table de Peutinger*, p. lxxx. table iii: Brambach in the *Rheinisches Museum*, 1868, vol. xxxiii. p. 262 sqq.): Chartres, Auxerre, Autun, Orleans, and Meaux, are bishoprics, and Paris an archbishopric: (some, probably later, MSS. of the *Notitia* add Nevers, which became a bishopric in the fifth century: see Brambach, *l. c.*): so in the province of Lugdunensis Secunda, Rouen is still an archbishopric, and the other *civitates* of the ancient province are bishoprics, Bayeux, Avranches, Evreux, Séez, Lisieux, and Coutances. Kuhn, *Ueber die Entstehung der Städte der Alten*, Leipsig, 1878, p. 439, says that the existence of a bishop in a given city is a proof of its having had municipal independence.

but required at certain periods to return and always liable to recall[20]. The important modification of this system by which such church officers became permanent is the result of endowment. For the endowment of a church, in either a small town or a country district, came to be regarded as constituting the duly appointed officers of that church tenants for life: they could not be ejected, except after due process of law, either by their congregations or by the bishop and his council: nor were they any longer dependent upon the bishop for their means of subsistence[21]. At one time the detach-

[20] Conc. Tarracon. A.D. 516, c. 7, requires all parish clergy to return to the bishop's church on Saturday evenings 'quo facilius die dominico solemnitas cum omnium praesentia celebretur:' 1 Conc. Arvern. A.D. 535, limits this necessary presence in the bishop's church to the clergy of oratories or chapels, and to the greater festivals: Conc. Emerit. A.D. 666, empowers a bishop to recall parish clergy from their parishes and attach them to his cathedral.

[21] Lands were originally given to the church of which a bishop was the immediate head, i.e. to what in later times would have been termed a cathedral or a diocese: unlike the ordinary oblations, which were divided in certain proportions between the bishop and the clergy, they were in the special disposition of the bishop (1 Conc. Aurel. A.D. 511, c. 14: so even of lands specially given for the endowment of parish churches, 3 Conc. Tolet. A.D. 589, c. 19, 4 Conc. Tolet. A.D. 633, c. 33), and from the point of view of a canonist the origin of ecclesiastical benefices is that 'ipsa bona ecclesiae quasi in quasdam portiones singulis titulis annexas dividi et a communi massa bonorum ecclesiae separari coeperunt' (Van Espen, *Jus Eccles. Univ.* pars ii. Sect. iv. Tit. i. 3). The usufruct of certain of these lands was granted by a bishop to the clergy either of his own church or of detached parishes: provision was made on the part of the church that the ordinary law of prescription should not apply (1 Conc. Aurel. c. 23, Conc. Epaon. A.D. 517, c. 18), and on the part of the grantees that the grant should not lapse on the death of the grantor (3 Conc. Aurel. A.D. 538, c. 17). How this system, in which the endowments were personal, fused with the system of endowing churches on private property, in which the Popes disallowed permanently-appointed presbyters (S. Greg. M. *Epist.* 2. 12, *ad Castor. Arim.* 9. 70, and 12. 12, *ad Passiv. Firman.* 9. 84, *ad Benen. Tundar.*: S. Zachar. Papae, *Epist.* 8 *ad Pippin.* c. 15, ap. *Codex Carolinus.* ed. Jaffé, p. 26, probably quoting pseudo-Pelag. Papae *Epist. ad Eleuther.* ap. Holsten. *Coll. Rom.* vol. i. p. 234), and developed into the later system of ecclesiastical benefices, in which particular lands were assigned in perpetuity to particular churches and in which also the holder of the benefice was immovable,

ment of such churches and their officers from the bishop threatened to be complete: but the legislation of the Carolingian kings restored the waning jurisdiction of the bishops [22]: the bishop of the district within which churches were situated was empowered to visit them and their clergy were compelled to receive him: he was entitled to receive certain specified dues, to enquire into the degree to which the clergy conformed to ecclesiastical rules, to hold courts of discipline, and to perform that part of the baptismal ceremonies which had come to be regarded in the Western Church as his special function [23]. And so grew up those relations

except upon a sentence of an ecclesiastical court, confirmed by the Roman See, (*Decret. Eleuth.* c. 2, Hinschius, *Decret. Pseudo-Isid.* p. 125), is a question of too great intricacy to be discussed here: reference may be made to the general history of 'beneficia' in Roth, *Geschichte des Beneficialwesens*, Erlangen, 1850, and to Hinschius, *Das Kirchenrecht der Katholiken u. Protestanten in Deutschland*, Berlin, 1878, Bd. ii. pp. 293, 366.

[22] This is an inference partly from the fact mentioned above, note 18, that presbyters were frequently appointed to and ejected from parishes without reference to the bishop, and partly from the repetition, which would have been unnecessary if the rule had been generally acknowledged, of the enactment that presbyters shall be subject to their bishop: e.g. Pippin. *Capit. Vern. duplex*, A.D. 755, c. 8, Pertz, i. 24, 'ut omnes presbyteri qui in parrochia sunt sub potestate episcopi debeant de eorum ordine et nullus presbiter non praesumat in illa parrochia nec baptizare nec missas celebrare sine jussione episcopi in cujus parrochia est:' so Karlomann, *Capit.* A.D. 742, c. 3, Pertz, vol. i. p. 17: Pippin. *Capit. Suession.* c. 4, *ibid.* p. 21; Karol. M. *Capit. General.* A.D. 769, c. 8, *ibid.* p. 33. So also in the Pseudo-Isidorian Decretals, *Epist. Clem. I.* c. 36, ed. Hinschius, p. 41, c. 70, *ibid.* p. 57.

[23] The visitation of detached churches by the bishop within whose district they were situated, is found as early as the fourth century, in e.g. Alexandria (S. Athanas. *Apol. c. Arian.* c. 65, vol. i. p. 143), and in Gaul (Sulp. Sever. *Dial.* 2. 3, ed. Halm. p. 183: Conc. Taurin. A.D. 401, c. 2). The earliest express enactment is probably 2 Conc. Brac. A.D. 572, c. 1, which requires bishops to go round their dioceses and examine their clergy 'quomodo ordinem baptismi teneant vel missarum et quaecumque officia quomodo peragantur;' after which they are to assemble the people and warn them to flee from idols and from mortal sins. The rule is recognised and repeated, though different objects are assigned for the visitation, in 4 Conc. Tolet. A.D. 633, c. 36, Conc. Emerit. A.D 666, c. 11, Karlomann. *Capit.* A.D.

between the bishop of the central church and the officers of detached churches which have lasted without essential modification until modern times.

While the parochial system was thus shaping itself the bishop's church preserved the main features of its original constitution.

In early times, as we have seen, the bishop was not what he has in many respects come to be in later times, in the position of a monarch, but in that of the president of a council. The presbyters who sat round him, the deacons who stood immediately below him, were integral elements in ecclesiastical administration. Without the assent of his council he could not legitimately either deal with the church funds, or administer discipline, or appoint persons to church office. On the death of a bishop the earliest system of church government revived: the council administered ecclesiastical affairs with a complete authority [24]. Before the final establishment of the parochial system all the presbyters and deacons over whom the bishop presided were ordinary members of that council. The fact that some of them were temporarily detached to minister in separate churches did not destroy the closeness of their

742, c. 3, Pertz, vol. i. p. 17, Pippin. *Capit. Suession.* A.D. 744, c. 4, *ibid.* p. 21. Karoli M. *Capit. General.* A.D. 769, c. 7, *ibid.* p. 32: but at the same time provision was made against the tendency of bishops to exact excessive fees and to require excessive hospitality; 2 Conc. Brac. A.D. 572, c. 2, 7 Conc. Tolet. A.D. 646, c. 4, Karoli M. *Capit. Langobard.* c. 5, Pertz, vol. i. p. 110, Karoli II. *Synod. ap. Tolos.* A.D. 844, c. 4, *ibid.* p. 379, Hludowic. *Convent. Ticin.* A.D. 855, c. 16, *ibid.* p. 432.

[24] This is shown by the action of the presbyters and deacons of Rome on the death of Fabian, and by Cyprian's letter to them (S. Cyprian. *Epist.* 30 (31), 9 (3), pp. 549, 488, ed. Hartel).

relation to the original church. When the bishop of Rome came to have a preponderating influence in Western Christendom, his council became so important that some of the greatest dignitaries in Christendom were willing to become, in name at least, parish clergy in Rome, in order to have a voice in it. And hence it is that, in at least the theory of its constitution, the college of Roman parish clergy, who have retained in the name 'Cardinal' the original designation of the permanent clergy of all parishes, has preserved to this day the outline of the primitive type[25].

In the greater part of the rest of Christendom another system grew up inside the primitive system. It arose out of the practice, of which I have already spoken, of the clergy living together in the bishop's house[26]. In Gaul and Spain that practice tended in

[25] The term 'cardinalis' (from which the verb 'incardinare') was transferred from the civil service of the Empire to denote a *fixed* officer (for its civil use see Bocking, *Notit. Dignit. Orient.* c. 5. 2, vol. i. pp. 24, 205). There is no early evidence of its having been originally applied to other than presbyters and deacons: but in the eleventh century it is used of acolytes (*Comment. Election. Greg. VII.* ap. Jaffé, *Monum. Gregor.* p. 9), and of the seven bishops of neighbouring sees who officiated by turns in the church of St. John Lateran, and who were consequently 'Ecclesiae Lateranensis cardinales' (S. Petr. Damian. *Epist.* 2. 1, ap. Migne, *Patrol. Lat.* vol. cxliv. p. 254: the uncertain authority of the Liber Pontificalis *Vit. Steph.* III. (IV.) vol. ii. p. 284, assigns an earlier date to the creation of these cardinal bishops). In the letters of Gregory the Great (e.g. lib. 1. 15, 79), and elsewhere, the word is in ordinary use for the permanent clergy of a parish, and it is found as a common title in all the great churches of Christendom: e.g. Constantinople, Milan, Naples, Cologne, Treves, Compostella, and London (see Muratori, *Antiq. Ital.* vol. v. p. 163, and Hinschius, *Das Kirchenrecht,* Bd. 1. p. 318). The admission of prelates and others from various parts of Christendom to the positions which properly belonged to the actual clergy of the city of Rome dates from the time when the holders of those positions came to have the uncontrolled election of the most important personage in Christendom. The modern restriction of the term to the Roman College dates from 1567, when Pius V formally disallowed its use in any other sense.

[26] See Lecture VI, p. 162. The later canon law based the practice upon a sup-

the sixth and seventh centuries to become general. It was fostered partly by the facilities which it offered for guarding the celibacy of the clergy, and partly by the introduction of that important change by which instead of church officers being freely chosen by the several communities from their adult members, youths were dedicated early in life to the service of the Church. The bishop's house was thus partly a monastery, though without a monastic rule, and partly a school at which younger clerks were taught and trained [27]. Those who so lived in it, whether old or young, bore the name which had originally been applied to all who were on the church-roll, and who were in receipt of church-funds—that of 'canonici [28].' In

posed letter of Clement of Rome (*Epist. Clement. quinta*, ap. Hinschius, *Decretales pseudo-Isid.* p. 65).

[27] 2 Conc. Tolet. A.D. 531, c. 1, 4 Conc. Tolet. A.D. 633, c. 24: 2 Conc. Vasens. A.D. 529 requires all parish presbyters to receive into their houses and to train the younger clerks.

[28] The word *canon* was used in the late Latin for the fixed contribution of corn or other produce paid by a province to Rome, e.g. 'Canon Aegypti,' Vopisc. *Vit. Firm.* c. 5, and hence for the total amount of such contributions which was available for distribution in fixed rations among the Roman populace, e.g. Cod. Theodos. 14. 15, 2, 6, Lamprid. *Vit. Elagab.* c. 27; Spart. *Vit. Sever.* c. 8. It was consequently used to denote the list of persons who were entitled to fixed allowances from the church funds: this list, which was sometimes also called 'matricula' (e.g. Conc. Agath. A.D. 506, c. 2; 4 Conc. Aurel. A.D. 541, c. 13; Conc. Autissiod. A.D. 578, c. 3.) comprehended not only the clergy but also other church officers (e.g. the steward and the 'paramonarius,' Conc. Chalc. c. 2) and the virgins (Socrat. *H. E.* 1. 7, p. 47): probably also the poor, for although there is no early evidence, the terms 'in matricula positi,' 'matricularii' (which Chrodegang, *Regul. Canon.* c. 34 uses as a synonym for 'canonici'), are used by a late writer for pensioners who received regular allowances (pseudo-*Testamentum S. Remig. Rem.* ap. Flodoard, *Hist. Eccles. Rem.* 1. 18). The derivative 'canonicus' is only found in use of clerks, but it is used of all orders, e.g. of singers, Conc. Laod. c. 15; of readers, 2 Conc. Turon. A.D. 567, c. 19; and of the clergy collectively, 3 Conc. Aurel. A.D. 538, c. 11: and there may be a relic of an earlier use in the fact that laymen were sometimes *ex officio* canons, e.g. the Roman Emperor was a canon of St. John Lateran and of Aix-la-Chapelle, and the Count of Anjou was a canon of St. Martin at Tours. At

course of time sums of money were left for the support of the common table: the 'canonici' came to have funds apart from the allowances which, in accordance with primitive practice, the bishop made from the general funds of the church [29]: they thus came to be more or less independent of the bishop, and to act for certain purposes without regard to him [30]. In the eighth century the influence of monasticism introduced a new element into the corporate life of the 'canonici.'

Orleans Our Lord Himself was enrolled as 'primus canonicus,' and the 'duplex honor distributionis' which was assigned to Him was given to the poor (Saussaye, *Annales Eccles. Aurelian.* lib. i. c. 13, Paris, 1615).

[29] Those who lived together received 'praebendas,' 'portiones,' which were not sums of money but specified quantities of victuals, from the church offerings. That this continued to be the ordinary rule in the ninth century is shown by the direction of the pseudo-Isidorian decretals (*Epist. Urbani prima*, c. 3, 6, ed. Hinschius, pp. 144, 145). But in the meantime there had grown up in some dioceses the practice of leaving funds for the support of a common table (Greg. Turon. *H. F.* 10. 31, of Bishop Baldwin of Tours, 'hic instituit mensam canonicorum:' id. *Vit. Patr.* c. 9 'ad convivium mensae canonicae'): and these funds were administered by the canons themselves (Flodoard, *Hist. Eccles. Rem.* 2. 11, of St. Rigobert, 'canonicam clericis religionem restituit ac sufficientia victualia constituit et praedia quaedam illis contulit, necnon aerarium commune usibus eorum instituit:' the earliest authentic document is probably the confirmation by Lothair II of the rights which Archbishop Gunthar had granted to the canons of Cologne, quoted from Ennen u. Eckertz, *Quellen zur Geschichte d. Stadt Köln*, Bd. i. 447 by Hinschius, *Das Kirchenrecht*, Bd. ii. p. 55). It was of course an integral part of the idea of a 'vita communis' that such funds should be held in common, and this was at first the case, the revenues being divided equally and the number of canons sometimes varying with their amount (see Dürr, *De Capit. Claus.* c. 11, in Schmidt, *Thes. Jur. Eccl.* iii. 149). But in time there grew up the practice of regarding a particular estate as furnishing the 'praebendam' or 'victum' for a particular canonry, and of assigning the income and management of the estate to the holder of the canonry, 'non ratione dominii, cum non sint capaces, sed solum ratione administrationis' (Barbosa, *De Canonicis*, ed. Lugdun. 1634, p. 8): the earliest instance is probably that of the canons of Cologne whose rights in this respect were confirmed by the Synod which was held there in A.D. 873, Mansi, vol. xvii. p. 275; Hinschius, *Das Kirchenrecht*, Bd. ii. p. 55.

[30] E.g. they had the right of making statutes (see Hinschius, Bd. ii. p. 131), of exercising a certain limited jurisdiction (*ibid.* p. 145), and in certain cases of coöpting members into their own body (see the confirmation of the rights of the canons by the Synod referred to in the preceding note, quoted *ibid.* p. 55).

Side by side with those who thus lived in the bishop's house, controlled only by the general rules of the Church, were the monks and clergy who lived in monasteries under the stern rule of St. Benedict. The contrast was often so strong that a pious French bishop framed a rule for the 'canonici' which was almost as strict as the rule for monks[31]. Henceforth, in most Churches of the West, the 'canonici' of the bishop's house became 'regulares,' i.e. canons living under a rule[32]: and about the same time they were divided into two classes, of whom ultimately the senior class, i.e.

[31] The 'regula canonicorum' was drawn up by Chrodegang of Metz about A.D. 760 (Paul. Diacon. *Gesta Episc. Metens.* ap. Pertz, M. H. G. *Script.* vol. ii. p. 268), chiefly on the model of the rule of St. Benedict (see Rettberg, *Kirchengesch. Deutschlands*, Bd. i. 496) for the clergy of his own church (it will be found in its original form in Mansi, *Concilia*, vol. xiv. p. 313; Walter, *Fontes Jur. Eccles.* p. 20: a much longer rule which, though attributed to Chrodegang, is evidently of later date, will be found in Mansi, vol. xiv. p. 332; D'Achery, *Spicilegium*, vol. i. p. 565; Harzheim, *Concil. Germ.* vol. i. p. 96). But the rule which was most widely adopted was not the rule of Chrodegang, but one based upon it which is commonly ascribed to Amalarius, and which was authorized by the Council of Aix-la-Chapelle in A.D. 816 (it will be found in Mansi, vol. xiv. pp. 153 sqq.; Harzheim, *Concil. German.* vol. i. p. 430).

[32] There was an attempt in the Frankish domain to make the 'regular' life compulsory. Pippin. *Capit. Eccles.* A.D. 789, c. 72, 'similiter qui ad clericatum accedunt quod nos nominamus canonicam vitam, volumus ut illi canonice secundum suam regulam omnimodis vivant et episcopus eorum regat vitam, sicut abbas canonicorum.' There is a series of similar enactments in the following century, Karoli M. *Capit.* A.D. 802, c. 22, Pertz, vol. i. p. 94; Conc. Mogunt. A.D. 813, c. 9, Mansi, vol. xiv. p. 67; Conc. Rem. A.D. 813, c. 8, *ibid.* p. 78; 6. Conc. Arelat. A.D. 813. c. 6, *ibid.* p. 60; 3 Conc. Turon. A.D. 813, c. 23, *ibid.* p. 86; Hludowic, *Capit. Aquisgran.* A.D. 817, c. 3, Pertz, vol. i. p. 206; Hludowic et Hlothar. *Capit. Aquisgran.* A.D. 828, *ibid.* p. 327; Conc. Meld. A.D. 845, c. 53, Mansi, vol. xiv. p. 831; Karoli II, *Convent. Ticin. II*, A.D. 876, c. 8, Pertz, vol. i. p. 531. In some of these cases only life in community was enjoined without the mention of a rule: what this meant is clear from e.g. 3 Conc. Turon. A.D. 813, c. 23, 'canonici et clerici civitatum qui in episcopiis conversantur consideravimus ut in claustris habitantes, simul omnes in uno dormitorio dormiant, simulque in uno reficiantur refectorio quo facilius possint ad horas canonicas celebrandas occurrere et de vita et conversatione sua admoneri et doceri: victum et vestimentum juxta facultatem episcopi accipiant ne paupertatis occasione compulsi per diversa vagari ac turpibus se implicare negotiis cogantur.'

the presbyters and deacons, alone retained the name [33]. But before two centuries had passed the name was almost all they did retain of the ancient 'vita communis.' Living not together but in separate houses, administering each for himself the revenues of his estate, discharging their duties by the agency of 'vicars,' and no longer giving their superfluity to the poor, the canons of the middle ages were legitimate objects of satire and of lament [34].

The clergy of country parishes and dependent towns were still, in theory, members of the bishop's council: once at least in every year that council had to be gathered together and they were bound to be present at it [35]. But for the most part they were permanently

[33] The distinction between *canonici seniores* and *c. juniores*, i.e. between those who were in major and those who were in minor orders, is found in the Rule of Chrodegang, e.g. c. 23, 29. The former came in time to be called *c. majores, ordinarii, cathedrales*, or *capitulares*: the latter were *domicelli, domicellares*, who were subdivided into *emancipati* and *non emancipati* according as they had or had not passed through the prescribed course of education.

[34] E.g. Bishop Yves of Chartres says 'communis vita in omnibus ecclesiis paene defecit' (D. Ivon. Carnot. *Epist.* 213, ap. Migne, *Patrol. Lat.* vol. clxii. p. 217): Urban II says 'prima [sc. vita canonicorum] decalescente fervore fidelium jam paene omnino defluxit' (B. Urban II. *Epist. ad clericos quosdam regulares*, ap. Mansi, *Concilia*, vol. xx. p. 713). Peter Damiani (*Contra clericos regulares proprietarios*, vol. iii. p. 483 ed. Caiet.; *De communi vita canonicorum*, *ibid.* p. 514) and others (e.g. Gerhoh von Reichersberg, *Liber de corrupto Ecclesiae statu*, ap. Baluze, *Miscell.* vol. ii. p. 197) threw the blame on the laxity of the rule itself: and a stricter rule was introduced which was drawn from the works of St. Augustine. But although there was a revival of the asceticism of the older canonical life, it was partial and temporary: there were indeed many societies of Augustinian, or as they now came to be exclusively called, 'regular' canons, but the canons of most cathedral chapters were 'secular,' administering their own estates and living not in community but in the world (for instances of the adoption of the Augustinian rule in cathedrals see Hinschius, *Das Kirchenrecht*, Bd. ii. p. 58).

[35] Pippin. *Capit. Vern. dupl.* A.D. 755, c. 8, Pertz, M. H. G. *Legum*, vol. i. p. 25, 'omnes presbiteri ad consilium episcopi conveniant.' In the *Modus tenendi synodos per Angliam*, Wilkins, *Concilia*, vol. iv. append. p. 784, a year's suspension is the penalty for non-attendance.

detached: they had no longer any ordinary place in the bishop's church: and they administered their own revenues, reserving for the bishop only a small and specified portion[36]. The ordinary functions of ecclesiastical administration were discharged by the bishop and the canons of his church: in place of the earlier phrase 'the bishop and presbyters,' we find the phrase 'the bishop and canons:' and it was not the general council of a diocese but the canons of the cathedral church—collectively known by the monastic title 'capitulum,' or 'chapter'—who administered the affairs of a diocese during a vacancy in the see and elected a new bishop[37].

The difference between parochial and cathedral clergy was still further widened when the former were grouped into districts, and when each district came to have its own organization. Just as the cathedral had its archpresbyter and its archdeacon, so in the districts

[36] In early times the bishop had the same control over the revenues of detached churches which he had over his own. In the sixth century a Spanish Council first enacted that the bishop's share in the *offerings*, i.e. one-third, should be devoted in parish churches to repairs and lights (2 Conc. Brac. A.D. 572, c. 2: so in the following century, Conc. Emerit. A.D. 665, c. 4; 16 Conc. Tolet. A.D. 693, c. 5): and this seems to have become the general rule. But though there is no doubt that the control of church lands and of tithes also passed from the hands of the bishops to that of the incumbents of parishes, the question *when* it did so belongs to the obscure history of ecclesiastical benefices (see above, note 21), and the facts which bear upon it are too intricate to be given here.

[37] For these and other facts in relation to the early history of cathedral chapters reference may be made to Fermosini, *De potestate capituli sede vacante necnon sede plena et quid possint episcopi per se aut debeant cum capitulo exequi*, Lugdun. 1666; Barbosa, *De canonicis et dignitatibus aliisque beneficiariis eorumque officiis in choro et capitulo*, Lugdun. 1634; Muratori *De Canonicis* in his *Antiquitates Italicae*, vol. v, pp. 183 sqq. The best modern account is that of Hinschius, *Das Kirchenrecht*, Bd. ii. pp. 59, 124, 228, 601; see also Richter, *Lehrbuch des katholishen u. Evangelischen Kirchenrechts*, ed. Dove, 1880, pp. 440 sqq.

into which a diocese came to be divided there was a rural archpresbyter and a rural archdeacon [38]. The latter, who had in the meantime ceased to be a deacon, but who, preserving the ancient close connexion between the bishop and the deacons, was in a special sense the bishop's deputy, had precedence over the rural archpresbyter, and a jurisdiction, at first delegated and temporary, afterwards ordinary and permanent, over a district in which several archpresbyteries or 'rural deaneries' were comprised [39].

[38] The division into *decaniae* (later also *archipresbyteratus, capitula ruralia*) dates from the middle of the ninth century and was the subject of formal enactments, viz. Karoli II. *Synod. ap. Tolos.* A.D. 844, c. 3, Pertz, vol. i. 378; Hludowic. *Convent. Ticin.* A.D. 850, c. 13, Pertz, vol. i. p. 399. Like the dioceses themselves, the deaneries seem, at least in the Frankish domain, to have followed the political subdivisions: see Sohm, *Die altdeutsche Reichs- und Gerichts-verfassung*, Wiemar, 1871, Bd. i. p. 203. The division into *archidiaconatus* commenced in the tenth century but was not completed until the twelfth (the documents in which Hadrian I is made to confirm the subdivision of the diocese of Strasburg into archdeaconries in A.D. 774 are forgeries, Rettberg, *Kirchengesch. Deutschlands*, Bd. ii. pp. 69, 611). Hinschius, Bd. ii. p. 189, refers to Landau, *Die Territorien in Bezug auf ihre Bildung u. Entwickelung*, Gotha, 1854, pp. 387 sqq., for evidence that the archdeaconries, like the other ecclesiastical divisions, followed political lines.

[39] The archdeacon sometimes took precedence of the archpresbyter in a cathedral as well as in a diocese: e.g. at Brescia, Ughelli, *Italia Sacra*, vol. iv. p. 521. The capitular officers of provost and dean were held sometimes by the one and sometimes by the other: e.g. the archdeacon was provost in the later version of the Rule of Chrodegang (D'Achery, *Spicil.* vol. i. p. 567), and at Liege, Treves, Mayence, Ratisbon, and elsewhere: he was sometimes dean at Cologne (Ennen u. Eckertz, i. 558, 598), and at Bayeux (Ordericus Vit. iii. 12): an archpresbyter was provost at Passau (Hansiz, *Germania Sacra*, vol. i. Coroll. vii), but usually, and at last always, dean (according to the canonists the jurisdiction of the modern dean is wholly due to the fact that he is *ex officio* archpresbyter, Barbosa, *De Canonicis*, c. 4. 32, p. 43). The independent jurisdiction of the rural archdeacons probably dates from the end of the twelfth century: in the course of the following century their position had become so obnoxious to the bishops, upon whose jurisdiction they trespassed, as to lead to the appointment of other officers, *officiales principales, vicarii generales*, to fill the place, which was once specially that of the archdeacons, of the bishop's agents and intermediaries (see Hinschius, Bd. ii. pp. 195, sqq.; Richter, ed. Dove, p. 453).

In this way it is that the organization which existed in the Middle Ages, and which in its essential features has remained to the present day in our own and other Churches, is linked by direct historical continuity with the organization of primitive times. The differences between the two extremes of the series are great: but they were the growth of a thousand years—the thousand years of change and storm which elapsed between the sixth century and the sixteenth.

And here the examination which I proposed at starting comes to an end.

The main propositions in which the results of that examination may be summed up are two—

(1) That the development of the organization of the Christian Churches was gradual:

(2) That the elements of which that organization were composed were already existing in human society.

These propositions are not new: they are so old as to have been, in greater or less degree, accepted by all ecclesiastical historians. For it is admitted by all such historians that at least *some* of the features of the complete organization did not exist in primitive times, but have been since added. It is also admitted that at least *some* of the elements of the organization are found outside it, in previously existing institutions.

But in dealing with them I have arrived at and set forth the view, in regard to the first of them, that the development was slower than has sometimes been supposed, and, in regard to the second, that not only some but *all* the elements of the organization can be traced to external sources. The difference between this view and the common view is one of degree and not of kind. The one no less than the other assumes the organization of the Church to be divine: but while the one accounts for certain phenomena of ecclesiastical history by a special and extraordinary action of the Holy Spirit, the other is rather in harmony with the belief that God acts in the realm of grace, as He acts in the realm of nature, by the mediation of general and far-reaching laws. It appears necessary to point out the existence of this relation between the two views of which I have spoken, because there is a confusion in the minds of some persons between the *fact* of divine operation and the *mode* of that operation, and a complete identification of the fact with some particular mode, which causes them to regard the questioning of that mode as equivalent to a questioning of the fact itself. But although it appears necessary to point this out, there is the less reason for enlarging upon it, because few of those who are here will have forgotten the subtle force with which the great living Father of modern Oxford theology, speaking in this place through the mouth of its greatest preacher, exposed the similar confusion of thought which exists in many minds in regard to the history of the Creation. What the theologian says to the man of science in regard to that Creation is, 'Nothing that you have proved, or can prove, about the mode in which God made the world, interferes with the truth that He did make it:' and what the theologian says also to the historian is, 'Nothing that you have shown, or can show, about the mode in which the organization of the

Church was developed interferes with the truth that God did organize it.' On the other hand, just as the man of science may say in reply, 'I am ready to allow that God made the world, but I claim the right to show, if I can, from the records which the world contains, how and in what order He made it:' so the historian may say, 'I am ready to allow that the Church is of divine institution: but I claim the right to show, if I can, from the facts of history, how and in what order God instituted it.' In the one case as in the other the appeal lies not to the opinions of eminent persons, but to ascertained and ascertainable facts. The divine plan must be inferred not *a priori*, from a conception of what He was likely to do, but *a posteriori*, from the investigation of what He has actually done. And if the timid souls who tremble at every fresh discovery of science, or at every newly-ascertained fact of history, could rise to the larger faith of earlier days, they would see in the close analogy between the development of the Christian societies and the development of the natural world, a corroboration of the belief that the Author of the one is also the Author of the other, and that the one no less than the other belongs not to those things which are rapidly formed and swiftly pass, but to that loftier sphere in which, though the development is slow, the result is eternal.

But as, on the one hand, the view that the framework of the Christian societies was slowly developed out of existing elements, so far from being inconsistent with, is rather confirmatory of, the belief in its divine origin: so, on the other hand, it tends to diminish the importance of some of the controversies which have existed respecting it, and which have separated one community of Christians from another.

On the hypothesis that the constitution of the Christian societies was settled by the Apostles in their lifetime, and that what was so settled was intended to be the form of all Christian societies for all time to come, different groups of Christians have at various times separated themselves from the main body, and claimed, in some cases not without reason, to be recurring to a more primitive type. And those who have opposed them, for the most part accepting the same major premiss, have endeavoured to show by arguments which have sometimes been marked by more of enthusiasm than of either logical force or historical probability, that this or that institution is not new but old.

But if the ultimate verdict of those who are competent to judge be in favour of the general view which has been advanced in these Lectures, the contentions on the one side and on the other, in regard to the minor premisses of the argument, will be beside the point: nothing will be really gained by showing that this or that element of Church government is more primitive than another: nothing will be really lost by the admission that this or that element in the great aggregate of historical developments is later than another. That for the preservation of which we have to contend is not so much ancient form as historical continuity.

For in reality the preservation of ancient form is impossible. We have received from our fathers the splendid inheritance of a vast and complex civilization

—a mighty aggregate of beliefs and practices and institutions, which have grown with the world's growth, and shaped themselves to the varying needs of successive generations. It is given to each generation to revise and reform the present: but it is not given to it to bring back the past. The web of history is being woven in the loom of time. The shuttles of incident fly quick, and each of them is irrevocable. We are not, and we cannot be, what our fathers were. We differ from them in ten thousand modes of thought, in ten thousand features of social circumstance. The attempt artificially to restore an ancient institution is futile from the nature of the case, because even if restored it stands alone, out of the relations which once gave it a meaning and a power. In that great product of the laws of God which we call human society, as in that other great product of the laws of God which we call the animal world, the succession of existence is not the succession of identical organisms, but a continuity of species, a unity of type. The type remains, but it embodies itself in changing shapes: and herein the history of the Christian Churches has been in harmony with all else that we know of God's government of the world; the large variations of form in one age as compared with another tend to show that the form was meant to be elastic, and that the importance which has frequently been attached to *fixity* of form has been exaggerated.

That there should be form of some kind is not only inevitable but desirable: it may be admitted to the full that the unity for which our Lord prayed is a 'unity of the Spirit,' a 'unity of the faith and of the knowledge of the Son of God,' rather than a unity of organization: and yet it would appear as though, in the divine economy which has made human nature what it is, it were owing in no small degree to the fact of its organization that Christianity fills the place which it does fill in the history of the world.

But the fact of the necessity and desirability of form is no proof of the necessity and desirability of this or that particular form. Nor is the fact that a particular form was good for a particular age a proof that it is also good for another age. The history of the organization of Christianity has been in reality the history of successive readjustments of form to altered circumstances. Its power of readjustment has been at once a mark of its divinity and a secret of its strength. Nor, if we look at it merely in its human aspect, is there any sublimer spectacle in all the vast landscape of history than this Tree of God, striking its roots deeper and deeper into the deep strata of human life, changing from age to age the fashion of its branches, and changing also the hue of its blossom, and assimilating to itself all the nurture which comes from the winds of God that blow and from the dew of heaven that falls.

In the first ages of its history, while on the one hand it was a great and living faith, so on the other hand it was a vast and organized brotherhood. And, being a brotherhood, it was a democracy: the 'multitude which no man could number' stood before the throne of God bound together in an equal union by the tie of a common sonship, a common kingship, and a common priesthood.

When the Roman Empire fell, and the Western World passed beneath the dominion of the vigorous races who had no long past of organized administration upon which Christian administration could be moulded, democracy gave way to monarchy. Democracy was almost as impossible as it would be to entrust the government of the mission communities of the South Sea Islands to the new converts from Fetichism.

And now, at the close of the nineteenth century, the Christian societies find themselves surrounded by new conditions. There are new intellectual conditions, and new social conditions. The question which presses for answer, and which will not be evaded, is how much of the form which grew out of, and was good for, earlier and different circumstances, must be retained or abandoned now. The contingency which has to be faced is that the intellectual forces of the civilized world may be arrayed against Christianity as once they were in its favour: and that the social forces which are drawing men into combination may draw them into combinations in which Christianity will have no part. For these contingencies the Church of Christ is prepared. It survived Gnosticism, and it will survive Agnosticism. It survived polytheism, and it will survive atheism. It survived the disruption of European society when the Roman Empire fell to pieces, it will survive the possible disruption of European society when, if ever, labour wins its victory over capital, and socialism over aristocracy. But the survival of the Church of Christ—that is, of 'the whole congregation of Christian people dispersed throughout the world'—

is not necessarily the survival of this or that existing institution. After each of its earlier struggles there was at least this mark of conflict, that there was a re-adaptation of form. The supremacy of the episcopate was the result of the struggle with Gnosticism, the centralization of ecclesiastical government was the outcome of the breaking up of the Empire. And if the secret of the past be the key to the future, the institutions of Christianity are destined in the providence of God, in the days that are to come, to shape themselves in new forms to meet the new needs of men. To the general character of those forms many indications point. It would seem as though, in that vast secular revolution which is accomplishing itself, all organizations, whether ecclesiastical or civil, must be, as the early Churches were, more or less democratical: and the most significant fact of modern Christian history is that, within the last hundred years, many millions of our own race and our own Church, without departing from the ancient faith, have slipped from beneath the inelastic framework of the ancient organization, and formed a group of new societies on the basis of a closer Christian brotherhood and an almost absolute democracy.

But, whatever be the form in which they are destined to be shaped, the work which the Christian societies, as societies, have to do, in the days that are to come, is not inferior to any work which has lain before them at any epoch of their history. For the air is charged with thunder, and the times that are coming may be times of storm. There are phenomena beneath the surface of society of which it would be hardly possible to overrate the significance. There is a widening separation of class from class: there is a growing social strain: there is a disturbance of the political equilibrium: there is the rise of an educated proletariat. To the problems which these phenomena suggest Christianity has the key. Its unaccomplished mission is to reconstruct society on the basis of brotherhood. What it has to do it does, and will do, in and through organization. At once profoundly individual and profoundly socialistic, its tendency to association is not so much an incident of its history as an essential element of its character. It spiritualizes that ineradicable instinct which draws man to man and makes society not a convention but a necessity. But the framing of its organization is left to human hands. To you and me and men like ourselves is committed, in these anxious days, that which is at once an awful responsibility and a splendid destiny—to transform this modern world into a Christian society, to change the socialism which is based on the assumption of clashing interests into the socialism which is based on the sense of spiritual union, and to gather together the scattered forces of a divided Christendom into a confederation in which organization will be of less account than fellowship with one Spirit and faith in one Lord—into a communion wide as human life and deep as human need—into a Church which shall outshine even the golden glory of its dawn by the splendour of its eternal noon.